Cash Management & Credit Control

Combined text

NVQ Accounting Unit 15
AAT Diploma Pathw

D1354424

Michael Fardon

Aubrey Penning

osborne BOOKS

Published by Osborne Books Limited
Unit 1B Everoak Estate
Bromyard Road
Worcester WR2 5HP
Tel 01905 748071
Email books@osbornebooks.co.uk
Website www.osbornebooks.co.uk

Design by Richard Holt
Cover image from Getty Images

Printed by the Bath Press, Bath

British Library Cataloguing in Publication Data
A catalogue record for this book is available from the British Library

ISBN 1 872962 97 1

Contents

Acknowledgements

The authors wish to thank the following for their help with the production of the book: Ruth Brown, Mike Gilbert, Rosemarie Griffiths and Claire McCarthy. Special thanks must go to Roger Petheram for reading, checking and contributing ideas in the writing process. Thanks must also go to George Johnston of Barclays Capital Bank and Graeme Gibson of the Royal Bank of Scotland for advising on the sections of the book which deal with economics and bank lending issues.

The publisher would like to thank Dun & Bradstreet and Experian for granting permission for the reproduction of website pages and the Royal Bank of Scotland for providing sample bank facility letters and allowing them to be illustrated in this text.

Lastly, the publisher is indebted to the Association of Accounting Technicians for permission for the reproduction of extracts from the Accounting Standards, expired simulations and the sample simulation, Lucent Limited.

Authors

Michael Fardon has extensive teaching experience of a wide range of banking, business and accountancy courses at Worcester College of Technology. Earlier in his career he worked in a major international bank, dealing with UK and overseas lending. He now specialises in writing business and financial texts and is General Editor at Osborne Books. He is also an educational consultant and has worked extensively in the areas of vocational business curriculum development.

Aubrey Penning co-ordinates the AAT courses at Worcester College of Technology and has written extensively for Osborne Books. He has many years experience of teaching accountancy on a variety of courses in Worcester and Gwent. He is a Certified Accountant, and before his move into full-time teaching he worked for the health service, a housing association and a chemical supplier.

Introduction

Cash Management and Credit Control has been written to cover the requirements of NVQ Unit 15 and Diploma Pathway Unit 15 'Operating a Cash Management and Credit Control System'.

Cash Management and Credit Control is a very practical and up-to-date book covering two very different areas of study: cash budgets and credit control. Students should be encouraged to appreciate that the cash budget links directly with Unit 9 (NVQ route) and Unit 33 (Diploma Pathway). Credit control is a vital function of every organisation that sells a product or service on credit; students should be encouraged to draw on their own experience when studying this area.

Cash Management and Credit Control is a 'combined text' which contains two main sections:

- A **tutorial section** containing eleven chapters covering the Unit 15 performance criteria and 'knowledge and understanding' requirements. The chapters contain:

    - a clear text with worked examples and Case Studies

    - a chapter summary and key terms to help with revision

    - student activities – with answers to selected questions at the end of the book

- A **practice simulation** section containing three full length simulations, based on AAT originals, including the guidance simulation – Lucent Limited – published when the New Standards were first introduced.

Osborne Tutor Packs

The answers to simulations and selected chapter activities are available in a separate *Tutor Pack*. Please contact the Osborne Books Sales Office on 01905 748071 for details of how to obtain this Tutor Pack.

Osborne website www.osbornebooks.co.uk

The Osborne Books website has proved popular for its free downloads. Visit the Resources Section for forms and computer files to help with studying.

Managing cash flows

- the reasons why cash is different from profit
- the ways in which working capital and the cash cycle operate
- the sources and uses of cash in a business
- which people to consult in the business about cash flows
- the various formats for cash flow statements

PERFORMANCE CRITERIA COVERED

unit 15 OPERATING A CASH MANAGEMENT AND CREDIT CONTROL SYSTEM

element 15.1

Monitor and control cash receipts and payments

A Monitor and control cash receipts and payments against budgeted cash flows

B Consult appropriate staff to determine the likely pattern of cash flows over the accounting period and to anticipate any exceptional receipts or payments

KNOWLEDGE AND UNDERSTANDING COVERAGE

1 The main types of cash receipts and payments: regular revenue receipts and payments; capital receipts and payments; drawings and disbursements; exceptional receipts and payments

12 Form and structure of cash budgets

24 Cash flow accounting and its relationship to accounting for income and expenditure

26 Understanding that the accounting systems of an organisation are affected by its organisational structure, its administrative systems and procedures and the nature of its business transactions

WHY CASH IS DIFFERENT FROM PROFIT

Throughout your studies in accounting you will have been mainly concerned with systems that plan, record and monitor income and expenditure – the net result of which is profit (or loss). In this unit we have a different focus – we are going to examine how the fundamental resource of cash can be budgeted, monitored and controlled.

accounting for profit

Profitability is the amount by which **income** exceeds **expenditure**, and can be seen as the increase of overall wealth of the business. In order to account for the income and expenditure that are used to calculate profit we often use cash-based receipts and payments as a starting point, but then make substantial adjustments, by using techniques such as

• taking account of amounts owed and owing (debtors and creditors)

• adjusting for accruals and prepayments

• depreciating fixed assets

• creating and adjusting provisions (for example provisions for bad debts)

The increased business wealth known as profit is reflected in the net result of all the assets and liabilities in the balance sheet. This is the 'accruals' system of accounting with which you are already very familiar, and the basis for double-entry accounting.

accounting for cash

Cash receipts and payments are normally recorded in a business's cash book. The balance of the cash book represents just one of the business assets (or possibly liabilities) that is shown in the balance sheet. Throughout this unit, when using the term 'cash' we will mean the cash book balances relating to business bank accounts as well as actual amounts of notes and coins.

In the same way, the cash receipts and payments that we will refer to throughout the text will also include amounts received into or paid from bank accounts. These transactions will include receipts and payments using cheques and BACS (direct payments, standing orders and direct debits), as well as notes and coins.

Receipts and **payments** are expressions that relate just to cash items, and do not incorporate any of the adjustments that are used to calculate **income** and **expenditure** when calculating profit (see above). We must be careful to understand the distinction between these two sets of terms.

the importance of 'cash'

What we are going to learn to plan, monitor and control – what we have just defined as **cash** – is therefore the amount of **money** that the business has in a form that it can use virtually immediately. This is sometimes referred to as money in a **liquid** form, from which we get the idea of liquidity. Cash is just as important to a business as profit, since

- the daily operations of a business depend on being able to receive funds and make payments as they become due, and

- the ultimate survival of a business depends on having sufficient cash to meet its obligations

Unlike profit, which could vary if different accounting policies were applied, cash is a matter of fact. If a business is £10,000 overdrawn at the bank then the amount owing is not simply a 'book entry', but an issue that may require immediate action – depending on the business's agreement with the bank.

WORKING CAPITAL AND THE CASH CYCLE

Working capital is the part of the net resources of the business that is made up of current assets minus current liabilities.

You will be familiar with the way that these categories are shown on a balance sheet. The total working capital shown on a balance sheet is also known as 'net current assets'.

Working capital involves the circulation of the elements of stocks, debtors, cash and trade creditors, and the value of these elements will typically change on a daily basis. Contrast this to the way that fixed assets change only occasionally.

The circulation of working capital can be illustrated by the cash cycle:

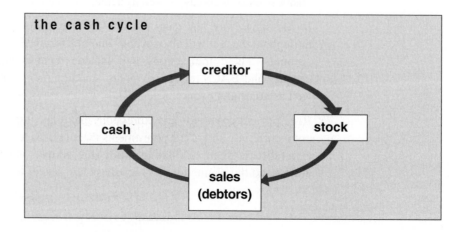

the cash cycle

The diagram on the previous page relates to a simple **trading situation**, and illustrates how creditors (or suppliers) provide goods for resale on credit in the form of stock. When the stock is sold on credit this generates an increase in the amount of debtors (and the sale is recognised under accruals accounting). As the debtors pay the amounts owing to the business this increases the cash balance of the business. This means that cash is then available to pay the creditors.

The same cycle applies to **manufacturing** organisations, except that the stock that is bought must be turned into finished goods before it can be sold, by using labour and other resources that must also be paid for.

Creditors will not usually want to wait to receive payment until the cash cycle is complete and the debtors have paid their accounts. This means that businesses must plan to have sufficient resources available in working capital – in particular in cash – to pay creditors on time.

calculating the cash cycle

Generally speaking, the shorter the cash cycle, the fewer resources will be needed, as the business is making better use of its working capital. We can demonstrate this by calculating the length (in time) of the cash cycle.

The cash cycle can be measured as the time from when payment is made for raw materials or stock until the time that payment is received for goods sold.

Example 1: 5 month cash cycle

A firm receives raw materials at the end of April, and pays for them one month later. The raw materials are processed during May, and the finished goods are held in stock until the end of August, when they are sold on two month's credit. The customer pays on time.

We can show the cash cycle for this example in the form of a time line as follows.

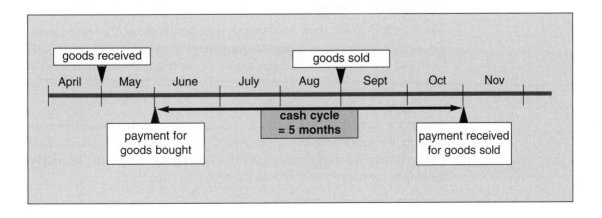

As we can see from the above diagram, the cash for the raw materials is paid out at the end of May. The money is received from the sale of the finished goods at the end of October. This gives a time for the cash cycle of five months.

Example 2: 2 month cash cycle

Suppose the firm in Example 1 had acted as follows: The raw materials that were received at the end of April were paid for on two month's credit. The finished goods were held in stock until the end of July when they were sold on one month's credit, and the customer paid on time.

This would give a cash cycle time of two months as demonstrated in the following diagram.

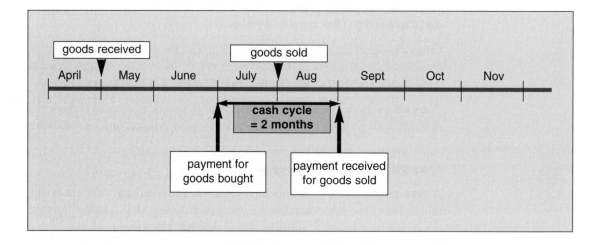

The business in Example 1 has to wait 5 months for the cycle to complete and the money that it has paid out to come back in. In the second example the wait is only 2 months.

The examples above show only sample information about one set of goods. Because firms operate continuously the pattern would be repeating over and over, and this would affect the amount of money that the firm would need to tie up in the cash cycle. The longer the cash cycle the more money is tied up in working capital; the shorter the cash cycle, the less money is tied up.

You may well be familiar with some of the accounting ratios that can be used to help us judge whether a business's working capital is being used efficiently, and whether there are any signs of liquidity problems. We will be looking at the use of ratios later in the book (see Chapter 8).

SOURCES OF CASH – CASH RECEIPTS

There are three main types of cash receipt:

- **regular revenue receipts**

  These arise from the operating activities of a business – the selling of the goods or services that the business provides

- **capital receipts**

  These relate to the proceeds of the sale of fixed assets – both tangible items like buildings or plant, and intangible assets such as investments.

- **exceptional receipts**

  These include 'exceptional' items such as the receipt of loans from the bank, or the proceeds of the sale of a major part of the business.

We will describe each of these three types in turn.

regular revenue receipts

For a trading organisation these amounts will be mainly the proceeds of the sales that the business has made. Other organisations may have revenue receipts in the form of government funding (for example in the National Health Service) or regular donations (for example charities). In this book we will concentrate on commercial organisations. The sales that these businesses make will be either:

- **cash sales** – money received immediately the sale is made, or
- **credit sales** – where the customer is allowed time to pay

When we go on to draw up cash flow statements we must be careful to distinguish between these receipts, and to calculate correctly the time at which the cash will be received.

capital receipts

Businesses dispose of fixed assets from time to time, and these transactions generate cash receipts that need to be accounted for. The disposal of fixed assets may have been planned to link with the acquisition of replacement fixed assets.

exceptional receipts

Businesses need an initial investment when they start up, to provide them with the resources that they need to operate. They may also need further investment later on, particularly if they wish to expand their activities. Investment either comes from the owner(s) of the business, or through loans. For a sole trader or partnership business, capital is introduced by the owners of the business, and a limited company raises equity finance by the issue of shares to the original owners and to new investors. Businesses may also borrow money from banks, other institutions and possibly from individuals. Occasionally businesses may sell off whole sections of their operations, which will bring in cash.

All these transactions will generate major cash receipts, and will be planned well in advance.

USES OF CASH – CASH PAYMENTS

An organisation has to pay at some time for all the goods and services that it buys, as well as paying tax and rewarding the owners and those who have lent money. Cash payments can be categorised into:

* **regular revenue payments**

    Paying for the operational needs of the organisation, the goods and services that are regularly used.

* **capital payments**

    Paying for the acquisition of fixed assets.

* **payments to the providers of finance and other disbursements**

    These include drawings (for a sole trader or partnership), dividends to the shareholders of a limited company, and interest to lenders, as well as tax payments.

* **exceptional payments**

    These include major investments, such as the acquisition of a new business. Also included would be the repayment of substantial financing.

We will describe each of these four types of payment in turn.

regular revenue payments

The regular revenue payments that a commercial organisation needs to make can be broadly divided into the following categories.

* **payments for goods for resale and raw materials**

    A **trading organisation** will need to purchase the goods that it wishes to sell. The amount and timing of these purchases will take account of the forecast sales, as well as the required level of stocks. Since the supplier may well offer to sell on credit, the timing of the payments will need to be calculated carefully. In the case of a **manufacturer** of goods for resale the planned production schedule will need to be taken account of so that the raw materials will be bought at the right time.

- **payments for labour costs**

  Apart from the smallest sole traders or partnerships, all organisations employ staff to carry out the operations of the business. This can include staff involved in the indirect (overhead) functions of the business as well as the direct labour force. Staff are usually paid in the same period that the work is carried out, but the complexities of income tax and national insurance may also need to be considered, and any overtime, bonuses or pay rises accurately accounted for.

- **payments for expenses**

  These are the other operational costs that are needed to keep the organisation functioning. Examples would include rent, rates and insurance, communication costs, stationery, and all the other items that are essential for the smooth running of a business (or not-for-profit organisation). One item of expenditure that is not translated into a cash payment is the depreciation charge for fixed assets. Since this is only a 'book-entry' used to help establish profit, and is not actually paid out, it does not form a cash flow.

capital payments

Capital payments may need to be made from time to time in respect of the acquisition of fixed assets. These may be made immediately the item is bought, or may be spread over a period of time, for example through a hire purchase or leasing arrangement. The fixed asset acquisition will have been planned through the capital budget to ensure that it is made at the optimum time for the business.

payments to providers of finance and other disbursements

Providers of capital and finance for a business will usually expect their reward to be made in the form of a payment. These payments will depend on the type of finance involved, and on any agreement between the parties. The following are the main types of payment:

- **drawings by sole traders or partners**

  These are often regular amounts taken out of the business in anticipation of profits earned. There is often no formal arrangement as to the frequency or amounts drawn, and the owners of the business may need to judge what are suitable amounts based on both their personal needs and those of the business.

- **dividends paid to shareholders of a limited company**

  These payments form the main reward for investing in the shares (along with the prospect of future growth in share value). For 'ordinary' shares, an interim dividend is often paid part way through the financial year, with a final dividend paid after the end of the year, when the profit figures have been finalised. Such payments are often made at the same times each year, although they can vary in amount, or may not be made at all if that is in the interests of the company. If the company has issued 'preference shares' then the owners of these shares will be entitled to regular dividends of amounts that are established from the outset.

- **interest payments to lenders**

    When an organisation has borrowed money from an institution (or an individual) an agreement will have been reached as to the amount and timing of interest payments. For a repayment loan, the regular repayments of parts of the amount borrowed will usually be made at the same time as the interest payments. Payments will typically range from monthly to annually and will need to be planned and implemented accurately. Interest is different from ordinary share dividends in that an organisation will be committed to making interest payments in full and on time, no matter how poor its profitability.

- **other disbursements**

    Other disbursements include tax payments – Value Added Tax for registered businesses, and Corporation Tax for limited companies, as well as PAYE payments to the Inland Revenue. Note that the income tax liability of sole traders and partnerships is the responsibility of the individual owners, and is not a business expense. It will be paid out of their drawings.

exceptional payments

These by definition will only arise occasionally, and could include the following:

- **payments for the acquisition of a new business**

    Businesses sometimes expand by acquiring other businesses and a payment for an acquisition would be considered an exceptional payment. Buying a business that is already operating can be an effective way of achieving rapid growth. The acquired business may be a limited company (in which case the shares would be acquired) or a sole trader or partnership, which would involve coming to a financial arrangement with the owner(s). Alternatively it could involve acquiring just a part of the business.

- **payments in respect of financing**

    Where a loan that was previously taken out is to be repaid in a lump sum, this is an exceptional payment. The timing will have to be carefully planned so that there are sufficient funds available to make the payment. The same sort of situation could arise if capital is repaid to the owners of a business.

sources and uses of cash – a summary

The following diagram summarises the sources and uses of cash discussed in the last few pages.

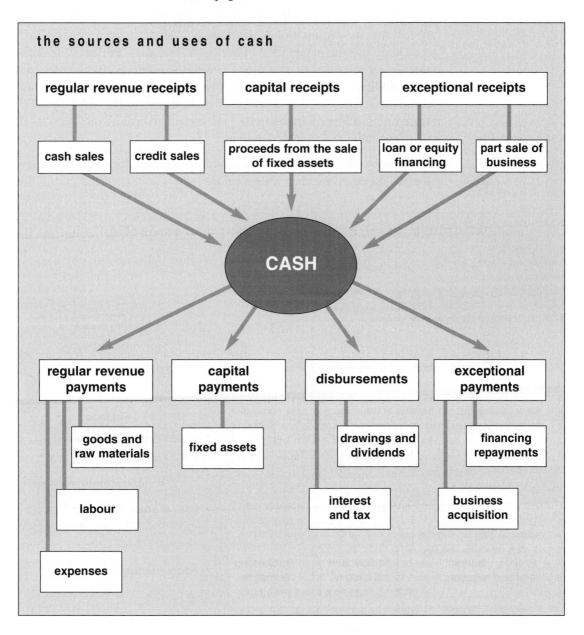

the sources and uses of cash

PEOPLE AND DEPARTMENTS TO CONSULT ABOUT CASH FLOWS

In a typical business there are a variety of people who may need to be consulted when planning, monitoring or controlling cash flows. Using the categories of receipts and payments shown in the diagram on the previous page, we will now discuss briefly the personnel that are most likely to hold information or otherwise need to interact with those who are managing cash.

Since all organisations are different, the following can only be of a very general nature. Remember that the accounting systems of an organisation are affected by its organisational structure, its administrative systems and procedures and the nature of its business transactions. For example each organisation will have its own structure with the positions having roles and responsibilities that are geared to the organisation's needs. Further information on how the organisational structure works in a specific organisation will be contained in the policies and procedures documentation and in the individuals' job descriptions.

We will now outline a possible organisational structure for a manufacturing business, based on the chart shown below.

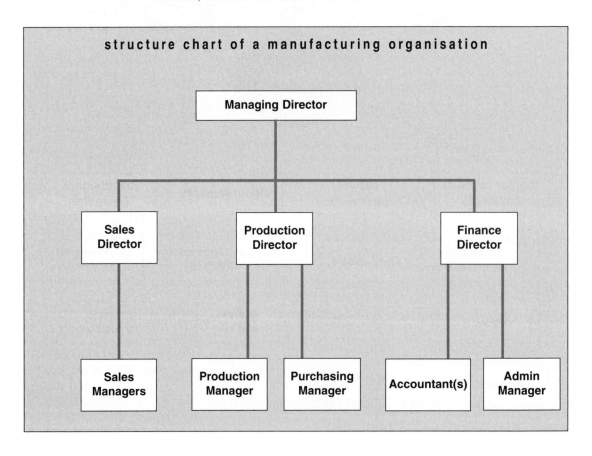

The directors and managers would be responsible for agreeing the organisation's budgets, possibly through a formal budget committee. The main budgets would typically include:

- sales budget

- production budget

- materials budget

- labour budget

- functional budget

- capital budget

- master budget (budgeted profit & loss account and balance sheet)

- cash budget

In the next chapters we will see in detail how the data from the other budgets are used in the cash budget. At this stage we will just refer to how the individuals responsible for the budgets can help with providing data on expected cash flows. Throughout the following discussion, the individuals referred to may delegate some of their responsibilities to their subordinates.

data for regular revenue receipts

Data for sales receipts – both cash and credit – will come from the sales budget. The sales budget is prepared by the Sales Director (in consultation with the Finance Director). Cash sales will generate instant cash, but sales made on credit will also require information about typical credit periods. This information may be obtained from the Finance Director or his/her team. When planning cash flows it will be important to use reliable estimates of how long it takes customers to pay – which is not always the same as the agreed credit terms!

data for capital receipts

Capital receipts will only take place on an irregular basis, but the amounts may be large. The sale of fixed assets will usually be planned through the capital budget, in conjunction with the acquisition of new fixed assets. The Production Director is likely to have the required information on the disposal of production related fixed assets, and the Finance Director will usually control the sale of investments.

data for exceptional receipts

When exceptional items like the raising of finance need to be accounted for (through capital injection or loans), this will usually have been planned by the Finance Director.

data for regular revenue payments

The purchase of goods and raw materials is normally carried out by the Purchasing Manager. The materials budgets (both for usage and purchase of materials) will have been developed in conjunction with the production budget. The Purchasing Manager and the Production Manager will have worked together to ensure that the right items are acquired at the right time. The Purchasing Manager or the Accountant will have information on credit typically taken.

The payment of labour costs related to manufacture will be laid out in the labour budget, and is controlled by the Production Manager. The Administration Manager (or Accountant) may deal with other salaries and wages that are agreed in the relevant functional budgets, along with expense payments.

data for capital payments

The acquisition of fixed assets will have been authorised in the capital budget, following proposals by the Production Director or Finance Director. The terms of payment will usually be set out in the budget following recommendations by the Finance Director's team.

data for disbursements

The Finance Director will usually have information on dividends and interest payments and taxation.

data for exceptional payments

The acquisition of new businesses will be agreed by the Managing Director with the other Directors. The detail of the payments may well have been delegated to the Finance Director's team, who will plan and organise the relevant amounts. Any repayments of capital to shareholders or lenders will also have been planned at a high level in the organisation, and the Finance Director will have agreed the arrangements.

THE FORM AND STRUCTURE OF CASH FLOW STATEMENTS

In order to effectively budget, monitor and control cash flows, the information must be compiled in a suitable format. There are two main formats that can be used to show cash flows.

- the cash flow summary format
- the receipts and payments format

Both formats have their own strengths and weaknesses.

cash flow summary format

This format demonstrates how cash is to be generated from operations, and shows to what use it is to be put. This format is effectively the same as the historical cash flow statement as detailed in Financial Reporting Standard 1 that you may have studied in financial accounting. In order to use this format as a budget, a budgeted balance sheet will need to be drafted at the end of the period (as well as one at the beginning) so that a comparison can be made. This comparison of data from the two balance sheets forms the basis of an important part of this type of cash flow statement.

The format of this statement is shown on the next page.

Although this format provides a simple analysis of the budgeted cash flows over the period as a whole, it does not provide the level of detail that is needed to manage cash effectively. In particular, by concentrating on the year as a whole it does not identify any peaks and troughs of cash that will occur during the period. This format has its strengths and weaknesses:

Strengths

- It gives a simple summary of the sources and uses of cash over the whole budget period.
- It can be produced quickly and easily once a budgeted profit and loss account and balance sheet have been drawn up.

Weaknesses

- It does not show peaks and troughs of cash within the period, and is therefore not suitable for detailed cash planning.
- It cannot be used to compare with actual cash movements until after the whole period is ended – making monitoring ineffective.

While it is useful that you are aware of this type of cash flow statement, and its strengths and weaknesses, we are not going to study its use any further in this Unit. Instead we are going to concentrate on the receipts and payments format (see pages 17-18). This is a far better tool for monitoring and controlling cash receipts and payments.

FUNDZFLOH LIMITED

BUDGETED CASH FLOW STATEMENT FOR THE YEAR ENDED 31 DECEMBER 20-5

	£	£
Net cash inflow from operating activities		89,000
Returns on investments and servicing of finance:		
Interest received	10,000	
Interest paid	(5,000)	
		5,000
Taxation:		
Corporation tax paid		(6,000)
Capital expenditure and financial investment:		
Payments to acquire fixed assets	(125,000)	
Receipts from sales of fixed assets	15,000	
		(110,000)
Acquisitions and disposals:		
Purchase of subsidiary undertakings	(–)	
Sale of a business	–	
		–
Equity dividends paid:		(22,000)
Cash outflow before use of liquid resources and financing		(44,000)
Management of liquid resources:		
Purchase of short-term investments	(250,000)	
Sale of short-term investments	200,000	
		(50,000)
Financing:		
Issue of share capital	275,000	
Repayment of capital/share capital	(–)	
Increase in loans	–	
Repayment of loans	(90,000)	
		185,000
Increase in cash		91,000

Reconciliation of operating profit to net cash inflow from operating activities	
Operating profit	75,000
Depreciation for year	10,000
Decrease in stock	2,000
Increase in debtors	(5,000)
Increase in creditors	7,000
Net cash inflow from operating activities	89,000

RECEIPTS AND PAYMENTS FORMAT

The receipts and payments format can be used to monitor and control cash flows through each month (or week) of the budget period. It shows the predicted movement of the organisation's cash (typically the business bank account) by showing:

A   the source and amounts of expected receipts – with an overall total 'Total Receipts'

B   the amounts of anticipated payment for each type of cash outflow – with an overall total 'Total payments'

C   'Cashflow for Month' (calculated as A – B)

D   the opening bank balance ('brought forward') for each month (or week, etc)

E   the closing bank balance ('carried forward') for each month, (C + D)

Note that the closing bank balance for one month is the same as the opening bank balance for the next month.

This format is illustrated below, in this case set out in a spreadsheet.

CORIANNE LIMITED				
CASH BUDGET				
	JANUARY £	FEBRUARY £	MARCH £	APRIL £
Receipts				
Sales Receipts	3,000	3,000	4,000	4,000
Capital	10,000			
TOTAL RECEIPTS	13,000	3,000	4,000	4,000
Payments				
Purchases	5,000	1,750	1,750	
Fixed Assets	4,500	5,250		
Rent/Rates	575	575	575	575
Insurance	50	50	50	50
Electricity	25	25	25	25
Telephone	150	15	15	15
Stationery	10	10	10	10
Postage	15	15	15	15
Bank charges	100		75	
Advertising	150	30	30	30
TOTAL PAYMENTS	10,575	7,720	2,545	720
CASHFLOW FOR MONTH	2,425	- 4,720	1,455	3,280
Bank Balance *brought forward*	-	2,425	- 2,295	- 840
Bank Balance *carried forward*	2,425	- 2,295	- 840	2,440

notes on the format

As you can see, the basic format can easily be tailored to the individual requirements of an organisation by inserting additional lines to deal with specific receipts and/or payments. Because each category of receipt and payment is shown separately, it can be used to monitor these specific items. However, this format can be more time-consuming to create than a cash flow statement (see page 16), although it is an ideal application for a computer spreadsheet because formulas can be used to carry out the calculations and the results of any changes can be viewed instantly.

The strengths and weaknesses of this format can be summarised as follows:

Strengths

- It gives a detailed picture of the inflows and outflows of cash within each month (or week, etc) within the budget period.

- It shows monthly cash balances, and therefore allows peaks and troughs of cash within the period to be anticipated and managed.

- It can be used to monitor actual cash movements as they occur, and to produce easy to understand variances.

- It is ideally suited to the use of a spreadsheet model.

Weaknesses

- It requires accurate information relating to the timing of each category of receipt and payment.

- It is more time-consuming to construct than a cash flow summary statement.

In the three chapters that follow we will examine in detail how this receipts and payments format can be used in practice, incorporating the complications that you are likely to come across in the workplace or in simulations.

Chapter Summary

- Cash is a simpler concept to grasp than profit. Whereas profit is measured by the difference between income and expenditure (which relate to accruals accounting), cash flows are simply based on receipts and payments of cash or bank transactions.

- The amount of working capital that an organisation needs depends upon the length of the cash cycle. This is a measure of how much time elapses between the time that cash is paid for goods (or materials) and the time that cash from sales of the goods is received.

- Cash receipts in a business arise from regular revenue receipts (typically cash or credit sales), capital receipts from the sale of fixed assets, other disbursements and exceptional receipts from sources like financing.

- Cash is used to pay for regular revenue commitments such as materials, labour and expenses, as well as the acquisition of fixed assets and the occasional exceptional items.

- There are a variety of staff in the business who will hold information about cash receipts and payments, and these people should be consulted regularly to utilise their expertise. These individuals will usually have helped to create the budgets that form the sources of the data used in the cash budget.While most organisations will be structured in similar ways and employ people in similar roles, it should always be remembered that structures and roles will have been tailored to the needs of the organisation, and this will have an impact on the choice of person who would need to be approached about a specific issue.

- Cash flow statements can be produced in 'cash flow' format (like FRS1 statements) or in receipts and payments format. While the former is simpler to produce, it lacks the detail necessary for monitoring and control purposes. The receipts and payments format is a little more complicated to produce, but is a far better tool for these purposes.

<table>
<tr><td>

Key Terms

</td><td>

accruals accounting

</td><td>

the traditional system of accounting in which income is compared with expenditure to arrive at the profit over a period of time

</td></tr>
<tr><td></td><td>

cash accounting

</td><td>

the system of accounting for receipts and payments in cash or through bank accounts – effectively a part of a normal accounting system

</td></tr>
<tr><td></td><td>

working capital

</td><td>

the current assets minus the current liabilities of an organisation – also known as net current assets

</td></tr>
<tr><td></td><td>

cash cycle

</td><td>

the circulation of value through working capital as cash is paid out, and eventually received back again – the length of the cash cycle can be measured in days

</td></tr>
<tr><td></td><td>

liquidity

</td><td>

the ability of an organisation to pay its liabilities as they become due – it involves keeping sufficient current assets in money or in a form that will quickly convert to money

</td></tr>
<tr><td></td><td>

receipt

</td><td>

the inflow of money in cash (or into the bank account)

</td></tr>
<tr><td></td><td>

payment

</td><td>

the outflow of money in cash (or from the bank account)

</td></tr>
<tr><td></td><td>

revenue receipts/payments

</td><td>

receipts or payments of money that relate to the ongoing operations of the business, and not to items that have a long term economic benefit such as fixed assets

</td></tr>
</table>

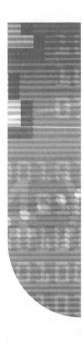

capital receipts/payments   receipts or payments of money that relate to the acquisition or sale of fixed assets in a business

exceptional receipts/ payments   receipts or payments of money that do not occur regularly or frequently

cash flow summary format   a cash flow format equivalent to an FRS1 historical cash flow statement

receipts and payments format   a cash flow format that shows opening balances, receipts, payments, and closing balances for each month (or week, etc.) within the budget period – the most suitable format for monitoring and controlling cash flows

Student Activities

answers to the asterisked (*) questions are to be found at the back of this book

1.1* A firm receives raw materials at the end of January on one month's credit, and pays for them on time. The raw materials are processed during February, and the finished goods are held in stock until the end of May, when they are sold on two month's credit. The customer pays on time.

Required

(a)   Draw a line diagram and calculate the cash cycle in months.

(b)   Calculate the cash cycle in months if the firm bought on two months' credit but sold on one month's credit.

1.2* Kool Limited, a trading company, is comparing the working capital from the budgeted balance sheet with the actual figures.

	Budget £	Actual £
Current Assets:		
Stocks:	20,000	50,000
Debtors	40,000	80,000
Bank	50,000	0
	110,000	130,000
Less Current Liabilities:		
Creditors for Purchases	30,000	50,000
	80,000	80,000

The following information has been obtained about the actual performance:

•   The credit controller has been off sick, so no one has been chasing debtors for the past few weeks. This has doubled the debtors.

•   An order of £20,000 worth of purchases was delivered before the above balance sheet date instead of afterwards as requested.

•   An additional £10,000 worth of purchases was bought and paid for earlier in the year when a supplier offered a special price. The goods have not yet been sold.

Required

Explain how each of the above pieces of information help to account for the differences between the budgeted parts of working capital and the actual figures.

1.3*   A trainee in the accountancy department has made the following statements about cash management:

1   Accounting for profit involves comparing receipts with payments, whereas accounting for cash involves comparing income and expenditure.

2   If the cash cycle of one business is longer than that of another business that is similar in other respects, then the first business will generally need more working capital.

3   If goods are kept in stock for a long time, and debtors are slow to pay there will be less cash available for other purposes.

4   Exceptional receipts should always be ignored when creating a cash budget.

5   A variety of people in the organisation should be consulted when creating a cash budget. The person to contact regarding a specific issue may vary according to the structure of the particular organisation.

6   A cash flow summary statement has the advantage of showing in detail the expected peaks and troughs of cash.

7   Monitoring and controlling cash flow is best carried out using a receipts and payments format of cash statement.

Required

Identify the statements above that are true.

1.4   Each of the following points relates *either* to a cash flow summary statement *or* to a receipts and payments format cash statement.

1   Gives a simple summary of the sources and uses of cash over the whole budget period.

2   Does not show peaks and troughs of cash within the period, and is therefore not suitable for detailed cash planning.

3   Gives a detailed picture of the inflows and outflows of cash within each month (or week, etc.) within the budget period.

4   Shows monthly cash balances, and therefore allows peaks and troughs of cash within the period to be anticipated and managed.

5   Is ideally suited to the use of a spreadsheet model.

6   Cannot be used to compare with actual cash movements until after the whole period is ended – making monitoring ineffective.

7   Requires accurate information on the timing of each category of receipt and payment.

Required

Identify the points that relate to a cash flow summary format of cash statement, and the points that relate to a receipts and payments format.

PERFORMANCE CRITERIA COVERED

unit 15 OPERATING A CASH MANAGEMENT AND CREDIT CONTROL SYSTEM

element 15.1

Monitor and control cash receipts and payments

D   Prepare cash budgets in the approved format and clearly indicate net cash requirements.

KNOWLEDGE AND UNDERSTANDING COVERAGE

1   The main types of cash receipts and payments: regular revenue receipts and payments; capital receipts and payments; drawings and disbursements; exceptional receipts and payments.

12   Form and structure of cash budgets.

13   Lagged receipts and payments.

PREPARING A CASH BUDGET FOR A NEW BUSINESS

In this chapter we are going to see how we can build up a cash budget using the receipts and payments format that we looked at briefly at the end of Chapter 1.

We will start by looking at the cash budget for a new trading organisation, so that we can get a clear idea of the main principles. We will also see how the cash budget fits in with the budgeted profit and loss account and balance sheet. Later on we will see how we can build on our technique to develop cash budgets for existing businesses by incorporating data from the opening balance sheet.

In the next chapter we will look at cash budgets for manufacturing organisations, and examine how issues of production budgets and stock levels are dealt with. We will also see how some simple statistical techniques can help us.

the basic process – linking with other budgets

The data that we use to create all our budgets must be consistent so that all our budgets are based on the same assumptions. We will find that much of the data for a cash budget can be found in a **budgeted profit and loss account**, if this has already been prepared. However, the key to accurate cash budgets is to remember that receipts and payments are based on **when the receipts and payments occur**, and therefore most of the figures in the budgeted profit and loss account will need analysing or modifying.

When we receive or pay cash at a different time to the recording of the sale, purchase or expense, this is known as **lagging**. It is these lagged figures – based on the time of receipt or payment – that we will use in our cash budget. For example, if credit sales of £10,000 were made in January, on two months' credit, then the money would be received in March. Although the sale would be recorded in the profit and loss account in January, it must appear in the March column in the cash budget.

A cash budget will not show any non-cash items that appear in the budgeted profit and loss account – the most common example of this is depreciation. There are also items that will appear in the cash budget, but are not shown in the budgeted profit and loss account. These are capital items (purchase or disposal of fixed assets), disbursements like drawings and tax, and exceptional items like financing (funds from equity or loans). These were discussed in the last chapter.

The diagram on the next page shows how the data in a simple cash budget links with the data used in other budgets.

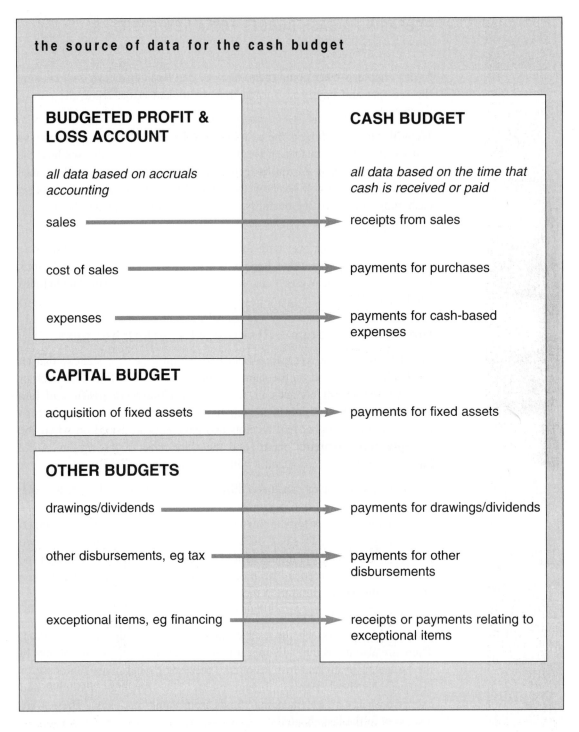

the source of data for the cash budget

BUDGETED PROFIT & LOSS ACCOUNT	**CASH BUDGET**
all data based on accruals accounting	*all data based on the time that cash is received or paid*
sales	receipts from sales
cost of sales	payments for purchases
expenses	payments for cash-based expenses
CAPITAL BUDGET	
acquisition of fixed assets	payments for fixed assets
OTHER BUDGETS	
drawings/dividends	payments for drawings/dividends
other disbursements, eg tax	payments for other disbursements
exceptional items, eg financing	receipts or payments relating to exceptional items

We will now use a Case Study to show how a simple cash budget can be produced for a new business, using the sources of data shown in the diagram above.

Case Study

FIRST TRADE:
SIMPLE CASH BUDGET

Jim First is planning to start a trading business. He has prepared the following budgeted profit and loss account for the initial four months trading.

Jim First: Budgeted Profit & Loss Account

	£	£
Sales		22,000
less cost of sales:		
opening stock	0	
purchases	21,000	
less closing stock	(7,000)	
		14,000
Gross profit		8,000
less:		
cash expenses	4,000	
depreciation	1,000	
		5,000
Net profit		3,000

Jim also provides you with the following information regarding his plans:

- **Sales** are to be made on two months' credit. The sales figures in the budgeted profit & loss account are based on monthly sales as follows:

	£
Month 1	4,000
Month 2	6,000
Month 3	5,000
Month 4	7,000
Total sales	22,000

- **Purchases** made in the first month must be paid for immediately. Subsequent purchases will be on one month's credit. The purchases figure in the budgeted profit and loss account is made up as follows:

	£
Month 1	6,000
Month 2	6,000
Month 3	4,000
Month 4	5,000
Total purchases	21,000

- Cash expenses are based on paying out £1,000 in each of the first four months of the business.

- Equipment is to be bought for £15,000 in the first month of the business. The depreciation shown in the budgeted profit and loss account is based on depreciating these fixed assets at 20% per year on a straight-line basis.

- Jim has £25,000 to invest in the business in month 1. The business has no opening cash balance.

- Jim wishes to withdraw £2,000 from the business in month 4.

Required

Prepare a cash budget in receipts and payments format for the first four months trading of First Trade.

Solution

The cash budget is prepared in the following way.

- The capital invested is entered as a receipt in month 1.

- The receipts from sales are entered on the appropriate line, taking account of the two months' credit by lagging the receipts by two months, ie sales for months 1 and 2 are received in months 3 and 4. Note that the sales made in months 3 and 4 do not appear on this cash budget as the money will not be received until months 5 and 6.

- The payments for purchases and expenses are entered into the appropriate lines, using the data on payment terms. Remember that the first month's purchases are paid for in month 1 and subsequent purchases are given one month's credit.

- The payments for fixed assets and drawings are entered as appropriate.

- The receipts and payments totals are completed, and each month's cash flow is calculated (ie total receipts minus total payments).

- The bank balance brought forward for month 1 is inserted (here it is zero).

- The carried forward bank balance for each month is calculated in turn. This is based on the calculation for each month using the formula:

cash flow for month + bank balance brought forward = bank balance carried forward

The closing bank balance (bank balance carried forward) for one month is then entered as the opening bank balance for the following month (bank balance brought forward).

FIRST TRADE – CASH BUDGET FOR MONTHS 1 TO 4

	Month 1 £'000	Month 2 £'000	Month 3 £'000	Month 4 £'000
Receipts:				
Initial Investment	25			
Receipts from Sales	-	-	4	6
Total Receipts	25	-	4	6
Payments:				
Purchases	6	-	6	4
Expenses	1	1	1	1
Fixed Assets	15	-	-	-
Drawings	-	-	-	2
Total Payments	22	1	7	7
Cash Flow for Month	3	(1)	(3)	(1)
Bank Balance brought forward	0	3	2	(1)
Bank Balance carried forward	3	2	(1)	(2)

We can see from the cash budget that if everything goes according to plan, Jim's business bank balance will be £3,000 in credit at the end of month 1, but will fall to an overdrawn balance of £2,000 by the end of month 4.

Jim would therefore need to arrange suitable finance if he wishes to follow this budget.

He should also consider the impact of things not going according to plan. For example sales may be lower than forecast and expenses may be higher. This 'what-if' planning process is called sensitivity analysis, and in Chapter 4 we will see how to deal with this issue, taking advantage of the flexibility offered by computer spreadsheets.

LINKS WITH THE BUDGETED BALANCE SHEET

cash budget and master budget

A full set of budgets for an organisation will include a **budgeted balance sheet** as at the end of the budget period, as well as a **budgeted profit and loss account** and **cash budget**.

The budgeted balance sheet is based on the same format as the historical balance sheet produced for Financial Accounting purposes, but is based in the future. It is a statement of the **expected assets**, **liabilities** and **capital** at the end of the budgeting period. Because this document will tie in with the other two main budgets, it will incorporate the profit generated in the budgeted profit and loss account, and the final cash or bank balance as predicted in the cash budget.

The budgeted profit and loss account and the budgeted balance sheet are together known as the **master budget**.

subsidiary budgets

There are also a number of other **subsidiary budgets** that often have to be created in more complex businesses in order to build up sufficient information to create the master budget and the budgeted cash flow statement. Examples of these are the sales budget, the production budget, and the materials usage budget. You will have examined the use of these budgets if you have studied the unit 'contributing to the planning and control of resources'. We will look in more detail at how the data from these budgets is used in the cash budget in the next chapter.

cash budget and budgeted balance sheet

In order to understand fully how the cash budget works, we need to be able to create a budgeted balance sheet either in full, or in extract form. By creating a full budgeted balance sheet we can also check that the budgets that we have created link together properly and that the final result balances.

Of particular importance are the following links between the cash budget and the budgeted balance sheet at the end of the budget period.

- The debtors figure in the budgeted balance sheet will represent the credit sales made that have not yet been received in cash. These are typically the sales for the final period(s) where receipts do not appear in the cash budget.

- The cash/bank figure in the budgeted balance sheet will be taken directly from the final cash/bank balance in the cash budget. If this is a negative figure it will be recorded as an overdraft under current liabilities.

- The trade creditors figure in the budgeted balance sheet will represent the credit purchases (and possibly expenses) that were made in the budget period, but are unpaid at the period end. In a similar way to sales, these are typically the purchases or expenses for the final period(s) that do not appear in the cash budget.

We will now continue the previous Case Study to see how the budgeted balance sheet can be developed in practice.

Case Study

FIRST TRADE:
PREPARING A BUDGETED BALANCE SHEET

Jim First is planning to start a trading business (see pages 27 to 29). He has prepared a budgeted profit and loss account for the initial four months trading that showed a budgeted profit of £3,000. A cash budget has also been prepared that shows an overdrawn bank balance of £2,000 at the end of month 4. The data shown on pages 27 to 28 is also relevant.

Required
Prepare a budgeted balance sheet as at the end of month 4.

Solution
The budgeted balance sheet is as follows, with notes showing how each figure was arrived at.

FIRST TRADE – BUDGETED BALANCE SHEET AS AT THE END OF MONTH 4

	£	£	£
Fixed Assets	Cost	Dep'n	Net book value
Equipment (1)	15,000	1,000	14,000
Current Assets			
Stock (2)		7,000	
Debtors (3)		12,000	
		19,000	
Less **Current Liabilities**			
Trade Creditors (4)	5,000		
Bank Overdraft (5)	2,000		
		7,000	
			12,000
Total Net Assets			26,000

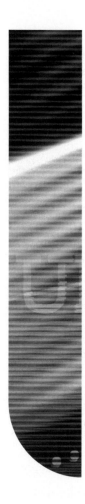

Financed by:

Capital Invested	25,000
Add Budgeted Profit (6)	3,000
Less Budgeted Drawings (7)	(2,000)
Total Capital	26,000

Notes

(1)   The fixed assets were bought in month 1. They are valued at cost, less the depreciation as shown in the budgeted profit & loss account, since this is also the cumulative depreciation.

(2)   The stock figure is the closing stock used in the budgeted profit & loss account.

(3)   The debtors figure is made up of the sales for months 3 and 4 (£5,000 + £7,000). The proceeds of these sales will not have been received within the budget period, since the sales are made on 2 months' credit.

(4)   The trade creditors figure is the month 4 purchases that are not due to be paid until month 5.

(5)   The bank overdraft is the final closing balance on the cash budget.

(6)   The budgeted profit is as recorded on the budgeted profit & loss account.

(7)   The budgeted drawings are as recorded in the cash budget.

Examine the above figures and notes carefully to ensure that you understand fully how the figures were arrived at. Note that the budgeted balance sheet should balance when the data is used consistently.

PRACTICAL ISSUES RELATING TO CASH BUDGETS

dealing with 'split' receipts

Sometimes receipts from a month's sales may not all be received at the same time. This may be because either

- some sales are made on a cash basis, and
- some customers are allowed different credit terms to others, or
- the budget is to take account of a percentage of sales being paid for late

The principle of dealing with this situation in both the cash budget and the balance sheet is identical to that already used, but there will be a little more calculation required.

The best way to deal with the cash budget is to use additional line(s) to account for the different assumed credit terms. If this is not possible due to the layout that is imposed, a separate working will serve the same purpose.

We will use a worked example to demonstrate the principle.

worked example: 'split receipts'

A new company has projected sales (all credit sales) as follows:

Month 1	£200,000
Month 2	£250,000
Month 3	£320,000

It is assumed that 80% of each month's sales will be received one month later, and the remaining 20% in the following month (ie two months after the sale).

An extract from the cash budget can be drawn up as follows:

	Month 1	Month 2	Month 3
	£'000	£'000	£'000
Receipts from sales:			
(1 month's credit)	-	160 [1]	200 [2]
(2 month's credit)	-	-	40 [3]
Total receipts from sales	-	160	240

Workings [1] £200,000 x 80%

[2] £250,000 x 80%

[3] £200,000 x 20%

The debtors figure in the budgeted balance sheet as at the end of month 3 would be made up as follows:

Part of month 2 sales	£50,000	(£250,000 x 20%)
All of month 3 sales	£320,000	
Total debtors	£370,000	

The same principle would apply if purchases were to be paid using varying credit terms, although this situation is less common.

dealing with discounts

If businesses offer discounts to debtors for prompt payment (or take advantage of those offered by creditors) this will have an impact on the cash budget. The key to remember is that the amount of any discount will reduce the amount received or paid, and the receipts or payments must therefore be adjusted accordingly.

worked example: dealing with discounts

For example, suppose a business offers a 3% discount if its debtors pay in the month of sale, but no discount if they pay on two months' credit. If the business estimates that

50% of its customers will take advantage of this discount, then it would have the following receipts relating to June sales of £100,000, and July sales of £120,000:

	June	July	Aug	Sept
	£	£	£	£
Receipts – Current Month's Sales	48,500	58,200	-	-
Receipts – Two Months' Credit	-	-	50,000	60,000

Note that the sales receipts for June and July are calculated by working out half of the month's sales and deducting 3%.

dealing with bank account interest

In the previous Case Studies we have ignored any bank interest, ie

- interest received from positive cash balances
- interest payable on a bank overdraft

Although interest calculations in practice would probably be based on daily bank balances, using monthly balances will usually provide a satisfactory estimate of the interest payments involved.

In the next worked example we assume that bank interest is received or paid monthly, based on the closing bank balance at the end of the previous month. One issue to be careful about is to check whether the interest quoted is based on monthly or annual rates. If the percentage rate is monthly, this can be applied directly to the balance, but where the rate is annual (the normal situation) it must first be divided by 12 to arrive at a monthly rate before the interest is calculated.

Because interest amounts are likely to be relatively small some rounding may be required. It is certainly never worth estimating interest amounts in less than whole pounds. It is also worth double-checking that your decimal point is correct when calculating the interest!

worked example – dealing with bank interest

Suppose the following cash budget figures had been calculated before taking account of bank interest.

The bank will pay interest at 0.5% per month on a closing credit balance of the previous month, and charge interest at 1.0% per month on overdrawn balances.

The bank balance at the end of the previous December is £10,000.

	January £	February £	March £
Total Receipts (before any interest)	6,500	4,500	6,000
Total Payments (before any interest)	15,000	6,500	7,000

The bank interest would be accounted for in the cash budget as follows:

	January £	February £	March £
Receipts (before any interest)	6,500	4,500	6,000
Interest Received	50	8	-
Total Receipts	6,550	4,508	6,000
Payments (before any interest)	15,000	6,500	7,000
Interest Paid	-	-	4
Total Payments	15,000	6,500	7,004
Cash flow for Month	(8,450)	(1,992)	(1,004)
Balance brought forward	10,000	1,550	(442)
Balance carried forward	1,550	(442)	(1,446)

The order of calculation is clearly important since the interest on each balance has an impact on the next month's balance, which in turn affects the next interest amount. Each month's cash balance must therefore be finalised before the next month's figures are finalised.

If you are using a budgeted profit and loss account for the same period, it will also be necessary to treat any interest as income or expenditure. This of course will have an impact on net profit, and if a draft figure has been calculated it will need revising.

Note that banks may credit or debit the bank account with interest on a quarterly basis. The calculation of the interest would be carried out in the same way.

a note on debenture interest

Some businesses are financed by fixed interest loans known as debentures. You may be told, for example, that a business has issued £10,000 of 5% Debenture Stock. It will need to account in the profit and loss account for paying 5% x £10,000 = £500 interest. This will also need to be accounted for as a payment on the relevant date(s) in the cash budget.

DEALING WITH SIMPLE STOCK MOVEMENTS

In the last Case Study both the individual purchase figures and the closing stock figure were provided for the sake of making things easy. In some situations we may need to use our knowledge of how stock operates to calculate some of the figures that we will need for our budgets.

Later on in this book we will look at developing cash budgets for traditional manufacturing organisations. As an introduction to the issue of stock movements, we will now use another Case Study that is based on a new business. This time the data is slightly more complex, and we will need to calculate the stock levels as well as produce master budgets and a cash budget.

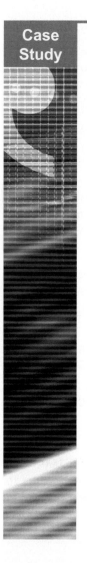

Case Study

CAMPER-FANS
PREPARING INITIAL BUDGETS

situation

Kylie and Jed are planning to start a business selling used camper vans. They will buy their stock from a hire company, recondition the mechanicals, and sell them on to young travellers who want cheap but reliable transport and accommodation. They have agreed to buy at a fixed price of £3,000 for the high mileage vans, and the sellers can supply as many as they are likely to need, at least in the short term.

They plan to start the venture in January, and spend January and February preparing the first few vehicles for sale. They have then estimated as best they can the sales levels for the coming months as follows:

Estimated sales	
March	2 camper vans
April	3 camper vans
May	4 camper vans
June & subsequent months	4 camper vans

The sales will all be on a cash basis for £5,000 each. Purchases of the vans will also be for cash, but the parts to recondition the mechanical parts (estimated at £400 per van) will be supplied on one month's credit. They will buy the necessary parts at the same time as the vans. They plan to buy 3 vans in January, and build up their stock so that by the end of February and each following month there will be enough vans ready for sale to satisfy the estimated demand of the following two months. In this way they hope to have enough on display to offer prospective customers a reasonable choice.

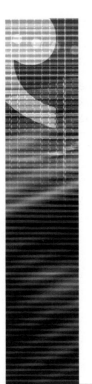

Kylie and Jed have found suitable premises with a small garage to work on the vehicles and a forecourt area. The rent is £4,000 per year, payable annually in advance. They will immediately equip the garage with tools costing £1,000, which should last about 4 years.

Other costs of running the business are estimated at £400 per month, all payable in the month that they are incurred.

Kylie and Jed have £20,000 cash as initial capital, and hope that any further finance required can be provided by a temporary bank overdraft facility. They will each draw £800 from the business per month in the first year. They wish to ignore bank interest in this initial set of budgets.

required

Draft a set of master budgets and a cash budget for the first six months of the business for Camper-Fans.

solution

The best place to start the calculations is to work out how many vans will need to be bought each month to comply with their stock requirements. This will be useful for all the main budgets, and will be vital to complete the cash budget. It can be carried out in the form of a table, as follows:

Numbers of Camper Vans:

Month	Opening Stock	Purchases	Sales	Closing Stock
Jan	0	3	0	3
Feb	3	2	0	5
March	5	4	2	7
April	7	4	3	8
May	8	4	4	8
June	8	4	4	8
		21	13	

The figures in the table are worked out as follows. The sales figures for each month are inserted first. Then the January purchases are inserted from the Case Study. For each month the following will be true (in numbers of vans):

Opening Stock + Purchases – Sales = Closing Stock

Therefore the closing stock in January will be 3 vans, (0 + 3 – 0 = 3) which will also form the opening stock in February. Since the closing stock in February needs to be 5 vans to satisfy the demand in March and April, the February purchases must be 2. The closing and opening stocks are then calculated for each of the remaining months, and the purchases calculated accordingly.

Notice that totals of purchases and sales have been included, and that these also comply with the above equation for the six months as a whole:

Opening Stock + Purchases – Sales = Closing Stock (ie 0 + 21 – 13 = 8)

Now that the movements of camper vans have been worked out, the budgeted profit and loss account and cash-flow statements can be prepared. Workings have been shown to clarify the sources of the figures, together with references to the explanatory notes but these would normally be excluded from the finished document.

Camper-Fans

Budgeted Profit & Loss Account for first 6 months

	£	£
Sales (13 vans at £5,000)		65,000 (1)
Less cost of vans sold:		
(13 vans at (£3,000 + £400 parts))		44,200 (2)
Gross Profit		20,800 (3)
Less Expenses:		
Premises Rent (£4,000 x 6/12)	2,000 (4)	
Depreciation of Equipment		
(£1,000 x 25% x 6/12)	125 (5)	
Other Costs (£400 x 6 months)	2,400 (6)	
		4,525
Budgeted Net Profit		16,275

Notes

1   The sales figure relates to the income of the budgetary period. In this case the money from these sales would also be received in the period, (but this would not necessarily be the case).

2   Here the cost of sales relates to the same 13 camper vans that will be sold in the period. An alternative form of presentation would have been to show the value of the purchases of vans plus parts, less the value of closing stock. This would provide the same cost of sales figure.

3   The gross profit represents the profit made on the 13 vans before deducting the running costs of the business. It therefore agrees with 13 x (£5,000 – (£3,000 + £400))= £20,800. The cost of labour has been excluded in this case since it is provided by the owners of the business (Kylie and Jed), and will therefore appear as drawings.

4   Although £4,000 rent has been paid for, the full amount relates to a 12 month period. It is therefore fair to incorporate only 6 months rent in this budget.

5   The £1,000 worth of equipment is estimated to last 4 years. The £125 therefore represents 6 months' depreciation (£1,000 x 6/48). The cost is spread over the expected useful life of the equipment.

6   The other costs are cash based running costs that will appear both in this budget and in the cash budget.

Camper-Fans

Cash budget for the first six months

Details	Jan (£)	Feb (£)	March (£)	April (£)	May (£)	June (£)
Receipts:						
Capital Invested	20,000					
Cash Sales (1)	0	0	10,000	15,000	20,000	20,000
Total Receipts	20,000	0	10,000	15,000	20,000	20,000
Payments:						
Camper Vans (2)	9,000	6,000	12,000	12,000	12,000	12,000
Parts (3)	0	1,200	800	1,600	1,600	1,600
Rent (4)	4,000					
Other Costs (5)	400	400	400	400	400	400
Equipment (6)	1,000					
Drawings (7)	1,600	1,600	1,600	1,600	1,600	1,600
Total Payments	16,000	9,200	14,800	15,600	15,600	15,600
Cash Flow for Month	4,000	(9,200)	(4,800)	(600)	4,400	4,400
Bank Balance b/f	0	4,000	(5,200)	(10,000)	(10,600)	(6,200)
Bank Balance c/f	4,000	(5,200)	(10,000)	(10,600)	(6,200)	(1,800)

Notes

1   Since all the sales are for cash, the receipt will occur in the month that the sale is made. The figures are based on the numbers of camper vans to be sold at £5,000 each.

2   The ex-hire vans are purchased for cash. The figures are taken from the table produced at the start of this solution, at £3,000 each.

3   The parts are bought at £400 for each van at the same time as the van is purchased. They are bought on 1 month's credit, and therefore the figures in the cash budget are lagged by one month (eg parts bought in January are paid for in February).

4   The year's rent is paid in January.

5   'Other Costs' are paid in the month that they relate to.

6   Equipment (a capital expenditure item) is paid for in January.

7   Drawings of £800 each for Kylie and Jed are taken monthly.

The final main budget statement to be completed is the budgeted balance sheet. This cannot be completed until the other two documents have been finished, since their results feed into it. The balance sheet is shown here, followed by explanatory notes.

Camper-Fans
Budgeted Balance Sheet as at the end of June

	£	£	£
Fixed Assets:			
	Cost	Dep'n	Net Book Value
Equipment (1)	1,000	125	875
Current Assets:			
Stock of Camper Vans (2)		27,200	
Debtors (3)		0	
Prepayments (4)		2,000	
		29,200	
Less Current Liabilities:			
Creditors for Parts (5)	1,600		
Bank Overdraft (6)	1,800		
		3,400	
			25,800
Total Net Assets			26,675
Financed by:			
Capital Invested			20,000
Add Budgeted Profit (7)			16,275
Less Budgeted Drawings (8)			(9,600)
			26,675

Notes

1   The equipment is shown at cost less accumulated depreciation. Here the only depreciation so far is that for the first 6 months.

2   The stock of camper vans at the end of June is valued at cost; (the buying price of £3,000 plus the parts of £400) x 8 camper vans. The labour cost has been excluded since it forms drawings in this Case Study. Other stock valuation bases are also possible.

3   There are no debtors since all sales are on a cash basis.

4   The prepayments figure of £2,000 represents the rent for the second six months that has already been paid. It was excluded from the budgeted profit and loss account, and is an asset in the business at the end of June.

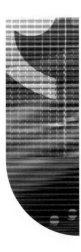

5   The creditor for parts has arisen because the parts are bought on credit. This figure represents the amount of parts bought in June, but not to be paid for until July, and therefore not shown in the cash budget.

6   The bank overdraft figure is the closing June balance taken from the cash budget.

7   The budgeted profit is taken from the budgeted profit & loss account.

8   The budgeted drawings are the amounts taken from the business by Kylie and Jed in the six months. The figure is the same as the one shown in the cash budget.

DEALING WITH ESTABLISHED BUSINESSES

In this chapter so far we have seen how a cash budget and budgeted balance sheet can be prepared for a new business. If we need to prepare these documents for a business that is already trading the main principles are identical. The only extra factor to account for is the cash impact in this budget period of transactions that occurred in the previous budget period. These will typically be:

• receipts in this period from sales made in the last period, and

• payments in this period related to purchases or expenses incurred in the last period

Since these amounts will show up as debtors or creditors in the balance sheet at the end of the previous period, we can normally pick up the data from this source. We will then just need to check when the cash receipt or payment is expected to occur to be able to insert the right figures into our cash budget.

For example, if we are producing a cash budget for January to March, we will need information about the debtors and creditors at the end of the previous December.

Suppose the December debtors figure is £20,000, made up of November sales of £12,000 and December sales of £8,000. If the credit customers pay on two months' credit, we will need to include in our cash budget:

• £12,000 receipt in January (in respect of November sales), and

• £8,000 receipt in February (in respect of December sales)

If we are provided with a balance sheet at the end of the preceding period, then the cash / bank figure shown there will form the opening cash balance figure for our cash budget. We will now use a Case Study to see how this approach fits alongside the techniques that we used earlier.

MOORE TRADING:
BUDGETS FOR AN ESTABLISHED BUSINESS

situation

Jane Moore has been trading for several years. She has prepared the following budgeted profit and loss account for the first four months trading of her year 10. Jane sells goods on two months' credit, and pays for purchases on one months' credit.

Budgeted Profit & Loss Account, January - April Year 10

	£	£
Sales		30,000
less cost of sales:		
opening stock	5,000	
purchases	21,000	
less closing stock	(6,000)	
		20,000
Gross profit		10,000
less:		
cash expenses	4,000	
depreciation	2,000	
		6,000
Net profit		4,000

Jane also provides you with the following information regarding her plans for the part of year 10 covered by her budgets.

• The sales figures in the budgeted profit & loss account are based on monthly sales as follows:

	£
January	6,000
February	7,000
March	8,000
April	9,000
Total sales	30,000

- The purchases figure in the budgeted profit and loss account is made up as follows:

	£
January	4,000
February	6,000
March	6,000
April	5,000
Total purchases	21,000

- Cash expenses are based on paying out £1,000 in each of the first four months year 10.

- The depreciation shown in the budgeted profit and loss account is based on depreciating equipment at 20% per year on a straight-line basis. Equipment that cost £20,000 was purchased in January of year 9. Further equipment is to be bought for £10,000 in January year 10.

- Jane wishes to withdraw £1,500 from the business in each of the months of February and April in year 10.

- Bank interest is to be ignored.

The draft balance sheet has already been prepared as at the end of year 9, and an extract is shown here. Notes on the balance sheet follow on the next page.

Moore Trading

Balance Sheet Extract as at 31 December Year 9

	£	£	£
Fixed Assets			
	Cost	*Dep'n*	*Net*
Equipment	20,000	4,000	16,000
Current Assets:			
Stock		5,000	
Debtors		11,000	
Bank		10,000	
		26,000	
Less Current Liabilities:			
Trade Creditors		4,000	
			22,000
Total Net Assets			38,000

Notes on the balance sheet:

- The debtors relates to sales of £6,500 in November and £4,500 in December. These sales are on two months credit.

- The trade creditors relate to December purchases. Payment is due to be made in January.

- The business is financed entirely by the capital account.

Required

Prepare a cash budget for the first four months of year 10, and a budgeted balance sheet as at 30 April, year 10.

Solution

Moore Trading: Cash Budget for January to April of Year 10.

	January £	February £	March £	April £
Receipts				
Receipts from year 9 sales	6,500	4,500	-	-
Receipts from year 10 sales	-	-	6,000	7,000
Total Receipts	6,500	4,500	6,000	7,000
Payments				
Purchases made in year 9	4,000	-	-	-
Purchases made in year 10	-	4,000	6,000	6,000
Expenses	1,000	1,000	1,000	1,000
Fixed Assets	10,000	-	-	-
Drawings	-	1,500	-	1,500
Total Payments	15,000	6,500	7,000	8,500
Cash Flow for Month	(8,500)	(2,000)	(1,000)	(1,500)
Bank Balance brought forward	10,000	1,500	(500)	(1,500)
Bank Balance carried forward	1,500	(500)	(1,500)	(3,000)

The receipts and payments figures arising from each year have been shown here as separate lines for clarity, but this is not always required. The opening balance in January of £10,000 is taken from the bank balance in the balance sheet extract.

Make sure that you can see where each figure in the cash budget has come from, before examining the budgeted balance sheet shown on the next page.

Moore Trading

Budgeted Balance Sheet as at 30 April Year 10

	£	£	£
Fixed Assets			
	Cost	*Dep'n*	*Net Book Value*
Equipment (1)	30,000	6,000	24,000
Current Assets:			
Stock (2)		6,000	
Debtors (3)		17,000	
		23,000	
Less **Current Liabilities**			
Trade Creditors (4)	5,000		
Bank Overdraft (5)	3,000		
		8,000	
			15,000
Total Net Assets			39,000
Financed by:			
Capital account as at 31 December year 9 (6)			38,000
Add budgeted profit for four months			4,000
			42,000
Less drawings			(3,000)
			39,000

Notes

(1) The additional fixed assets are added to those previously acquired, and the depreciation shown is the cumulative amount.

(2) The stock figure is the closing stock from the budgeted profit and loss account.

(3) The debtors figure represents the credit sales made in March and April.

(4) Trade creditors represent the amount owed for April purchases.

(5) The bank overdraft is the final balance from the cash budget.

(6) The opening capital figure is the total net assets at 31 December.

- Most of the data that is used to prepare a cash budget is also used to prepare a budgeted profit and loss account. In a cash budget the receipts and payments are accounted for on the basis of the time at which the cash flows, rather than on an accruals basis. Some data from other sources is also used in a cash budget.

- When sales or purchases that are made on credit are inserted into a cash budget the entries are lagged based on the credit terms to be applied. For example receipts from sales made on two months' credit would be lagged by two months, and entered in the cash budget two months after the sale was made.

- The budgeted balance sheet at the end of the budget period links with the cash budget. It includes amounts under debtors and creditors that were not included in the cash budget because the receipt or payment of cash would not have taken place in the budget period.

- When preparing a cash budget for an existing business, the opening cash balance will often be taken from the balance sheet of the same date. Debtors and creditors shown on the same balance sheet will also need to be accounted for in the cash budget based on the expected dates of the receipt or the payment.

cash budget	a budget that sets out the inflows and outflows of cash in a budget period – the receipts and payments format is the most suitable form of cash budget for monitoring and controlling cash in a business.
lagging	accounting for the time difference between a credit sale or purchase and the cash receipt or payment.
budgeted profit & loss account	one of the main summary budgets that can be prepared for the budget period, in the same format as a historical profit and loss account.
budgeted balance sheet	normally prepared in the same format as a historical balance sheet – it is usually prepared on basis of the final day of the budget period
master budget	the combination of the budgeted profit & loss account and the budgeted balance sheet

Student Activities

answers to the asterisked (*) questions are to be found at the back of this book

2.1* Sonita is planning to open a retail shop. The following is her budgeted profit & loss account for the first four months of the business.

	£	£
Sales		40,000
less cost of sales:		
opening stock	0	
purchases	30,000	
less closing stock	(5,000)	
		25,000
Gross profit		15,000
less:		
cash expenses	8,000	
depreciation	2,000	
		10,000
Net profit		5,000

Sonita also provides you with the following information regarding her plans.

- Sales are to be made only for cash (not on credit). The figure in the profit and loss account represents £10,000 sales for each of the four months.

- Purchases made in the first month must be paid for immediately. Subsequent purchases will be on one month's credit. The purchases figure in the budgeted profit and loss account is made up as follows:

	£
Month 1	9,000
Month 2	8,000
Month 3	7,000
Month 4	6,000
Total purchases	30,000

- Cash expenses are based on paying out £2,000 in each of the first four months of the business.

- Equipment is to be bought for £30,000 in the first month of the business. The depreciation shown in the budgeted profit and loss account is based on depreciating these assets at 20% per year on a straight-line basis.

- Sonita has £35,000 to invest in the business in month one. The business has no opening cash balance.

- Sonita wishes to withdraw £1,000 from the business in each of the first four months of trading (a total of £4,000).

- Bank interest can be ignored.

Required

- Prepare a cash budget in receipts and payments format for the first four months trading of Sonita's business.

- Prepare a budgeted balance sheet as at the end of month four of the business.

2.2* Jim Smith has recently been made redundant; he has received a redundancy payment and this, together with his accumulated savings, amounts to £10,000. He has decided to set up his own business selling computer stationery and will start trading with an initial capital of £10,000 on 1 January. On this date he will buy a van for business use at a cost of £6,000. He has estimated his purchases, sales, and expenses for the next six months as follows:

	Purchases £	Sales £	Expenses £
January	4,500	1,250	750
February	4,500	3,000	600
March	3,500	4,000	600
April	3,500	4,000	650
May	3,500	4,500	650
June	4,000	6,000	700

He will pay for purchases in the month after purchase and expects his customers to pay for sales in the month after sale. All expenses will be paid for in the month in which they are incurred.

Jim realises that he may need bank overdraft facilities before his business becomes established. He asks you to help him with information for the bank and, in particular, he asks you to prepare the following:

Required

(a)   a month-by-month cash budget for the first six months

(b)   a budgeted profit and loss account for the first six months – for this he tells you that his closing stock at 30 June is expected to have a value of £3,250, and that he wishes to depreciate the van at 20% per annum.

(c)   A budgeted balance sheet as at 30 June

2.3   Sarah is planning to start a trading business. The following is her budgeted profit & loss account for the first three months of the business (before overdraft interest).

	£	£
Sales		50,000
less cost of sales:		
opening stock	0	
purchases	40,000	
less closing stock	(10,000)	
		30,000
Gross profit		20,000
less:		
rent	1,000	
cash expenses	6,000	
depreciation	2,000	
		9,000
Net profit		11,000

Sarah also provides you with the following information regarding her plans.

- Sales are to be made on credit. Although she will formally offer one month's credit, she wishes the budgets to assume that only 75% of the sales will be paid in this time, and 25% of the sales will take two months before the cash is received. The sales figure in the profit and loss account represents the following monthly sales:

Month 1	£10,000
Month 2	£16,000
Month 3	£24,000
	£50,000

- All purchases will be on one month's credit. The purchases figure in the budgeted profit and loss account is made up as follows:

Month 1	£10,000
Month 2	£14,000
Month 3	£16,000
Total purchases	£40,000

- The annual rent of £4,000 is payable at the start of month 1.

- Cash expenses are based on paying out £2,000 in each of the first three months of the business.

- Equipment is to be bought for £32,000 in the first month of the business. The depreciation shown in the budgeted profit and loss account is based on depreciating these fixed assets at 25% per year on a straight-line basis.

- Sarah has £40,000 to invest in the business in month one. The business has no opening cash balance.

- Sarah wishes to withdraw £2,000 from the business in each of the first three months of trading.

- Overdraft interest for each month is calculated at 1% of the month's overdrawn balance at the beginning of the month, and is paid during the month.

Required

- Prepare a cash budget in receipts and payments format for the first three months trading of Sarah's business.

- Prepare a budgeted balance sheet as at the end of month three of the business.

2.4   The balance sheet of Antonio's Speciality Food Shop at 31 August 2005 was:

	£ Cost	£ Dep'n	£ Net
Fixed assets	15,000	3,000	12,000
Current assets			
Stocks		5,000	
Debtors		800	
		5,800	
Less current liabilities			
Creditors	3,000		
Bank overdraft	1,050		
		4,050	
Working capital			1,750
NET ASSETS			13,750
FINANCED BY			
Antonio's capital			13,750

On the basis of past performance, Antonio expects that his sales during the coming six months will be:

September	October	November	December	January	February
£8,000	£8,000	£10,000	£20,000	£6,000	£6,000

Antonio allows credit to some of his regular customers, and the proportions of cash and credit sales are usually:

	Cash sales	Credit sales
November	80%	20%
December	60%	40%
All other months	90%	10%

Customers who buy on credit normally pay in the following month. Antonio's gross profit margin is consistently 25 per cent of his selling price. He normally maintains his stocks at a constant level by purchasing goods in the month in which they are sold: the only exception to this is that in November he purchases in advance 50 per cent of the goods he expects to sell in December.

Half of the purchases each month are made from suppliers who give a 2 per cent prompt payment discount for immediate payment and he takes advantage of the discount. He pays for the remainder (without discount) in the month after purchase.

Expenditure on wages, rent and other running expenses of the shop are consistently £2,000 per month, paid in the month in which they are incurred.

Fixed assets are depreciated at 10 per cent per annum on cost price.

Required

(a) • prepare a cash budget showing Antonio's bank balance or overdraft for each month in the half-year ending 28 February 2006

• prepare a budgeted profit and loss account for the six months to 28 February 2006

• prepare Antonio's balance sheet at 28 February 2006

(b) If Antonio's bank manager considered it necessary to fix the overdraft limit at £3,500, explain what Antonio should do in order to observe the limit.

2.5 Pete Still has been trading for several years. He has prepared the following budgeted profit and loss account for the first four months trading of 2006. Pete sells goods on two months' credit, and pays for purchases on one months' credit.

Still Trading Budgeted Profit & Loss Account, January – April 2006		
	£	£
Sales		60,000
less cost of sales:		
opening stock	9,000	
purchases	38,000	
less closing stock	(6,000)	
		41,000
Gross profit		19,000
less:		
cash expenses	8,000	
depreciation	5,000	
		13,000
Net profit		6,000

Pete also provides you with the following information regarding his plans for the first 4 months of 2006.

- The sales figures in the budgeted profit & loss account are based on monthly sales as follows:

	£
January	16,000
February	12,000
March	15,000
April	17,000
Total sales	60,000

- The purchases figure in the budgeted profit and loss account is made up as follows:

	£
January	8,000
February	9,000
March	10,000
April	11,000
Total purchases	38,000

- Cash expenses are based on paying out £2,000 in each of the first four months of 2006.

- The depreciation shown in the budgeted profit and loss account is based on depreciating equipment at 25% per year on a straight-line basis. Equipment that cost £30,000 was purchased in January of 2004. Further equipment is to be bought for £30,000 in January 2006.

- Pete wishes to withdraw £2,000 from the business in each of the months of February and April 2006.

- Bank interest can be ignored.

The draft balance sheet has already been prepared as at the end of December 2005, and an extract is shown on the next page.

Still Trading

Balance Sheet Extract as at 31 December 2005

	£	£	£
Fixed Assets	*Cost*	*Dep'n*	*Net*
Equipment	30,000	15,000	15,000
Current Assets			
Stock		9,000	
Debtors		21,000	
Bank		10,000	
		40,000	
Less Current Liabilities			
Trade Creditors		8,000	
			32,000
Total Net Assets			47,000

Notes

- The debtors relates to sales of £12,000 in November and £9,000 in December. These sales are on two months credit.

- The trade creditors relate to December purchases. Payment is due to be made in January.

- The business is financed entirely by the capital account.

Required

Prepare a cash budget for the first four months of 2006, and a budgeted balance sheet as at 30 April, 2006.

In this chapter we concentrate on the production of budgets for manufacturing businesses and examine some of the statistical techniques used for preparing the figures used in the budgeting process. We cover specifically:

- the preparation of production and resource budgets for a manufacturing business

- the preparation of a cash budget for a manufacturing business

- the use of time series analysis to estimate future trends

PERFORMANCE CRITERIA COVERED

unit 15 OPERATING A CASH MANAGEMENT AND CREDIT CONTROL SYSTEM

element 15.1
Monitor and control cash receipts and payments

B   Consult appropriate staff to determine the likely pattern of cash flows over the accounting period and to anticipate any exceptional receipts or payments.

C   Ensure forecasts of future cash payments and receipts are in accord with known income and expenditure trends.

D   Prepare cash budgets in the approved format and clearly indicate net cash requirements.

KNOWLEDGE AND UNDERSTANDING COVERAGE

12   Form and structure of cash budgets.

13   Lagged receipts and payments.

27   Understanding that recording and accounting practice may vary in different parts of the organisation.

31   An understanding of the organisation's relevant policies and procedures.

BUDGETS FOR MANUFACTURING BUSINESSES

links with your other studies

In this book so far we have concentrated on the way in which cash budgets can be prepared for trading organisations. In this section we will apply what we have learnt to the more complex situation of a manufacturing organisation. Some of the issues that we will look at here are also relevant to Unit 9 (NVQ route) and Unit 33 (Diploma Pathway), and you will find your studies of these Units complementary.

types of budget

Because a manufacturing organisation is typically more complex than a business that just buys and sells, there is a wider range of budgets that may be used to build up to the master budget and the cash budget. The budgets will all need to be based on the same set of assumptions about the way that the organisation operates, and will have been built up around estimates of the 'key budget factor' – usually the sales forecast. The budgets would typically include:

- **sales budget** – usually generated directly from the key factor forecast data.

- **production budget** – based on the sales budget together with the anticipated finished goods stock levels.

- **materials usage budget** – based on the production budget.

- **materials purchases budget** – based on the materials usage budget, together with the anticipated materials stock levels.

- **labour utilisation budget** – also based on the production budget.

- various **functional budgets** to support the operation, for example the administration budget, and the finance budget.

- a **capital expenditure budget** would also have to be developed in conjunction with the above revenue budgets to ensure that the agreed spending on new or replacement equipment etc was in place.

- the **cash budget** would then be developed to take account of the data in the above budgets, as we will see shortly.

The effect of all the revenue and capital budgets is finally consolidated into the **master budget**. This would take the form of a budgeted profit and loss account and balance sheet for the whole business.

a note on stock levels

You will have noticed several references in the above list of budgets to **stock levels**. Where stock levels are to remain constant the situation is simple. For example the production budget will be identical to the sales budget if the finished goods stock level is to remain unchanged. However if the stock level is to increase then the extra units of goods that will go into stock will need to be produced in addition to the units that are to be sold immediately. This is a concept that is important throughout budgeting, including the preparation of the cash budget.

The diagram below shows how the main budgets used in a manufacturing business fit together, and how the data is used in the cash budget.

This diagram, for the sake of clarity, concentrates on issues that are specific to the creation of a cash budget for a manufacturing business. Other data (eg disbursements, capital items and financing) also need to be accounted for in the cash budget, as discussed in the last chapter.

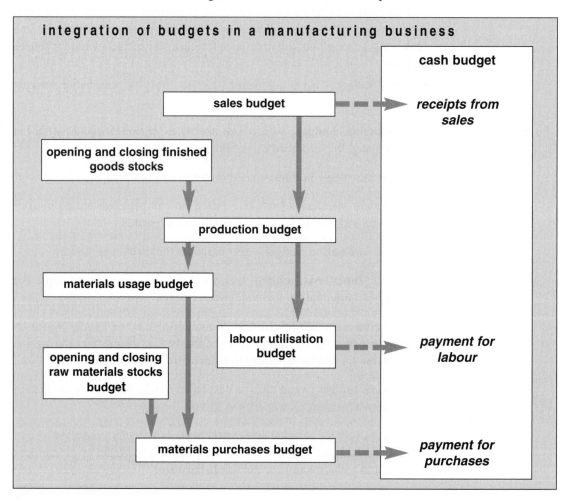

PREPARING A PRODUCTION BUDGET

As we can see from the diagram on the previous page, the budgets that provide sources for much of the data in the cash budget are:

- sales budget (as also seen in a trading business)
- labour utilisation budget
- materials purchases budget

Both the **labour utilisation** budget (also known as the **labour** budget) and the **materials purchases** budget rely on the production budget having been prepared, so we will now see how that is carried out.

The forecast of **sales units** (units that will be sold) will need to be developed first, as this is fundamental to the whole series of budgets. The level of actual production that is required will depend primarily on the required movement in finished goods stocks.

If you have studied Unit 9 (NVQ route students) you will be aware that rejection of production units is also an issue that should be considered when creating a production budget. In this unit we do not have to deal with that complexity, nor the wastage of raw materials. We will therefore need to plan to produce the units that we intend to sell, but we can budget to change stock levels ,ie:

- reduce our production by the intended fall in finished goods stock, or
- increase our production to build up our finished goods stock.

The **production budget** will project the number of units to be produced in a period using the formula:

> *Budgeted Sales Units*
> − *Opening Stock of Finished Goods*
> + *Closing Stock of Finished Goods*
> = *Production Budget*

This can be justified because:

- the opening stock of finished goods has already been produced, and can therefore be deducted from our calculation of what needs to be made, and
- the closing stock has yet to be made so needs to be added in to our total of goods to be produced

In summary:

- if stocks of finished goods are to increase, then production must be greater than sales
- if finished goods stocks are to remain constant, production will be the same as sales

budgets for materials usage and labour

After the production budget has been developed in units, we can then calculate the quantity of material we need to use and the amount of labour time required.

The **materials usage budget** is created to calculate the amount of raw material that will be used in production. The **labour utilisation budget** is usually based on labour time in hours, but it could be converted into an equivalent number of full-time employees. Any shortfall in the available number of personnel will become clear at this stage as will any anticipated requirement for overtime working. The payment of labour as calculated in the labour utilisation budget will feed directly into the cash budget.

The materials **purchases** budget can be created after the materials **usage** budget has been established. Here differences between the quantity of material to be consumed in production and the quantity to be purchased will depend primarily on the required movement in raw material goods stocks.

The reasoning follows a similar pattern to the one described for sales, finished goods and production. If we already have raw materials in the opening stock this amount does not have to be purchased, but the quantity that we plan to have in stock at the end of the period must be purchased in addition to the amount that will be used in production.

The **quantity of material purchased** (as recorded in the material purchases budget) will therefore equal:

Quantity of material to be used (per materials usage budget)

− *opening stock of raw materials,*

+ *closing stock of raw materials*

= *quantity of materials purchased*

The link between purchases and raw materials stocks can be summarised as:

- if stocks of raw materials are to increase, then purchases must be greater than materials usage
- if raw material stocks are to remain constant purchases will be the same as materials usage
- if raw materials stocks are to fall purchases will be less than materials usage

One vital reason for creating a materials purchases budget is that the information on the timing of purchases will feed into the cash budget, based on the time at which payments to suppliers will need to be made.

The Case Study that follows will illustrate the procedure used to prepare a production budget that is then used to prepare the materials usage and purchases budgets. The purchases budget will then provide the source of data for the cash budget.

Case Study

ANFIELD LIMITED:
PREPARING PRODUCTION AND MATERIALS BUDGETS

situation

A manufacturing company, Anfield Limited, makes a single product, the Trophy. The sales forecast for February is 5,900 units. Each unit of Trophy uses 5 kilos of Mersey and 3 kilos of Gatt.

The anticipated stocks at the beginning of February are:

Finished Trophies	1,400 units
Unused Mersey	350 kilos
Unused Gatt	200 kilos

The required stocks levels at the end of February are:

Finished Trophies	1,800 units
Unused Mersey	250 kilos
Unused Gatt	450 kilos

required

1   Produce the following budget figures for the month of February:

(a)   Production of Trophies (in units)

(b)   Materials usage of Mersey and Gatt (in kilos)

(c)   Materials purchases of Mersey and Gatt (in kilos)

2   Explain how the data produced in the above budgets will be used in the cash budget

solution

1 (a)   Production units =

Budgeted Sales Units	5,900	
– Opening Stock of Finished Goods	(1,400)	
+ Closing Stock of Finished Goods.	1,800	
Production units =	6,300	Trophies

(b)   Materials Usage

Mersey: 6,300 x 5 kilos	= 31,500	kilos
Gatt: 6,300 x 3 kilos	= 18,900	kilos

(c) Materials purchases:

Mersey:

Quantity of material to be used	31,500	kilos
– opening stock of raw materials,	(350	kilos)
+ closing stock of raw materials.	250	kilos
Required purchases of Mersey	31,400	kilos

Gatt:

Quantity of material to be used	18,900	kilos
– opening stock of raw materials,	(200	kilos)
+ closing stock of raw materials.	450	kilos
Required purchases of Gatt	19,150	kilos

2   The completed purchases budgets for Mersey and Gatt will be used to help prepare the cash budget. This will be done by valuing the quantities to be purchased, and lagging the results by the credit period obtained from the supplier.

budgets for consecutive periods, and links with the cash budget

The above Case Study was based on one period – the month of February, but the process is identical if we wish to generate a series of budgets for consecutive periods. Remember that the closing stock values for one period will be the same as the opening stocks for the next period, and so on.

It is also a straightforward matter to incorporate values as well as quantities in the budgets if standard costs (or alternative estimates of value) are available. It is then quite logical to see how the data will fit into a cash budget. We will demonstrate how this works with our next Case Study.

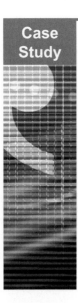

Case Study

HIGHBURY LIMITED: PREPARING CASH BUDGET DATA

situation

Highbury Limited produces a single product, the Highbury. Each Highbury has cost data as follows:

• 3 kilos raw material at £8.00 per kilo

• 2 hours labour at £6.00 per hour

The forecast sales level of Highburys for the first quarter of the next financial year is as follows:

January	11,800	units
February	12,400	units
March	12,100	units

The forecast stock levels on 1 January are:

    Finished Units of Highbury 5,800

    Raw materials   8,000 kilos.

Highbury Limited plans to reduce the raw material stock by 500 kilos in each month of the first quarter, and to increase the number of finished Highburys in stock by 2,000 each month in anticipation of a sales drive in the second quarter.

The following data is relevant to the cash budget.

* Highburys sell for £80 each, and sales are made on two months' credit.

* Purchases of raw materials are made on one month's credit.

* Labour costs are paid for in the month that they are incurred.

required

1   Produce the following budgets for each of the months of January, February and March.

   (a)   Production of Highburys (in units)

   (b)   Usage of Raw Material (in kilos and £)

   (c)   Purchases of Raw Material (in kilos and £)

   (d)   Labour Utilisation (in hours and £)

2   Using the information generated in Task 1, show extracts from the cash budget for January to May relating to sales receipts, payment for purchases, and payment for labour costs.

solution

Task 1

(a) Production of Highburys

	January	February	March
Forecast Sales Units	11,800	12,400	12,100
Less opening stock finished units	(5,800)	(7,800)	(9,800)
Add closing stock finished units	7,800	9,800	11,800
Production Units	13,800	14,400	14,100

The calculation could alternatively have been carried out by adding each month's increase in finished goods stock to the sales forecast.

(b) Usage of Raw Materials

	January	February	March
Production Units (per (a))	13,800	14,400	14,100
Usage Raw Materials (at 3 kilo per unit)	41,400 kg	43,200 kg	42,300 kg
Cost of Raw Materials Used (at £8.00 per kilo)	£331,200	£345,600	£338,400

(c) **Materials Purchases**

	January	February	March
Usage Raw Materials (per (b))	41,400 kg	43,200 kg	42,300 kg
Less opening stock of Raw Materials	(8,000 kg)	(7,500 kg)	(7,000 kg)
Add closing stock of Raw Materials	7,500 kg	7,000 kg	6,500 kg
Raw Materials Purchases	40,900 kg	42,700 kg	41,800 kg
Cost of Raw Materials Purchases (at £8.00 per kilo)	£327,200	£341,600	£334,400

(d) **Labour Utilisation**

	January	February	March
Production Units (per (a))	13,800	14,400	14,100
Utilisation of Labour (at 2 hours per unit)	27,600 hrs	28,800 hrs	28,200 hrs
Cost of Labour (at £6.00 per hour)	£165,600	£172,800	£169,200

Task 2: Cash Budget (Extract)

	Jan £	Feb £	March £	April £	May £
Receipts					
Sales			944,000	992,000	968,000
Payments					
Purchases of raw materials		327,200	341,600	334,400	
Labour	165,600	172,800	169,200		

In a full cash budget there would of course also be:

• receipts and payments relating to earlier transactions

• other categories of receipts and payments

• net cash flow for the month

• the bank/cash position at the beginning and the end of the month

dealing with overheads

Manufacturing overheads are dealt with in a cash budget in a similar way to trading expenses. They are usually mainly cash based, and may be paid for immediately, or on credit, according to the organisation's policy. If the overheads are described as fixed they will be the same irrespective of production levels. Variable overheads will depend upon the level of production as stated in the production budget for that particular month. A variable overheads cost will often be provided based on an amount per unit of production (eg £10 per unit produced).

a warning note on depreciation

One issue to watch out for is that where overheads include **depreciation** of fixed assets, this amount is not cash based, and therefore **must be deducted from the overheads** before the figure is inserted into the cash budget.

accounting policies

We will shortly use a further Case Study to consolidate our understanding of some of the issues covered so far. In this Case Study we will use the idea of 'standard costs', as you may have studied in Unit 8 'Contributing to the management of performance and the enhancement of value' (if you are taking the NVQ qualification). If you are not familiar with the term, just think of standard costs as costs worked out in advance for each product.

Accounting policies will vary between different organisations, and even within the same organisation the data will need to be obtained in various forms. If there is a formal system like standard costing in use throughout the organisation then data should be easy to collect for budgets. In other situations we may need to collect data from different sources, since the accounting practices may lead to fragmentation of information. For example forecast sales figures (in units) may be available from the Sales Director while sales prices may be authorised by the Managing Director. The credit terms on offer to customers and the level of discounts may be agreed by the Finance Director.

The policies and procedures of each organisation must therefore be taken into account when gathering together the data for budgets.

Case Study

JEAN-E-US:
PREPARING MANUFACTURING BUDGETS

situation

Jean-E-Us makes denim jeans that are sold to various clothing wholesalers. The company uses standard costing to help plan and control its costs.

The company is now preparing its budgets for the first three months of next year, and has provided the following data:

The standard cost of one pair of jeans is calculated as follows:

Direct materials: 3 square metres at £2.50 per square metre	£7.50
Direct labour: 45 minutes at £5.60 per hour	£4.20
Fixed overheads: £20,000 ÷ 2,500 pairs jeans per month	£8.00
Total standard cost per pair	£19.70

The jeans sell for £25.00 per pair to wholesalers on one month's credit.

Forecast sales levels are:		
	January	2,200 pairs
	February	2,500 pairs
	March	2,800 pairs
	April	2,200 pairs

The stock of finished jeans at the month-end is planned to equal half of the next month's forecast sales level.

The stock of raw materials held at each month-end is to be sufficient for half of the following month's production. At the end of March this stock is to be 3,750 sq metres.

Raw materials purchases are made on one month's credit.

The fixed overheads of £20,000 per month include £3,000 depreciation on existing fixed assets. There are no planned purchases of further fixed assets. All the other fixed overheads are paid for in the month they are incurred.

Bank interest at 0.4% per month is received monthly, based on the month's opening bank balance.

A summary of the balance sheet of Jean-E-Us at the end of December preceding the budget period is shown on the next page, with workings where necessary.

JEAN-E-US: SUMMARY BALANCE SHEET AS AT 31 DECEMBER		
	£	£
Fixed Assets: (Cost £144,000, cumulative depreciation £36,000)		108,000
Current Assets:		
Stocks: Finished goods (1,100 pairs at £19.70)	21,670	
Raw materials (3,525 square metres at £2.50)	8,813	
Debtors (re December sales)	62,500	
Bank	10,000	
	102,983	
Current Liabilities:		
Creditors (re December purchases)	18,750	
		84,233
Total Net Assets		192,233
Capital as at December 31		192,233

required

Prepare the following budgets for Jean-E-Us for the months of January, February and March, using standard costs where appropriate.

- Production budget (in pairs of jeans)
- Labour utilisation budget (in hours and £)
- Materials usage budget (in square metres of denim)
- Materials purchases budget (in square metres and £)

Using the data from these budgets, prepare a set of master budgets for the quarter, together with a cash budget in months.

solution

The **production budget** is worked out in pairs of jeans, taking account of planned finished goods stock levels, as follows:

	January	February	March
Forecast Sales	2,200	2,500	2,800
Less opening stocks	(1,100)	(1,250)	(1,400)
Add closing stocks	1,250	1,400	1,100
Production Budget	2,350	2,650	2,500

The **labour utilisation budget** (or labour budget) uses the pairs of jeans from the production budget, and multiplies it by the time for each pair of jeans (45 minutes). This time is then valued at the standard hourly rate (£5.60).

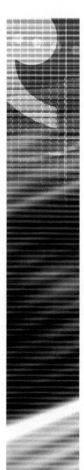

	January	February	March
Labour Budget (hours)	1,762.5	1,987.5	1,875
Labour Budget (£)	£9,870	£11,130	£10,500

The **materials usage budget** uses the pairs of jeans from the production budget, and multiplies it by the standard amount of denim needed to make each pair of jeans (3 square metres).

	January	February	March
Materials Usage Budget (square metres)	7,050	7,950	7,500

The **materials purchases budget** is worked out in square metres of denim, starting with the materials usage budget, and taking account of the required levels of raw materials stocks.

	January	February	March
Materials Usage Budget	7,050	7,950	7,500
Less opening stock of Raw Materials	(3,525)	(3,975)	(3,750)
Add closing stock of Raw Materials	3,975	3,750	3,750
Materials Purchases (square metres)	7,500	7,725	7,500
Materials Purchases (£)	£18,750	£19,312	£18,750

The cash budget can now be prepared using data from the previous balance sheet and that produced in the separate additional budgets.

Jean-E-Us – Cash Budget for the period January – March

	January £	February £	March £
Receipts:			
From Debtors/Sales (1)	62,500	55,000	62,500
Interest received	40	108	141
Total receipts	62,540	55,108	62,641
Payments:			
Creditors/Purchases (2)	18,750	18,750	19,312
Labour (3)	9,870	11,130	10,500
Fixed Overheads (4)	17,000	17,000	17,000
Total Payments	45,620	46,880	46,812
Cash Flow for month	16,920	8,228	15,829
Bank balance at beginning of the month (5)	10,000	26,920	35,148
Bank balance at the end of of the month	26,920	35,148	50,977

1   The January receipts are the December sales that are shown as debtors in the balance sheet at the end of December. The lagged receipts in February and March relate to the forecast sales at £25 per pair made in January and February respectively (to allow for the one month credit given on invoices).

2   The January payment is the creditor from the December balance sheet. The following two payments are from the materials purchases budget for January and February. Payments occur one month after purchase (again to allow for the one month credit terms).

3   The labour costs are taken from the labour utilisation budget. There is no time delay with these payments.

4   The fixed overheads relate to the monthly amount of £20,000, less the depreciation included in that figure of £3,000 per month.

5   The opening bank balance in January is taken from the balance sheet at the end of the preceding December.

The **budgeted profit and loss account** can be prepared. Because it is affected by interest received, it cannot be finalised until after the cash budget has been prepared.

Jean-E-Us: Budgeted Profit and Loss Account for January – March	
	£
Sales (7,500 pairs of jeans at £25)	187,500
Less cost of goods sold:	
(7,500 pairs of jeans at £19.70)	147,750
Operating Profit	39,750
Add Interest Receivable	289
Total Profit	40,039

This budget has been prepared in summary form for simplicity, but could be shown in more detail by using the separate elements of the standard costs. Since the planned production is 7,500 pairs of jeans, each pair absorbing £8, this will exactly cover the quarter's fixed costs of £60,000.

We can now complete the **budgeted balance sheet**. The document is shown below, followed by explanatory notes on the next page.

Jean-E-Us: Budgeted Balance Sheet as at 31 March			
	£	£	£
Fixed Assets	Cost	Dep'n	Net
Equipment (1)	144,000	45,000	99,000
Current Assets			
Stocks			
Finished Goods (2)	21,670		
Raw Materials (3)	9,375		
Debtors (4)	70,000		
Bank (5)	50,977		
	152,022		

continued on next page

Less **Current Liabilities**		
Creditors for Purchases (6)	18,750	
		133,272
Total Net Assets		232,272
Financed by:		
Capital at 31 Dec		192,233
Add Budgeted Profit (7)		40,039
		232,272

Notes

(1) The equipment depreciation is increased by the £3,000 x 3 months that relates to the budget period.

(2) Finished Goods stocks are based on those used in the production budget, valued at the standard cost of £19.70 per pair.

(3) Raw Materials stocks are the 3,750 square metres given in the case study (and used in the workings for the materials purchases budget), valued at standard cost of £2.50 per square metre.

(4) Debtors relates to the forecast March sales of 2,800 pairs of jeans at £25 per pair.

(5) The forecast bank balance is taken from the cash budget.

(6) The creditors amount is taken from the March purchases budget, since the payments are made on one month's credit.

(7) The budgeted profit is taken from the budgeted profit & loss account for the three months.

TIME SERIES ANALYSIS

When preparing a cash budget, or the forecasts on which it is based, there are some statistical techniques that may help us to arrive at valid estimates. You may have come across these techniques in other units that you have studied. If you have studied this area previously you should find that the next few pages cover familiar ground.

Time series analysis is concerned with numerical ways that the past can be used to forecast the future. The term **trend analysis** is also used to describe the technique that we will now examine. It is useful as a tool to help us to forecast future sales units, but it can also be used in other circumstances, as we will see later on in this section.

At its simplest, the idea is based on the assumption that data will continue to move in the same direction in the future as it has in the past.

For example, suppose the following are the number of pairs of shoes that are sold by a shoe manufacturer over the last few months:

Month 1	10,000
Month 2	11,000
Month 3	12,000
Month 4	13,000
Month 5	14,000
Month 6	15,000
Month 7	16,000

It does not require a great deal of arithmetic to calculate that if the trend continues at the previous rate then shoe sales could be forecast at 17,000 pairs in Month 8 and 18,000 pairs in Month 9. Of course this is a very simple example, and life is rarely this straightforward. It is also worth wondering for how long this rate of increase is sustainable.

Before we move on, we will examine the techniques available to forecast simple data. They will become very useful later.

When each monthly change is identical . . .

What you probably did was to see that in each month the sales were 1,000 pairs of shoes more than the previous month. Using the last known figure of 16,000 pairs of shoes in Month 7, we can then add 1,000 to arrive at a forecast of 17,000 pairs in Month 8, and so on.

Calculating the average monthly change . . .

A slightly more complicated technique could have been used to arrive at the same answer. If we compare the number of sales in Month 7 with the number in Month 1, we can see that it has risen by 6,000 pairs. By dividing that figure by the number of times the month changed in our data we can arrive at an average change per month. The number of times that the month changes is 6, which is the same as the number of "spaces" between the months, or the total number of months minus 1. Shown as an equation this becomes:

Average Monthly Sales Change   =

$$\frac{\textit{(Sales in Final Month – Sales in First Month)}}{\textit{(Number of Months – 1)}}$$

$$= \quad \frac{(16,000 - 10,000)}{(7 - 1)}$$

$$= \quad + 1,000 \ldots \text{which is what we would expect.}$$

The +1,000 would then be added to the sales data in Month 7 of 16,000 (the last actual data) to arrive at a forecast of 17,000 for Month 8.

This technique is useful when all the increases are not quite identical, yet we want to use the average increase to forecast the trend.

constructing a graph

The same result can be produced graphically. Using the same shoe shop example we can extend the graph based on the actual data to form a forecast line.

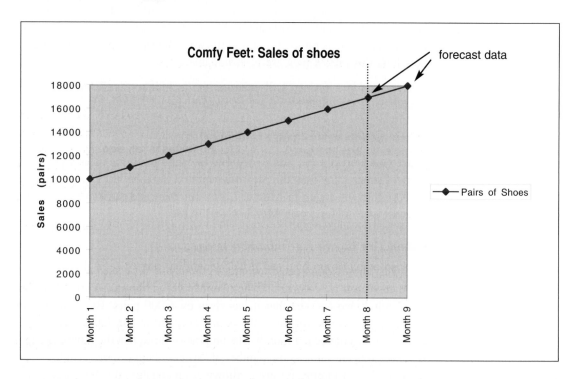

If in another situation the actual data does not produce exactly equal increases, the graph will produce the same answer as the average annual change provided the straight line runs through the first and last data points.

using a formula

The data in the example could have been expressed in the following formula:

$$y = mx + c$$

where

y is the forecast amount

m is 1,000 (the amount by which the data increases each month)

x is the number of months since the start month

c is 10,000 (which is the sales figure in the start month)

If we wanted a forecast for Month 8, we could calculate it as:

Forecast   = (1,000 x number of months since Month 1) + 10,000

y (the forecast) = (1,000 x 7) + 10,000

                  = 17,000, which is what we would expect.

This formula works because the formula is based on the equation of a straight line.

TIME SERIES AND SEASONAL VARIATIONS

In the last section we saw how simple historical data can be used to create an estimate or forecast of its future movement. To do this we assumed that there were no cyclical influences called **seasonal variations** that would have an impact on the data. We are now going to examine how historical data that we believe is affected by regular cyclical variations can be used to generate a forecast.

We can often use **moving averages** to analyse our historical data into its two main components of:

- the **trend** - the general direction that the data is moving, and

- the **seasonal variations** – the predictable movements in the data that occur in regular cycles

The technique of moving averages that we are going to demonstrate can be used to generate the following types of data for cash budgets in certain circumstances. In all these situations the technique will only provide valid data if the past movements of data provide a good basis for a forecast of the future.

- forecasts of sales units

- forecasts of prices

- forecasts of production levels

how do moving averages work?

A **moving average** is the term used for a series of averages calculated from a series of data (eg sales per month, labour costs per month) so that

- every average is based on the same number of pieces of data, (eg three pieces of data in a 'three point moving average'), and
- each subsequent average moves along that series of data by one piece of data so that compared to the previous average it
  - uses one new piece of data and
  - abandons one old piece of data

For example, suppose a factory used a manufacturing process that operated on a three-week cycle for technological reasons. At the end of each three-week period the production vessels are cleaned and the process starts again. Meanwhile as the operatives become more competent at controlling the process, output is gradually rising. The production figures for the last few weeks are as follows:

Week Number	Production Output (Tonnes):
1	20
2	46
3	27
4	23
5	49
6	30
7	26
8	52
9	33

As the three-week cycle will influence the output, we can calculate a three-point moving average, with workings as follows:

First moving average	(20 + 46 + 27) / 3	= 31
Second moving average	(46 + 27 + 23) / 3	= 32
Third moving average	(27 + 23 + 49) / 3	= 33
Fourth moving average	(23 + 49 + 30) / 3	= 34
Fifth moving average	(49 + 30 + 26) / 3	= 35
Sixth moving average	(30 + 26 + 52) / 3	= 36
Seventh moving average	(26 + 52 + 33) / 3	= 37

Notice how we move along the list of data. In this simple example with nine pieces of data we can't work out any more three-point averages since we have arrived at the end of the numbers after seven calculations.

Here we chose the number of pieces of data to average each time so that it corresponded with the number of points in a full cycle (in this case the three week production cycle of the manufacturing business). By choosing three points that correspond with the number of weeks in the production cycle we always had one example of the output of every type of week in our average. This means that any influence on the average by including a first week is cancelled out by also including data from a second week and a third week in the production cycle.

We must therefore always be careful to work out moving averages so that exactly one complete cycle is included in every average.

working out the trend line

By using moving averages we have worked out what is called the **trend line**, and we can use this to help with our forecast. A trend line is essentially a line showing a trend that can be plotted on a graph. When determining a trend line, each average relates to the data from its mid point, as is shown in the layout of the figures we have just calculated:

Week Number	Production (Tonnes)	Moving Average (Trend) (Tonnes)
1	20	
2	46	31
3	27	32
4	23	33
5	49	34
6	30	35
7	26	36
8	52	37
9	33	

This means that the first average that we calculated (31 tonnes) can be used as the trend point of week 2, with the second point (32 tonnes) forming the trend point of week 3 (see dotted lines). The result is that we

- know exactly where the trend line is for each period of time, and
- have a basis from which we can calculate 'seasonal variations'

calculating seasonal variations

Even using our limited data in this example we can see how **seasonal variations** can be calculated. They are **the difference between the actual data at a point and the trend at the same point**. These seasonal variations are shown in the right-hand column of the table below. The data used are the figures already calculated on the previous page. All the data are in tonnes.

Week Number	Production	Trend	Seasonal Variation
1	20		
2	46	31	+15
3	27	32	- 5
4	23	33	- 10
5	49	34	+ 15
6	30	35	- 5
7	26	36	- 10
8	52	37	+ 15
9	33		

We can see in this example that the seasonal variations repeat as follows:

- the first week in the production cycle always has an output of 10 tonnes less than the trend
- the second week in the production cycle has an output of 15 tonnes more than the trend, and
- the third week in the cycle regularly has a production output of 5 tonnes less than the trend

Note the way that plus and minus signs are used to denote the seasonal variations, and be careful to calculate them accurately:

- a plus sign in this case means that the actual production figure is higher than the trend (see week 2)
- a minus sign in this case means that the actual production figure is less than the trend (see week 3)

Using the same data we can now go on to forecast the production for future weeks by:

- estimating where the trend will be by the chosen week, and
- incorporating the seasonal variation based on the appropriate week in the cycle

The forecast production for weeks 10 – 12 is carried out as follows:

Week Number	Forecast Trend	Seasonal Variation	Forecast
10	39	- 10	29
11	40	+ 15	55
12	41	- 5	36

Here we can calculate the forecast trend easily, since it is consistently increasing by 1 tonne of output each week.

using forecast data in the cash budget

We can now see how this forecast data can be used in a cash budget. Using the data from the above example, we will assume:

- all output is sold immediately it is produced
- the selling price is £2000 per tonne
- sales are made on four weeks credit

The following receipts would appear in the cash budget for weeks 12 – 16.

	Week 12	Week 13	Week 14	Week 15	Week 16
Receipts from sales	£104,000	£66,000	£58,000	£110,000	£72,000

Note that due to lagging, the receipts in weeks 12 and 13 relate to the actual production in weeks 8 and 9. The forecast data for weeks 10 – 12 is used to calculate the receipts in weeks 14 – 16.

We will now use a Case Study to demonstrate how the same technique could be used to forecast price data for a cash budget.

Case Study

THE KNAWBERRY:
FORECASTING SEASONAL PRICES

situation

A supermarket obtains its supplies of the knawberry (a popular soft fruit) from three sources, depending on the time of year.

- In January – April it is bought from UK growers who raise the plants in glasshouses so that they will crop earlier than plants grown outdoors.
- In May – August it is obtained from UK farmers who grow the fruit outdoors.

- In September – December it is bought from overseas growers whose climate allows production at this time of the year.

Prices paid by the supermarket to the suppliers have been as follows over the last three years.

Year	Source	Price (per kilo)
1	UK glasshouse	£7
	UK outside	£4
	Overseas	£16
2	UK glasshouse	£10
	UK outside	£7
	Overseas	£19
3	UK glasshouse	£13
	UK outside	£10
	Overseas	£22

The monthly demand for the fruit (which will form the basis of the purchasing requirements) has already been calculated for the months of April – October of year 4, as follows:

April	1,600 kilos
May	1,900 kilos
June	2,500 kilos
July	2,600 kilos
August	2,400 kilos
September	2,000 kilos
October	1,200 kilos

All growers are paid on two months credit.

Required

- Using a three point moving average and seasonal variations, forecast the buying prices that will be payable in year 4.

- Show an extract from the payments section of the cash budget for June – November year 4 relating to the knawberry.

solution

Year	Source	Price	Trend	Seasonal Variation
		£	£	£
1	UK glasshouse	7		
	UK outside	4	9	- 5
	Overseas	16	10	+ 6
2	UK glasshouse	10	11	- 1
	UK outside	7	12	- 5
	Overseas	19	13	+ 6
3	UK glasshouse	13	14	- 1
	UK outside	10	15	- 5
	Overseas	22		

The trend in the prices is rising by £1 each 'season'. We can use this with the seasonal variations to forecast the prices in year 4.

Source	Forecast Trend	Seasonal Variation	Forecast
	£	£	£
UK glasshouse	17	- 1	16
UK outside	18	- 5	13
Overseas	19	+ 6	25

We can now use the demand data, together with the forecast prices and credit period to calculate our payments extract from the cash budget.

	June	July	Aug	Sept	Oct	Nov
	£	£	£	£	£	£
	25,600	24,700	32,500	33,800	31,200	50,000

Note that the amounts paid in June relate to April purchases (due to the credit period), and are therefore based on 1,600 kilos at £16. Similarly, the July – October payments are based on the UK outside prices and quantities in May to August. The November payment is for overseas goods bought in September at £25 per kilo.

Chapter Summary

- Budgets that are prepared for manufacturing organisations typically include Sales, Production, Material Usage, Material Purchases, and Labour Utilisation, together with other budgets including various functional budgets, capital expenditure budgets and cash flow budgets. These are coordinated and amalgamated to form a set of Master Budgets.

- Budgets for manufacturing organisations can be created by working from the forecast sales data to the production level by using anticipated finished goods stock levels. From the production budget the materials usage can be ascertained, and by incorporating the anticipated materials stock levels the materials purchases can be calculated.

- The cash budget uses data from the sales budget, the materials purchases budget and the labour utilisation budget, as well as other budgets, including the capital budget and various functional budgets.

- When compiling figures for the cash budget it is sometimes necessary to use statistical techniques to assist with forecasting. These include the use of moving averages to work out trends and seasonal variations.

Key Terms

production budget	the budget for a manufacturing organisation that determines the output to be made – it is usually expressed in units
trend analysis	a numerical technique for analysing historical data so that it can be used for forecasting future data – it involves identifying and separating seasonal and other variations so that the underlying trend can be ascertained
deseasonalised data	data that has had the effects of seasonal variations stripped away
seasonal variations	regular variations in data that occur in a repeating pattern

Student Activities

answers to the asterisked (*) questions are to be found at the back of this book

3.1* A manufacturing company that makes a single product is planning its activities for month 3 in the current year. The following data is available:

- Sales in month 3 are forecast at 2,600 units.

- Each completed unit requires 6 kilos of raw material.

- Planned stock levels are:

	Raw Materials	Finished Goods
At end of month 2	1,500 kilos	600 units
At end of month 3	1,800 kilos	500 units

Required

(a) Calculate the following budgets for month 3:

- production budget (in units)

- raw materials usage (in kilos)

- raw materials purchases (in kilos)

(b) Explain which of the above budgets would be used to help prepare a cash budget for the company, and how they would be used.

3.2* The Unit Company has prepared the following balance sheet extract as at 31 December 20-6.

	£	£	£
Fixed Assets	Cost	Dep'n	Net
Equipment	50,000	30,000	20,000
Current Assets			
Stocks: Finished Goods (20 units)		2,000	
Raw Materials (30 units)		1,200	
Debtors		10,000	
Bank		12,000	
		25,200	
Less **Current Liabilities**			
Creditors for Raw Materials		1,000	
			24,200
Less Long Term Liabilities			
8% Debentures			(30,000)
			14,200

- The following data relates to the first four months of 20-7:

	Jan	Feb	March	April
Sales (units)	20	22	23	25
Production (units)	22	21	22	24
Purchases (units)	21	24	25	22

- Costs are estimated as follows for these months:

Raw materials	£40 per unit
Labour	£60 per unit
Fixed Overheads	£1,000 per month (including depreciation of £200)

- Completed units sell for £200 each.

- Sales are made on two months credit.

- Purchases of raw materials are made on one month's credit, and the creditors amount at 31 December relates to December purchases.

- One unit of raw material is used to make one unit of finished product.

- Labour and cash fixed overheads are paid in the month incurred.

- Debtors at 31 December 20-6 are made up of:

November Sales	£6,500
December Sales	£3,500

- Finished goods are valued at variable costs only.

- Debenture interest is paid in January and June each year.

  Ordinary Dividends are to be paid in April at 50p per share, based on 20,000 shares.

  Bank interest can be ignored.

Required

- Prepare a cash budget for the months of January – April 20-7

- Calculate the value of the following elements of working capital of the business as at 30 April 20-7:

  - Stock of finished goods
  - Stock of raw materials
  - Debtors
  - Bank
  - Creditors for raw materials

3.3   The Shackshop is open 5 days a week (Tuesday to Saturday) and records the following cash sales over a three week period.

	Tues	Wed	Thurs	Fri	Sat
Week 1	£915	£960	£1040	£1080	£1080
Week 2	£940	£985	£1065	£1105	£1105
Week 3	£965	£1010	£1090	£1130	£1130

Required

(a)   Using a five point moving average, analyse this data into the trend and seasonal variations. (Note: a five point moving average works on the same principle as a three point moving average, but takes a series of averages of five numbers instead of three).

(b)   Use the data from (a) to forecast the cash sales for each day of week 4.

3.4   A company has analysed its sales in units over the last two years, and produced the following information:

Year	Quarter	Trend (No. Units)	Seasonal Variation (No. Units)
1	1	5,800	- 430
	2	5,870	- 350
	3	5,935	+880
	4	6,010	- 100
2	1	6,090	- 430
	2	6,165	- 350
	3	6,220	+880
	4	6,290	- 100

(a)   Calculate the average trend movement per quarter over the last two years.

(b)   Use the average trend movement to forecast the expected sales (in units) in quarters 3 and 4 of year 3.

3.5 The Magnum Manufacturing Company has prepared the following balance sheet extract as at 31 December 20-5.

	£	£
Current Assets		
Stocks: Finished Goods (50 units)	50,000	
Raw Materials (30 units)	9,000	
Debtors	90,000	
		149,000
Less **Current Liabilities**		
Creditors for Raw Materials	18,000	
Bank Overdraft	10,000	
		28,000
		121,000

- The following data relates to the first four months of 20-6:

	Jan	Feb	March	April
Sales (units)	75	70	80	75
Production (units)	65	70	75	80
Purchases (units)	70	75	70	73

- Costs are estimated as follows for these months:

Raw materials	£300 per unit
Labour	£600 per unit
Variable overheads	£100 per unit
Fixed Overheads	£36,000 per month (including depreciation £1,000)

- Completed units sell for £1,500 each.

  Sales are made on either:

  - no credit, with 2% discount, or

  - on two months credit, with no discount.

  Discounts are normally claimed for 60% of the sales.

- Debtors at 31 December 20-5 are made up of :

November Sales	£50,000
December Sales	£40,000

- Purchases of raw materials are made on one month's credit, and the creditors total at 31 December relates to December purchases.

- One unit of raw material is used to make one unit of finished product.

- Labour and overheads are paid in the month incurred.

- Finished goods are valued at variable costs only.

- Bank interest is received monthly at 0.4% per month of the closing bank balance of the previous month.

- Overdraft interest is paid monthly at 1.0% per month of the closing overdraft balance of the previous month.

Required

- Prepare a cash budget for the months of January to April 20-6

- Calculate the value of the following elements of working capital of the business as at 30 April 20-6:

  - Stock of finished goods

  - Stock of raw materials

  - Debtors

  - Bank

  - Creditors for raw materials

4 Using cash budgets

this chapter covers . . .

In this chapter we will examine the practical ways in which cash budgets – both in manual and computer model forms – can be used to monitor cash receipts and payments and to indicate the need for any corrective action. Specific areas covered include:

- using sensitivity or 'what-if' analysis to examine the impact of changes to the receipts and payments figures in a cash budget

- the usefulness of computer spreadsheets in calculating the effects of these changes

- the need to make allowances for inflation

- comparing the projections in cash budgets with actual results

- the need to take corrective action when cash flows do not go according to plan

PERFORMANCE CRITERIA COVERED

unit 15 OPERATING A CASH MANAGEMENT AND CREDIT CONTROL SYSTEM

element 15.1
Monitor and control cash receipts and payments

A   Monitor and control cash receipts and payments against budgeted cash flow.

E   Identify significant deviations from the cash budget and take corrective action within defined organisational policies.

KNOWLEDGE AND UNDERSTANDING COVERAGE

14   Basic statistical techniques for estimating future trends: moving averages, allowance for inflation.

15   Computer models to assess the sensitivity of elements in the cash budget to change (eg price, wage rate changes).

31   An understanding of the organisation's relevant policies and procedures.

SENSITIVITY ANALYSIS

In the last two chapters we have seen how cash budgets can be developed for various organisations, including manufacturing businesses. In this chapter we are going to see how we can make effective use of cash budgets, firstly to see how changes in cash flow would impact on them, and then by using the budgets to monitor and control actual results.

assumptions made in cash budgeting

In each Case Study and example we have used various assumptions that are reflected in the final budget. These assumptions are about issues like:

- selling prices charged
- credit terms offered, and whether receipts would be in line with them
- prices paid for purchases, expenses and fixed assets
- labour rates and the number of labour hours required
- how quickly payments need to be made

If any one of these assumptions turns out to be incorrect it would make a difference to the cash budget, and could even invalidate all the planning that has taken place.

the importance of sensitivity analysis

The problem that arises therefore is to determine how sensitive the cash budget is to possible changes in the initial assumptions. If a change in one assumption produced a cash difference of only a small amount we would not be too concerned. However sometimes a change in one assumption can lead to severe changes in the cash position. **Sensitivity analysis** helps us to determine which assumptions are critical and which have less impact. The technique investigates the impact that changes would have on the budget, so that we are aware of how the situation could vary from our expected position.

Sensitivity analysis is sometimes called 'what-if' analysis, and that really sums up what it does. The technique simply shows us what will happen to the budget if changes occur.

The procedure involves 'trying out' various alterations from our original assumptions to assess the impact. This can be done by changing one category of receipt or payment (for example – what if our purchase prices go up by 5%?), or using more than one change in combination (for example – what if our purchase prices go up by 5% and we have to pay for them after one month instead of two months?). You may be asked to carry out some sensitivity analysis in a given task, and we will look at the numerical techniques shortly. Before we do that it is worth examining an important practical tool for carrying out sensitivity analysis – the computer spreadsheet.

using a spreadsheet for sensitivity analysis

The format of a cash budget that we have been using in the last two chapters is very easy to reproduce on a computer spreadsheet, using formulas to carry out the arithmetic.

Once a spreadsheet is set up it is a simple matter to change any of the data, or to add lines for additional receipts or payments. The totals of receipts and payments will automatically adjust when changes are made, together with the bank/cash balances at the bottom of the budget. An example of a cash budget layout is shown on the opposite page. It is illustrated twice:

• a normal view, showing the figures (upper illustration)

• a view showing the formulas used (lower illustration)

Although the practical use of spreadsheets is difficult to incorporate into AAT simulations, the knowledge and understanding requirements of this Unit include computer modelling. The cash budgets that have been used in Case Studies and activities in the last two chapters of this book are all suitable for practice of using spreadsheets. You should at some stage discuss with your tutor what spreadsheets you can use as a basis for your budgets.

carrying out sensitivity analysis manually

The type of change to data that can be carried out in sensitivity analysis generally falls into one of three categories:

• **changes in underlying volumes**

 Here we mean changes in the sales units, or the production or purchase units. It could also apply to some extent to overheads or fixed assets (eg hiring or buying additional equipment not included in the original budget).

• **changes in prices**

 We will initially deal with some straightforward price changes, and then in the next section examine the impact of inflation and how to deal with it.

• **timing changes**

 We also need to see the impact when the receipts and payments are the same as the original cash budget, but they occur at different times. Examples would be allowing longer (or shorter) credit terms on sales, or paying for purchases or other outgoings at a different time than was originally planned.

	A	B	C	D	E	F	G
1	CORIANNE LIMITED						
2	CASH BUDGET						
3		JANUARY	FEBRUARY	MARCH	APRIL	MAY	JUNE
4		£	£	£	£	£	£
5	*Receipts*						
6							
7							
8	Sales Receipts	3,000	3,000	4,000	4,000	4,000	4,000
9							
10	Capital	10,000					
11	TOTAL RECEIPTS	13,000	3,000	4,000	4,000	4,000	4,000
12	*Payments*						
13	Purchases	5,000	1,750	1,750		1,750	1,750
14	Fixed Assets	4,500	5,250				
15	Rent/Rates	575	575	575	575	575	575
16	Insurance	50	50	50	50	50	50
17	Electricity	25	25	25	25	25	25
18	Telephone	150	15	15	15	15	15
19	Stationery	10	10	10	10	10	10
20	Postage	15	15	15	15	15	15
21	Bank charges	100		75			75
22	Advertising	150	30	30	30	30	30
23	TOTAL PAYMENTS	10,575	7,720	2,545	720	2,470	2,545
24	CASHFLOW FOR MONTH	2,425	- 4,720	1,455	3,280	1,530	1,455
25	Bank Balance *brought forward*	-	2,425	- 2,295	- 840	2,440	3,970
26	Bank Balance *carried forward*	2,425	- 2,295	- 840	2,440	3,970	5,425
27							

cash budget on a computer spreadsheet – showing figures

	A	B	C	D	E	F	G
1	CORIANNE LIMITED						
2	CASH BUDGET						
3		JANUARY	FEBRUARY	MARCH	APRIL	MAY	JUNE
4		£	£	£	£	£	£
5	*Receipts*						
6							
7							
8	Sales Receipts	3000	3000	4000	4000	4000	4000
9							
10	Capital	10000					
11	TOTAL RECEIPTS	=SUM(B6:B10)	=SUM(C6:C10)	=SUM(D6:D10)	=SUM(E6:E10)	=SUM(F6:F10)	=SUM(G6:G10)
12	*Payments*						
13	Purchases	5000	1750	1750		1750	1750
14	Fixed Assets	4500	5250				
15	Rent/Rates	575	575	575	575	575	575
16	Insurance	50	50	50	50	50	50
17	Electricity	25	25	25	25	25	25
18	Telephone	150	15	15	15	15	15
19	Stationery	10	10	10	10	10	10
20	Postage	15	15	15	15	15	15
21	Bank charges	100		75			75
22	Advertising	150	30	30	30	30	30
23	TOTAL PAYMENTS	=SUM(B13:B22)	=SUM(C13:C22)	=SUM(D13:D22)	=SUM(E13:E22)	=SUM(F13:F22)	=SUM(G13:G22)
24	CASHFLOW FOR MONTH	=SUM(B11-B23)	=SUM(C11-C23)	=SUM(D11-D23)	=SUM(E11-E23)	=SUM(F11-F23)	=SUM(G11-G23)
25	Bank Balance *brought forward*	0	=SUM(B26)	=SUM(C26)	=SUM(D26)	=SUM(E26)	=SUM(F26)
26	Bank Balance *carried forward*	=SUM(B24:B25)	=SUM(C24:C25)	=SUM(D24:D25)	=SUM(E24:E25)	=SUM(F24:F25)	=SUM(G24:G25)
27							

cash budget on a computer spreadsheet – showing formulas

There are two approaches to changing the cash budget data:

1   The whole cash budget could be redrafted. While this would be a simple matter when using a spreadsheet model, it would be very time-consuming manually, especially if there were several alternative options to consider.

2   The impact on the cash movements for each month could be calculated from just examining the changes proposed. This approach requires the application of some logic to the problem, but is a quicker technique than redrafting the whole budget.

The second technique is often required in AAT simulations, and we will now look in more detail at how this is carried out. The key is to look at each month separately, and calculate for that month

- any change in receipts, and
- any change in payments, that together result in
- a change in cash movement

The revised closing cash balance for that month can then be calculated, and carried forward to the next month. The exercise can be carried out in the form of a table.

We will use a straightforward example to demonstrate the process.

The following cash budget is taken from the Moore Trading Case Study used in Chapter 2, page 44. It is based on all sales being made on two months' credit. March sales are estimated at £8,000.

Moore Trading: Cash Budget for January to April of Year 10.

	January £	February £	March £	April £
Receipts				
Receipts from year 9 sales	6,500	4,500	-	-
Receipts from year 10 sales	-	-	6,000	7,000
Total Receipts	6,500	4,500	6,000	7,000
Payments				
Purchases made in year 9	4,000	-	-	-
Purchases made in year 10	-	4,000	6,000	6,000
Expenses	1,000	1,000	1,000	1,000
Fixed Assets	10,000	-	-	-
Drawings	-	1,500	-	1,500
Total Payments	15,000	6,500	7,000	8,500
Cash Flow for Month	(8,500)	(2,000)	(1,000)	(1,500)
Bank Balance brought forward	10,000	1,500	(500)	(1,500)
Bank Balance carried forward	1,500	(500)	(1,500)	(3,000)

Suppose that we wanted to see the impact of changing our terms of sale to one month's credit, with effect from January sales. For simplicity we will assume that all our customers comply with the revised terms. By following the procedure outlined above we would get the following results.

	January £	February £	March £	April £
'Old' Receipts from sales	6,500	4,500	6,000	7,000
'New' Receipts from sales	6,500	10,500	7,000	8,000
Changes to receipts	-	+ 6,000	+1,000	+1,000

Revised cash flow figures				
	January £	February £	March £	April £
Cash Flow for Month	(8,500)	4,000	0	(500)
Bank balance brought forward	10,000	1,500	5,500	5,500
Bank balance carried forward	1,500	5,500	5,500	5,000

In this example two month's sales receipts would arise in February, increasing the receipts for that month by £6,000. The changes in receipts for March and April result from receiving different month's sales than originally planned. The overall result is a new bank balance at the end of April of £5,000 instead of the original £3,000 overdrawn figure.

Note that using this technique it is only necessary to examine those lines in the cash budget that are subject to change. Here there was no impact on payments so there was no need to revisit those figures.

We will now present a Case Study incorporating more than one change to the cash budget data.

Case Study

THE SENSITIVE COMPANY: ASSESSING THE IMPACT OF BUDGET CHANGES

A cash budget has been prepared (see next page), based on various assumptions, including the following:

- Completed units sell for £200 each, on two month's credit.

- Raw materials purchases are made on one month's credit.

- Dividends paid are based on 50 pence per share.

	January £	February £	March £	April £
Receipts				
Receipts from year 20-6 sales	6,500	3,500	-	-
Receipts from year 20-7 sales	-	-	4,000	4,400
Total Receipts	6,500	3,500	4,000	4,400
Payments				
Raw Material Purchases	1,000	840	960	1,000
Labour	1,320	1,260	1,320	1,440
Fixed Overheads	800	800	800	800
Debenture Interest	1,200	-	-	-
Dividends	-	-	-	10,000
Total Payments	4,320	2,900	3,080	13,240
Cash Flow for Month	2,180	600	920	(8,840)
Bank balance brought forward	12,000	14,180	14,780	15,700
Bank balance carried forward	14,180	14,780	15,700	6,860

possible changes

The impact of a number of possible changes all occurring together needs to be assessed:

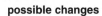

- The unit selling price is reduced to £195 each with effect from January, a £5 reduction from the current selling price of £200.

- Purchases of raw materials are to be paid for in the month of purchase (instead of one month later), and are subject to a 4% settlement discount. This takes effect from the January purchases. April purchases are to be £880 before discount.

- Dividends to be paid in April are based on 60 pence per share, instead of 50 pence per share.

required

Calculate the impact of **all** the possible changes on each month's closing bank balance.

solution

	January £	February £	March £	April £
Changes to Receipts	-	-	(100)	(110)
Changes to Payments				
'Old' purchase payments	1,000	840	960	1,000
'New' purchase payments	1,806	922	960	845
Changes to purchase payments	806	82	0	(155)
Change to dividend	-	-	-	2,000
Total changes to payments	806	82	0	1,845
Revised cash flow position				
Cash Flow for Month	1,374	518	820	(10,795)
Bank balance brought forward	12,000	13,374	13,892	14,712
Bank balance carried forward	13,374	13,892	14,712	3,917

In these calculations increases in receipts or payments have been shown as positive figures and reductions as negative figures (in brackets).

It is important to remember that a lower receipts figure has the same impact as a higher payments figure – ie a reduction in cash flow!

The detail recorded in the workings is a matter of personal preference, but you should show enough detail in your calculations to enable your working method to be checked.

ALLOWING FOR INFLATION

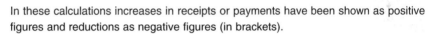

Because prices and costs change over time it is important to make sure that budgets take account of the most accurate estimates of the amounts that will apply in the budget period. This can either occur at the initial budget preparation stage, or as part of sensitivity analysis. Inflation will have a particular impact on:

* selling prices
* purchase prices
* expenses
* cost of fixed assets
* labour costs

selling prices

Because selling prices are set within an organisation it is possible to obtain information about future prices from the relevant personnel, as discussed in Chapter 1. However it is important to be aware that selling prices are subject to market forces as well as inflation, and it is vital to check that data that has been provided has been based on valid assumptions.

prices for purchases, expenses and fixed assets

Depending on the number of different suppliers that the organisation has, it may be possible to obtain information about expected price rises of individual inputs. For example, car manufacturers will be able to obtain market reports about likely movements in the price of pressed steel. Where substantial fixed assets are to be purchased the cost should be ascertained accurately in advance.

Where changes in costs cannot be investigated individually, index numbers (as described below) can be used to calculate the impact of expected price changes in different categories of cost. It should be remembered that an organisation may have diverse supplies and expenses, and it probably will not be sufficient to apply the same allowance for inflation to all costs. For example, business rates may well be increasing by a different percentage than raw materials.

labour costs

Like selling prices, wage rates are controlled by the organisation, although they are subject to external pressures such as the legal requirements of the Minimum Wage. Although wage cost indices are available for all industrial sectors, it is better to use information about the specific organisation – for example taking account of the timing and percentage of any anticipated wage rise.

USING INDEX NUMBERS

Index numbers are used to assist in the comparison of various numerical data over time. The traditional index that measures inflation by comparing the cost of a group of expenses typically incurred by households in the UK is the Retail Price Index (RPI). This has more recently been supplemented by the CPI (Consumer Prices Index). There are many other types of index numbers that have been created for specific purposes. For the measurement of cost changes some of the following types of index may be useful:

- the price of specific items, either based on the retail price or the cost to specific industries (eg the price of unleaded petrol)
- the average price of a group of items, usually using a weighted price (ie taking relative quantities into account) for example the average price per litre of all types of motor fuel
- the average wage rate for a particular job, or for all employment
- the currency exchange rates between specific currencies

Whatever type of index we need to use, the principle is the same. The index numbers represent a convenient way of comparing figures. For example, the Retail Price Index (RPI) was 82.61 in January 1983, and 183.1 in January 2004. This means that average household costs had more than doubled in the 21 years between. We could also calculate that if something that cost £5.00 in January 1983 had risen exactly in line with inflation, it would have cost £11.08 in January 2004. This calculation is carried out using the formula:

$$\text{Historical price} \quad \times \quad \frac{\text{Index of time converting to}}{\text{Index of time converting from}}$$

For example, the item that cost £5.00 in January 1983 would in January 2004 cost:

$$£5.00 \quad \times \quad \frac{183.1 \text{ (RPI in January 2004)}}{82.61 \text{ (RPI in January 1983)}}$$

$$= \quad £11.08$$

An organisation will clearly not be dealing with a 21 year time span when constructing a cash budget, but the principle of the use of index numbers remains the same.

You.may be told that the 'base year' for a particular index is a certain point in time. This is when the particular index was 100. For example the current RPI index was 100 in January 1987. You are unlikely to need to know the base year in the sort of calculations that are needed in budgeting.

use a specific index if possible

Index numbers referring to costs or prices are commonly used in the cash management process. If we want to use cost index numbers to monitor past costs or forecast future ones, then it is best and more accurate to use as specific an index as possible. For example, if we were operating in the food industry, and wanted to compare our coffee cost movements with the average that the industry had experienced, we should use an index that analyses coffee costs in the food industry. This would be much more accurate than the RPI, CPI or even a general cost index for the food industry.

a reminder about lagging

When incorporating an allowance for inflation, we must be careful to remember that price changes that occur in one month will only impact when the receipt or payment occurs. For example if we increase our selling prices by 5% in January, but sell our goods on two months' credit, it will not affect the cash budget until March.

Case Study

HIGH-RISE SUPPLIES:
ALLOWING FOR INFLATION IN THE CASH BUDGET

High-Rise Supplies, a trading company, has produced the following extract from its initial draft cash budget for the months of July – October, based on prices and costs at June levels.

Sales are made on two months' credit, purchases on one month's credit.

Expenses and labour costs are paid in the month they are incurred.

Rent is payable half yearly in advance.

High-Rise Supplies: Draft Cash Budget (extract) for the period July - October				
	July	August	September	October
	£	£	£	£
Receipts				
Sales	60,000	63,000	55,000	68,000
Payments				
Purchases	25,000	28,000	26,000	24,000
Labour	19,000	17,000	18,000	20,000
Rent	18,000	-	-	-
Expenses	12,000	12,000	12,000	12,000

The following information about price and cost changes is now available :

• Selling prices are due to increase by 3% from 1 July.

• Purchase prices are forecast to rise by 4% from 1 September.

• A pay rise of 2.5% has been agreed to take effect from 1 July.

• Rent is to rise to £40,000 per year with effect from 1 July.

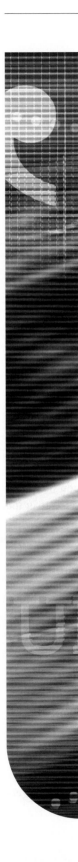

- Expenses are expected to follow the following forecast cost index

June	291.0
July	291.8
August	292.3
September	293.0
October	293.7

required

Revise the cash budget extract to incorporate appropriate allowances for price and cost changes.

solution

Revised Cash Budget (extract) for the period July - October

	July £	August £	September £	October £
Receipts				
Sales (1)	60,000	63,000	56,650	70,040
Payments				
Purchases (2)	25,000	28,000	26,000	24,960
Labour (3)	19,475	17,425	18,450	20,500
Rent (4)	20,000	-	-	-
Expenses (5)	12,033	12,054	12,082	12,111

Notes

(1) The sales price change impacts after 2 months.

(2) The purchase price change impacts one month after 1 September.

(3) The labour pay rise takes effect immediately.

(4) The rent rise to £40,000 per year = £20,000 per half year.

(5) Expenses rise each month in line with the forecast index. For example, August expenses are calculated as

$$£12,000 \times \frac{292.3 \text{ (August index)}}{291.0 \text{ (June index)}}$$

$$= £12,054$$

the overall impact of inflation

If inflation is higher than anticipated then the following generalisations can be made about its impact.

* selling prices can be increased

* buying prices, labour costs and expenses may increase

Depending on the structure of the business and the amount and timing of these increases, profit may well also increase. However each £1 of increased profit will not be worth as much as previously!

One other impact of inflation is that interest rates tend to move in the same direction as inflation. This means that when inflation is high interest rates are normally high. If the organisation has borrowed a substantial amount of money, this will add to its costs, whereas if the organisation has surplus funds it will generate more revenue from this source.

COMPARING THE CASH BUDGET WITH THE ACTUAL FIGURES

The cash budget, like any other budget, has a major advantage in that it can be used for monitoring and control. It would make no sense if the completed budget were simply locked away after completion and the organisation carried on regardless!

When making comparisons between the cash budget and the actual cash flow it is important to identify the reasons for any differences between budgeted and actual figures. These are the same factors that we looked at earlier in the chapter when considering sensitivity analysis:

* changes in underlying volumes

* changes in prices

* timing changes

It will not always be possible by just examining the two sets of figures to identify the exact reasons for any differences, but it should be possible to identify possible or likely reasons from the three categories listed above. It should also be possible to investigate the differences (or variances) further and obtain information about the causes.

It will be necessary to ask:

* which variances should be investigated?

* which variances require that action should be taken?

* which variances just need to be monitored?

We can use a similar approach to that used when monitoring other budgets or in standard costing. This is based on a few key questions:

- **is the difference significant?**

  If the difference between the budget and the actual cash flow is small it is unlikely to be worth investigating fully, unless there is a danger that it is the beginning of a trend that will become significant.

- **do we know the cause of the difference?**

  If we know the cause then we are in a strong position, even if action is subsequently needed. If the difference is significant and we do not yet know the cause, then we should find out more.

- **will the difference right itself anyway?**

  If the difference will automatically right itself – for example a late receipt from a major customer – then we may just need to monitor the situation.

- **will the difference recur?**

  A one-off variance can probably be managed, but if it is expected to recur, it may need different treatment. If the late receipt from the last example is a warning sign of the customer's inability to pay then it should lead to a re-examination of the trading relationship with that customer.

- **is the cause controllable?**

  Some situations are outside the control of the organisation, and time should not be wasted trying to achieve the impossible. If interest rate rises or a change in currency exchange rates have had an impact on cash flow, then a strategy will have to be developed to manage the situation. This may also involve amending the original budget.

The Case Study that follows demonstrates how to analyse possible causes of differences.

Case Study

CASH-GONE LIMITED:
EXAMINING CASH DIFFERENCES

Cash-Gone Limited is a trading company selling to the UK manufacturing industry.

The following figures compare the company's cash budget – as initially prepared for the period Oct-Dec – with the actual figures for the same period.

	Cash Budget			Actual Cash		
	Oct	*Nov*	*Dec*	*Oct*	*Nov*	*Dec*
	£'000	£'000	£'000	£'000	£'000	£'000
Receipts						
Cash Sales	20	20	20	20	19	15
Trade Debtors	50	40	50	45	45	35
Total Receipts	70	60	70	65	64	50
Payments						
Purchases	10	11	10	10	12	10
Wages	20	20	20	20	23	20
Rent	5	5	5	5	5	5
Administration	10	10	10	10	10	9
Fixed Assets	0	30	0	38	2	0
Total payments	45	76	45	83	52	44
Monthly Cash Flow	25	(16)	25	(18)	12	6
Bank balance brought fwd	10	35	19	10	(8)	4
Bank balance carried fwd	35	19	44	(8)	4	10

required

Summarise the differences for each category of receipt and payment between the forecast and the actual data, and suggest possible causes for each difference.

solution

- **Receipts from Cash Sales: £6,000 less than budgeted**

  The actual receipts are down by £1,000 in November and by £5,000 in December. Since these are cash sales the cause cannot be a timing difference, but must result from a difference in cash sales volume. Since the major difference is in December this could be the result of the original forecast not estimating accurately the sales in this month where many businesses shut down for long periods.

- **Receipts from Debtors: £15,000 less than budgeted**

  The actual receipts are down by £5,000 in October, but greater by the same amount in November – this could be a possible timing difference only due to delayed receipts. In December the receipts are £15,000 fewer than budgeted. This could be a timing difference, or could be due to lower sales in the relevant period.

- **Payments for Purchases: £1,000 more than budgeted.**

  Since only November payments differ from the budget, a timing difference seems unlikely. It could be due to increased stocks, or to a price rise. Since sales are not higher than in the budget it cannot be due to demand.

- **Payment for Wages: £3,000 more than budgeted.**

    Since this occurs only in November it appears to be a one-off difference rather than a pay increase or more employees. It could relate to overtime working or possibly a bonus that was not originally planned.

- **Payment for Administration: £1,000 less than budgeted.**

    The payment is lower only in December. This could be a timing difference to be caught up with in January, or maybe a saving that will be repeated in future months.

- **Payment for Fixed Assets: £10,000 more than budgeted.**

    The total cost is £10,000 higher than budgeted, and the larger part of this payment is made one month earlier than planned. This could point to an earlier acquisition, or less available credit than planned. In addition, the price could be higher than planned, or more assets or higher specification assets could have been purchased.

The overall net difference is a reduction in cash of £34,000. This accounts for the difference between the budgeted and actual closing December cash balances.

TAKING CORRECTIVE ACTION

The types of action that can be taken when cash budget variances have been identified will depend on the causes of those differences. It is also worth remembering that some issues may involve major decisions in the organisation at a high level – for example altering credit control policies. While we may recommend such changes, we will rarely be in a position to implement them personally.

As already discussed, only significant variances should be a cause for action. What is a significant variance could be an issue for company policy, and could be measured in amounts of cash, or percentages of the budget figures. Unless small variances are thought to be indicative of a future trend, or are the result of two significant but opposite variances then action should not be required.

In the table on the next page are some examples of typical causes of cash budget variances, and possible actions that could be followed to remedy the situation.

The table concentrates on adverse causes, but action could also be taken to maximise the benefit from favourable situations.

causes of cash variances	possible actions
Receipts from credit sales delayed	Improve credit control Offer discounts for prompt payment
Sales volumes reduced	Improve product Improve marketing Reduce selling price
Purchase volumes increased	Improve stock control Reduce wastage
Purchase prices increased	Negotiate better prices Change suppliers
Payments made prematurely	Negotiate longer credit terms Ensure available credit is taken
Labour costs increased	Increase labour efficiency Reduce absenteeism Reduce overtime working Negotiate flexible contacts

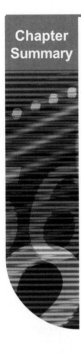

**Chapter
Summary**

- Sensitivity analysis involves examining what happens to a budget when changes are made in the assumptions on which it is based. It is also known as 'what-if' analysis, and can be carried out using a spreadsheet or with manual calculations. Manual calculations are easier if they focus only on the parts of the budget that are subject to change.

- Inflation affects selling prices, purchase prices and expenses. Index numbers can be used to measure and predict inflation – including the Retail Price Index and Consumer Prices Index. When using index numbers the best approach is to use an index that is as specific to the costs involved as possible.

- Cash budgets can be monitored and controlled by comparing the actual cash figures with the budget and then calculating any differences (or variances). Once the causes of significant variances have been established, corrective action can be taken as appropriate.

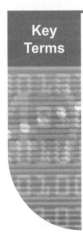

**Key
Terms**

sensitivity analysis   examining the budget to determine how sensitive it is to the various assumptions on which it has been prepared

index numbers   a sequence of numbers used to compare data, usually over a time period

variance   the financial difference between the budgeted data and the actual data – in a cash budget the variances relate to differences in receipts or payments

Student Activities

answers to the asterisked (*) questions are to be found at the back of this book

---

Note
Some of the activities on the next three pages are suitable material for processing on a computer spreadsheet.

4.1* The following cash budget has been prepared, based on various assumptions, including the following:

- completed units sell on two months credit
- raw materials purchases are made on one month's credit

	January £	February £	March £	April £
Receipts				
Receipts from sales	8,500	7,500	5,000	9,000
Receipt of Loan		20,000		
Total Receipts	8,500	27,500	5,000	9,000
Payments				
Raw Material Purchases	3,000	2,800	3,960	3,000
Labour	1,320	1,260	1,320	1,440
Fixed Overheads	1,800	1,800	1,800	1,800
Debenture Interest	1,200	-	-	-
Fixed Assets	-	24,000	-	-
Total Payments	7,320	29,860	7,080	6,240
Cash Flow for Month	1,180	(2,360)	(2,080)	2,760
Balance bf	10,000	11,180	8,820	6,740
Balance cf	11,180	8,820	6,740	9,500

The impact of both the following possible changes occurring now needs to be assessed:
- Three months credit offered on sales with effect from January sales.
- The fixed assets to cost £26,000, and to be paid for in January.

Required

Calculate the impact of the possible changes both occurring on each month's closing bank balance.

4.2* Sun-Rise Supplies, a trading company, has produced the following extract from its initial draft cash budget for the months of July to October, based on prices and costs at June levels.

Purchases are made on one month's credit.

Expenses and labour costs are paid in the month they are incurred.

Rent is payable half yearly in advance.

Draft Cash Budget (extract) for the period July to October				
	July	August	September	October
	£	£	£	£
Payments				
Purchases	25,000	28,000	26,000	24,000
Labour	19,000	17,000	18,000	20,000
Rent	18,000	-	-	-
Expenses	10,000	10,000	10,000	10,000

The following information is now available regarding price and cost changes:

- Purchase prices will rise by 2.5% from 1 August.
- A pay rise of 3.5% has been agreed to take effect from 1 October.
- Rent is to rise to £42,000 per year with effect from 1 July.
- Expenses are expected to follow the following forecast cost index:

June	150.0
July	151.2
August	151.4
September	152.0
October	152.1

Required

Revise the cash budget extract to incorporate appropriate allowances for price and cost changes.

4.3   The cash budget set out below has been based on various assumptions, including the following:

- Completed units sell on two month's credit.

- Raw materials purchases are made on one month's credit.

	January £	February £	March £	April £
Receipts				
Receipts from sales	8,500	7,500	5,000	9,000
Total Receipts	8,500	7,500	5,000	9,000
Payments				
Raw Material Purchases	3,000	2,800	3,960	3,000
Labour	1,320	1,260	1,320	1,440
Fixed Overheads	1,800	1,800	1,800	1,800
Total Payments	6,120	5,860	7,080	6,240
Cash Flow for Month	2,380	1,640	(2,080)	2,760
Bank balance brought forward	10,000	12,380	14,020	11,940
Bank balance carried forward	12,380	14,020	11,940	14,700

The impact of both the following possible changes occurring now needs to be assessed:

1   A discount of 5% is to be offered to customers who pay in the month of sale. 50% of sales will be received on this basis. The remainder will continue to pay in two months. This is to come into effect from January. March sales are expected to be £10,000, and April sales £12,000.

2   Raw material costs are due to rise by 7% with effect from those purchased in March.

Required

Calculate the impact of both the two possible changes occurring on each month's closing bank balance.

4.4   Cash-Change Limited is a trading company selling to the UK manufacturing industry. The following figures are an extract from a cash budget as initially prepared for the period April to June, together with the actual figures for the same period.

	Cash Budget			Actual Cash		
	April £'000	May £'000	June £'000	April £'000	May £'000	June £'000
Receipts						
Cash Sales	10	20	25	12	19	24
Trade Debtors	50	50	50	45	45	60
Payments						
Purchases	10	13	10	10	10	10
Wages	20	20	20	20	20	20
Rent	15	0	0	5	5	5
Administration	10	10	10	10	10	11
Fixed Assets	0	20	0	0	0	17

Required

Summarise the differences for each category of receipt and payment between the forecast and the actual data, and suggest possible causes for each difference.

5 Managing liquidity – the UK financial system

this chapter covers . . .

So far in this book we have looked in detail at the way in which organisations set up cash flow forecasts to budget for future inflows and outflows of cash and estimate their liquidity. Organisations need to be able to manage their liquidity and deal with:

- shortages of cash – by borrowing from banks

- surpluses of cash – by placing deposits with banks

This chapter provides the background knowledge needed to place this process of liquidity management in context and provide an understanding of how interest rates are arrived at, and how they affect organisations. The chapter covers:

- the structure of the banking system and the way in which banks themselves raise funds from the money markets

- the way in which the Government's monetary policy is carried out by the control of interest rates and inflation in order to provide stability in the economy

- the influence of these economic trends on an organisation's own liquidity management

PERFORMANCE CRITERIA COVERED

unit 15 OPERATING A CASH MANAGEMENT AND CREDIT CONTROL SYSTEM

element 15.2

Manage cash balances

D   Ensure account is taken of trends in the economic and financial environment in managing cash balances.

KNOWLEDGE AND UNDERSTANDING COVERAGE

2   The basic structure of the banking system and the money market in the UK and the relationships between financial institutions.

4   Types of marketable security (bills of exchange, certificates of deposit, government securities, local authority short term loans); terms and conditions; risks.

5   Government monetary policies.

THE BASIS OF LIQUIDITY MANAGEMENT

why is liquidity important?

the liquidity of a business is the availability of cash or assets which can easily be turned into cash

Without cash or liquidity a business can experience cash flow problems by running out of money to meet day-to-day requirements, for example – payments to trade creditors, paying wages and reducing the bank overdraft when requested to do so. In a worst case scenario the business can be bankrupted (made insolvent) because creditors – including the bank – who are not paid on time can take legal action in which the court can repay creditors by selling the assets of the business. Insolvency (the inability to pay debts as they fall due) is covered in Chapter 11 when we describe how a business can minimise its bad debt risks as part of credit control policy.

Remember that cash is crucial. A common saying worth bearing in mind is:

Turnover is vanity, profit is sanity, but cash is king!

liquidity management

It is crucial that a business **manages** its liquidity. **Liquidity management** involves:

- the management of cash inflows and outflows
- the arrangement of finance at the best terms obtainable when there is a cash shortfall
- the appropriate investment of any cash surplus to achieve maximum return

In the earlier chapters of this book we have examined the way in which organisations such as businesses set up cash flow forecasts and use sophisticated methods to forecast shortages and surpluses of cash over a period of time. As we have seen, these fluctuations can to some extent be smoothed out by managing timing efficiently, for example by scheduling payments to suppliers so that they are covered by receipts from debtors. The raising of finance and the investment of surplus funds are also aspects of liquidity management, and will be dealt with in the next two chapters.

First, however, it is important to put the individual business in the context of the financial system as a whole – in short, the workings of the banks and the setting of the level of interest rates which can seriously affect planning and operations.

BANKS AS FINANCIAL INTERMEDIARIES

the need for a banking system

It is easy to take banks for granted. But consider what would happen if they did not exist. Think again about the problems of cash flow and liquidity: suppose Business A needed £10,000 for the period of a month and Business B had £10,000 surplus cash. Would Business B lend to Business A? Would Business B know about Business A? Probably not. There are a number of problems:

- Business A might be a poor credit risk as a borrower
- Business B might only have the money available for two weeks
- they would need to work out the 'cost' of the loan which Business A would pay to Business B

Of course if there were banks, Business B could deposit the money and be paid interest and Business A could borrow the money and pay interest. It can be seen from this that banks form the useful function of **financial intermediaries** – they come between (intermediate) between depositors and borrowers.

There are many advantages to this arrangement:

- the **amounts** deposited and borrowed can be very flexible – Business A does not have to look around for someone who has £10,000 to lend, the loan from the bank may be funded by a number (an aggregate) of smaller deposits
- the **time period** of the loan does not have to rely on the time period of the deposit – there is what is known technically as 'maturity transformation'
- the **risk** to the depositor is low – the bank is unlikely to crash
- **known cost and reward** – the interest payable on the loan and the interest received for the deposit will be based on established market rates, providing a fair deal for borrower and depositor

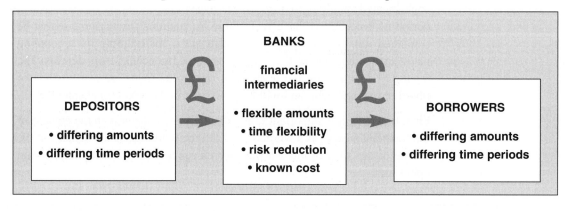

Banks are therefore very efficient financial intermediaries. The banking system not only provides its traditional service of money transmission, it also helps to provide a stable source of liquidity for organisations such as businesses. You should note that Building Societies are also financial intermediaries, although they mostly deal in the narrower field of personal savings and house finance.

The banking system as a whole includes a variety of institutions – and groups of companies – carrying out different functions:

- retail 'High Street' banks such as Barclays Bank, RBS and HSBC
- 'investment' banks or merchant banks, which deal with major company financing, investment advice and share issues, eg Barclays Capital Bank

The banking system, as we will see in the next section, has an important relationship with the UK Central Bank, the Bank of England.

THE BANK OF ENGLAND AND BANK LIQUIDITY

role of the Bank of England

The Bank of England is the UK's Central Bank. It carries out a number of functions, for example:

- it is banker to the Government – it holds accounts for Government departments
- it is banker to other banks – it holds accounts for other banks
- it is responsible for note printing, gold and foreign currency reserves
- it helps to influence interest rates in the economy – these rates are set with the aim of controlling the rate of inflation (see page 113)

If you want to find out more about the Bank of England, visit www.bankof england.co.uk, a very helpful and informative website.

banks and the Bank of England

The banks operating in the banking system provide each other with liquidity – ie cash balances – as they are regularly making large volumes of payments to each other and settling up with each other at the end of every working day.

But, like other businesses, the banks need a fail-safe source of liquidity. Just as businesses borrow from retail banks, the banks themselves can borrow funds when needed, provided on a daily basis. The money is provided by the Bank of England buying from the banks a variety of short-term securities (paper 'certificates') which are traded in the London **money markets.** These markets need some explanation.

UK money markets

A **money market** is what the term suggests – a market for borrowing money and investing money. Nothing, of course, is free: the cost of the money is the interest rate charged on the amount borrowed. Trading is carried out largely on computer screen and by telephone. There is no physical marketplace.

One of the major sterling money markets is the **interbank market**, which, as the name suggests, involves banks and other large institutions lending to each other over short periods, for example overnight or over one, three or six months. Note that there are no certificates issued for these loans.

Other money markets involve the issue of a variety of what are essentially IOU 'securities' or 'certificates' issued by reputable institutions, both governmental and commercial (retail and merchant banks, insurance companies, pension funds), when raising money. The institution agrees to pay a fixed interest rate on the certificates, which can then be 'sold' as an investment in the money markets before the maturity (repayment) date. Whoever has the certificate when it matures will receive the face value of that certificate from the issuer.

There are markets for the following types of 'security' or 'certificate', shown in the table below. The term 'short-term' typically applies to three or six month certificates. Notice that they are listed in the order of risk.

UK money markets in tradeable securities

type of market	issuer of security	description
gilts	UK Government	'gilts' (short for 'gilt-edged stock') are Government securities, ie certificates issued in return for long-term Government borrowing
treasury bills	UK Government	91 day certificates issued to provide short-term Government funding
local authority bills	local authorities	short-term bills issued by local authorities (eg County Councils, Metropolitan Councils in the UK)
Euro securities	EU central banks and Governments	securities issued within the EEA (European Economic Area) and also by major international institutions
certificates of deposit (CDs)	banks	short-term certificates issued by the banks for deposits received
bills of exchange	companies	short-term bills, normally guaranteed by banks (often merchant banks)
corporate bonds	companies	debt certificates (higher risk than bills)

a note on 'bills'

The table on the previous page mentions the term 'bill'. This is an abbreviation of **bill of exchange**, a traditional method of settling debt between traders, and another form of marketable security in the London money markets.

A bill of exchange is a document which sets out the amount and payment date of a debt. It might state, for example, that Company A owes Company B £50,000, and is due to pay that amount on 30 March. If Company B needed the money in advance it could sell the bill to Company C at a discounted price (say £49,500) and Company C would then receive £50,000 on 30 March from Company A. Sometimes banks will be prepared to guarantee payment of bills by adding their name to the document.

If this all sounds too complex, the important point to remember is that bills issued by reputable organisations are yet another way of investing surplus funds in the London money markets.

bank borrowing from the Bank of England

Each day the UK banks pass between themselves a large volume of payments relating to customer transactions, eg BACS payments and cheques. They trade on the inter-bank market (see previous page) making 'wholesale' deposits and borrowing short-term, according to their liquidity needs. They also invest funds in the 'marketable security' money markets, eg in gilts, treasury bills, CDs, and other types of bill. These investments are made so that the banks can remain liquid – they are in a position to be able to repay customer deposits because they are holding marketable securities which they can sell at short notice if they need to.

The balance sheet of a bank will therefore contain the following elements:

elements of a bank balance sheet (simplified)

liabilities	assets
customer deposits (amounts due to customers)	loans (amounts due from customers)
other creditors	investments, including • inter-bank market deposits • marketable securities from the London money market
capital & reserves	accounts with the Bank of England notes and coins

Banks are able to borrow from the Bank of England when they are in need of funds. The Bank of England does not lend money direct but instead either

- buys market securities (eg bills and CDs) outright from the banks

- buys market securities from the banks and agrees to sell back equivalent securities two weeks later in what is known as a **repo** (repurchase) agreement – effectively a two week loan

These transactions affect the assets side of the bank balance sheet (see previous page for full balance sheet) as follows:

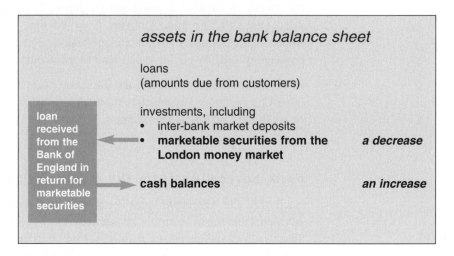

assets in the bank balance sheet

loans
(amounts due from customers)

loan received from the Bank of England in return for marketable securities

investments, including
- inter-bank market deposits
- **marketable securities from the London money market**   *a decrease*

cash balances   *an increase*

the 'repo' rate

The important point here is that the effective interest rate at which the banks obtain funds from the Bank of England – the **repo rate** – is a 'base' rate set by the Bank of England's Monetary Policy Committee (MPC). It is the rate which the Committee wishes to be used as a basis for all interest rates in the economy in its efforts to control inflation.

THE BANK OF ENGLAND AND MONETARY POLICY

One of the Bank of England's main purposes is 'maintaining the integrity and value of the currency'. The Bank achieves this primarily through monetary policy.

Monetary policy involves the control of the money supply (the amount of money) in the economy which in turn affects the rate of inflation. The object of monetary policy is to maintain price stability, as defined by the inflation target set by the Government. This will in turn help to achieve the economic goal of sustainable growth and employment.

High inflation can be damaging to the functioning of the economy. Low inflation – price stability – can encourage sustainable long-term economic growth.

the repo rate – a summary

The Bank of England aims to meet the Government's inflation target by setting short-term interest rates. Interest rate decisions are taken by the Monetary Policy Committee (MPC) of the Bank of England. Monetary policy operates by influencing the cost of money. The Bank of England sets an interest rate for its own dealings with the banks and other participants in the money markets (ie short-term lending) – the **repo rate** – and that rate then affects the whole pattern of rates set by the commercial banks for their savers and borrowers. This, in turn, affects spending and output in the economy, and eventually costs and prices.

CHANGES IN THE ECONOMIC AND FINANCIAL ENVIRONMENT

It is the aim of the Government to bring about stability in the economy by controlling inflation through interest rates. Organisations such as businesses often find it disruptive, however, if interest rates fluctuate:

the effect of a rise in interest rates on a business

If interest rates rise, financial planning is made more difficult:

- the cost of borrowing will increase – interest charges will increase and investment in the business will be discouraged
- a rise in interest rates is often associated with a rise in inflation, leading to a rise in the cost of raw materials and an increase in overheads
- the value of the currency will tend to rise in the short term, making exports less competitive but imported raw materials cheaper

On the other hand, if the business is very liquid and has funds to invest, the return will be greater as interest rates rise.

the effect of a fall in interest rates

If interest rates fall, the effects are generally positive – which is what the Government is aiming for:

- the cost of borrowing will decrease – interest charges will go down, borrowing will be cheaper and investment in the business will be encouraged, all of which is symptomatic of a healthy economy
- the rate of inflation will stabilise or even fall, leading to price stability or even a fall in the costs of raw materials and overheads

Chapter Summary

- Sufficient liquidity – the availability of cash or near-cash assets – in an organisation such as a business is essential for its survival.

- Liquidity management involves the careful timing of cash inflows and outflows, the arrangement of finance where required and the investment of surplus funds where appropriate.

- Banks are needed as financial intermediaries to service the needs of borrowers and investors so that amounts can be aggregated, time periods made flexible, risk minimised and the cost or return of the borrowing or investment quantified.

- The Bank of England carries out a number of important roles: banker to the Government, banker to the banks, note printing, maintaining gold and currency reserves, influencing interest rates as part of the monetary policy of the Government.

- Banks and other institutions trade actively in the UK money markets where money can be borrowed or invested, normally over the short term. The money markets include the interbank market (wholesale money deposits) and markets in tradeable securities, for example Government stocks, CDs, bills of exchange, local authority bills and Euro securities (see Key Terms for fuller details).

- Banks can raise funds from the Bank of England by trading marketable securities in return for cash on the basis that they will repurchase equivalent securities in approximately two weeks time from the Bank of England. This is known as a 'repo' transaction and is charged by the Bank of England at what is known as the 'repo' rate of interest.

- One of the Bank of England's functions is to help administer the monetary policy of the Government. This policy aims to adjust the supply of money in the economy in order to control the rate of inflation and the stability of the currency.

- Monetary policy is carried out by the Bank of England influencing interest rates (under the direction of the Monetary Control Committee) through the setting of the repo rate (base rate) at which the Bank of England lends to the financial system. This repo rate then affects the borrowing and investing rates throughout the economy.

- Organisations such as businesses are affected by the economic and financial environment which results from the operation of monetary policy. Generally speaking low interest rates are associated with low inflation and are beneficial – they enable businesses to borrow and invest in growth, which in turn is a sign of a healthy and stable economy.

Key Terms		
	liquidity	the availability of cash or assets which can easily be turned into cash
	liquidity management	the management of cash inflows and outflows, ensuring that finance is arranged where there is a cash shortfall and surplus funds are invested to achieve a return
	financial intermediary	a body that accepts deposits and lends money, enabling funds to move from depositors to borrowers in the most efficient way
	retail bank	a bank that offers financial services to the general public, also known as a 'High Street' bank
	merchant bank	a bank that deals with company financing and investments, also known as an 'investment' bank
	money market	a market in which institutions invest and raise 'money', either in the form of straightforward money balances or through tradeable securities (see below)
	tradeable securities	certificates issued by institutions (including the Government) in return for money received for a certain period of time; these certificates (see below for the different types) can be 'sold' to other institutions in the money markets before maturity
	gilts	also known as 'Government stock' or 'gilt-edged stock', gilts are certificates issued in return for money borrowed by the Government over the long term (ie periods of years)
	treasury bill	91 day certificate issued to raise short-term funding for the Government
	certificate of deposit	short-term certificate issued by the banks in return for money deposited; often referred to as CDs
	bill of exchange	a tradeable document issued by a company or local authority to provide evidence that an amount is owing to that company or local authority and has to be repaid on a certain date

repo agreement   a 'repurchase' agreement made between the Bank of England and banking institutions whereby the Bank of England buys acceptable tradeable securities on the basis that the institution will repurchase equivalent securities from the Bank of England, normally in two weeks time; it is in essence a short-term loan by the Bank of England

repo rate   the effective rate of interest charged by the Bank of England on a repo agreement – it is the 'base' rate set by the Bank of England's Monetary Policy Committee (under the direction of the Government) which is used to set rates of interest for borrowers and savers in the economy generally

monetary policy   Government policy which is used to adjust the amount of money in the economy by setting interest rates and attempting to control inflation

Student Activities

answers to the asterisked (*) questions are to be found at the back of this book

5.1*   There is a saying that 'cash is king'. Why is cash so important to a business that buys and sells on credit?

5.2*   (a)   Write down in your own words the meaning of 'liquidity'.

(b)   What action is a business likely to take if it encounters a shortfall of cash?

(c)   What action is a business likely to take if it has a surplus of cash?

5.3*   (a)   Write down in your own words what you understand by the phrase 'financial intermediary'

(b)   What are the four main advantages of financial intermediaries to investors and borrowers?

5.4* Which type of bank (retail or merchant) is most likely to be used by

(a) a private customer opening an account for receiving a salary and paying bills?

(b) a private customer applying for a mortgage loan for buying an apartment?

(c) a company wishing to raise money through the issue of shares?

(d) a company needing an account from which to pay its employees' salaries?

5.5* Describe four main functions of the Bank of England. If you want further information, visit www.bankofengland.co.uk

5.6* What type of tradeable security is issued by the Government for

(a) its short-term borrowing requirements

(b) its long-term borrowing requirements

5.7* Local Authority bills sometimes offer a slightly better interest rate than Treasury Bills over the same time period. Why?

5.8* Why should banks hold tradeable securities such as Treasury Bills among their assets?

5.9* How might a retail bank such as Barclays raise funds from the Bank of England if it finds that it needs cash at the end of the day in order to settle all its payment transactions?

5.10 Explain what the 'repo' rate is, and why it is so important in the implementation of the Government's monetary policy.

5.11 Describe two significant effects on a business of a rise in interest rates in the UK economy. How might this affect the liquidity of a business?

5.12 Describe two significant effects on a business of a fall in interest rates in the UK economy. How might this affect the liquidity of a business?

6 Managing liquidity – obtaining finance

this chapter covers . . .

Liquidity management involves the accurate forecast of shortages and surpluses of cash through the use of a cash flow forecast. It also requires the knowledge of what to do when these fluctuations occur – either borrowing to cover financial needs or investing surplus funds. In this chapter we will explain how shortages of cash are dealt with by arranging financing in the form of:

- bank overdrafts for short-term day-to-day requirements

- bank loans and other structured borrowing for longer-term requirements

Efficient liquidity management involves:

- arranging the right finance – the right loan for the right time period

- obtaining the best terms – ie fees and interest rates – from the lender

This chapter also examines the customer/banker legal relationship and the need for businesses to provide security to cover borrowing.

PERFORMANCE CRITERIA COVERED

unit 15 OPERATING A CASH MANAGEMENT AND CREDIT CONTROL SYSTEM

element 15.2

Manage cash balances

A Arrange overdraft and loan facilities in anticipation of requirements and on the most favourable terms available.

C Ensure the organisation's financial regulations and security procedures are observed.

D Ensure account is taken of trends in the economic and financial environment in managing cash balances.

E Maintain an adequate level of liquidity in line with cash forecasts.

KNOWLEDGE AND UNDERSTANDING COVERAGE

3 Bank overdrafts and loans; terms and conditions; legal relationship between bank and customer.

CASH FLOW AND LIQUIDITY

cash flow – a reminder

As we saw in the earlier chapters in this book, an organisation constructs a cash flow forecast, often using a spreadsheet:

- to project cash inflows and outflows
- to highlight cash shortages and cash surpluses
- to monitor the figures on a regular basis, comparing actual results with the projections

The illustration below shows the items that will typically be included on a cash flow forecast.

You should by now be familiar with the entries on the forecast, the arithmetic involved and the significance of the 'bottom line' in showing shortfalls and surpluses. If you need reminding, read Chapter 1 again.

	A	B	C	D	E	F	G
1	CORIANNE LIMITED						
2	Cash flow forecast for the six months ending June 2004						
3		JANUARY	FEBRUARY	MARCH	APRIL	MAY	JUNE
4		£	£	£	£	£	£
5	Receipts						
6							
7							
8	Sales Receipts	3,000	3,000	4,000	4,000	4,000	4,000
9							
10	Capital	10,000					
11	TOTAL RECEIPTS	13,000	3,000	4,000	4,000	4,000	4,000
12	Payments						
13	Purchases	5,000	1,750	1,750		1,750	1,750
14	Fixed Assets	4,500	5,250				
15	Rent/Rates	575	575	575	575	575	575
16	Insurance	50	50	50	50	50	50
17	Electricity	25	25	25	25	25	25
18	Telephone	150	15	15	15	15	15
19	Stationery	10	10	10	10	10	10
20	Postage	15	15	15	15	15	15
21	Bank charges	100		75			75
22	Advertising	150	30	30	30	30	30
23	TOTAL PAYMENTS	10,575	7,720	2,545	720	2,470	2,545
24	CASHFLOW FOR MONTH	2,425	- 4,720	1,455	3,280	1,530	1,455
25	Bank Balance *brought forward*	-	2,425	- 2,295	- 840	2,440	3,970
26	Bank Balance *carried forward*	2,425	- 2,295	- 840	2,440	3,970	5,425

liquidity – a reminder

the liquidity of a business is the availability of cash or assets which can easily be turned into cash

As we saw at the beginning of the last chapter, without cash or liquidity a business can experience cash flow problems by running out of money to meet day-to-day requirements, for example – payments to trade creditors, paying wages and reducing the bank overdraft when requested to do so. If sufficient liquidity is not provided, the business can become insolvent, in other words it will not be able to repay its debts as they become due.

This may happen through **overtrading**. This is when a business which buys and sells on credit does not realise that when there is a big increase in the volume of orders, it will need extra cash to purchase stock and pay creditors. The irony here is that the business appears to be profitable, but if it cannot pay its debts to creditors, it is in danger of becoming insolvent.

There are two points which arise from this:

- profitability is not the same as liquidity – if you have not got the cash, you can forget the profit
- it is in this situation that the **financing** of the cash shortage becomes critical

THE FINANCING SOLUTION

It is important to appreciate that the financing solution – whether it is provided by a bank or by another financial institution – must be the right form of finance and suitable for the purpose. For example:

- the **time period** – is the finance needed for the short-term or the long-term – for days, months or for years?
- the **purpose** – is the finance needed for acquiring assets such as computers or warehousing, or is it to fund working capital requirements such as paying creditors and wages?
- the **amount** – is the amount enough for the purpose and can the organisation or business show that it can repay it?

There is no point in an ice cream trader obtaining a long-term fixed loan to finance stock for the summer season or for a car showroom using a short-term loan to pay for an extension which it wants to pay for over a period of years. Admittedly these are extreme examples, but they do illustrate a point.

Your assessments will often ask you to compare a short-term financing solution such as a bank overdraft with a longer-term facility such as a fixed loan. We will therefore classify financing solutions along these lines.

SHORT-TERM FINANCING SOLUTIONS

The main forms of short-term finance include:

- overdraft
- invoice discounting
- factoring

There are various interpretations of what 'short-term' means. In this chapter we will use the term to refer to periods of up to twelve months.

overdraft

An overdraft is an arrangement ('facility') between a bank and a customer which allows the customer to borrow money on a current account up to a specified amount ('limit').

Overdrafts are available to personal and to business customers. Students will be very familiar with them! Negative figures on the bottom of a cash flow forecast indicate an overdraft.

The **features** of an overdraft include:

- interest is calculated on a daily basis and charged at an agreed rate (usually a fixed percentage above the bank's 'base' rate) monthly or quarterly, but only on the amount that is borrowed

- the customer is also likely to have to pay an arrangement fee based on a percentage of the overall 'limit', ie the maximum amount that can be borrowed

- the overdraft 'facility' is agreed for a set time period, often six or twelve months, after which it can be reviewed by the bank and renewed with an appropriate limit to reflect activity on the current account

- a 'healthy' overdraft will swing from borrowing into credit on a regular basis – if the balance sticks at an overdrawn position for any length of time near the limit, it may be that the customer is in financial trouble (a working capital shortage) or is using the overdraft for longer term borrowing (eg fixed asset purchase)

- business overdrafts are normally secured, ie the bank will require some form of security, eg a charge over the customer's business or private assets or a guarantee from someone else (see pages 132-133 for further details of providing security) – but note that personal overdrafts are normally unsecured

- a business overdraft is nowadays normally a **committed overdraft**, ie it is granted for a fixed period of time and is only repayable on demand if the borrower becomes bankrupt; note that a committed overdraft is not the same as a personal overdraft which is strictly repayable on demand

The main **advantage** of an overdraft is that it is very flexible:

- the customer only borrows what is needed for the short-term – by issuing cheques and then paying in receipts to repay the borrowing
- the customer only pays interest on what is borrowed, which helps reduce the overall interest charge
- the overdraft limit may be raised by the bank with the minimum of formality (subject to its normal lending criteria) if the customer needs extra working capital – for example a shop stocking up in the period before Christmas

The often-quoted **disadvantage** of an overdraft is that it is repayable on demand. But, as mentioned on the previous page, this is only likely to happen with a business overdraft if the bank is going to call in the Receiver when the business looks like it is becoming insolvent. So, for most practical purposes, this disadvantage becomes rather academic.

invoice finance

One major problem facing organisations that supply goods or services on credit is simply that of getting the money in on time. Debtors have a handy habit of saying things like 'the cheque is in the post' or 'we seem to have lost the invoice – can you fax a copy?' when they want to delay payment or when they do not have the funds to pay. The subject of credit management forms the basis for Chapters 8 to 11 of this book.

Businesses can be made insolvent when their debtors do not pay on time – liquidity dries up, the overdraft goes up to the limit and the business cannot then issue the cheques it desperately needs to pay. This can happen when a business is expanding too fast (overtrading) or when it is unlucky and a major customer becomes insolvent, leaving unpaid cheques to push up the overdraft balance.

Invoice finance is one solution to this problem. This can take two forms:

- **invoice discounting**
- **factoring**

We will describe these in turn.

invoice discounting

Here a finance house (normally a subsidiary company owned by a bank) lends money against the invoices received by selected debtors of the business, but the business continues to operate its own credit management system.

The **features** of this scheme are:

- the finance house will be prepared to set up invoice discounting for a business which has good credit management procedures in place (the finance house will examine its credit control procedures)
- when an invoice is issued to a debtor, details are passed to the finance house
- the finance house will immediately lend between 60% to 90% of the invoice value to the business that issued the invoice
- repayment is made when the invoice has been settled by the debtor
- the finance house charges interest on the amount borrowed and also charges an administration fee

The **advantages** of this scheme are:

- the debtor does not know that money has been borrowed against the invoice
- a significant cash flow advantage to the business issuing the invoices
- flexibility – the invoice finance keeps up with growth in the business – the greater the total value of eligible invoices, the greater the amount of available finance

factoring

Factoring is the process where a finance house lends money against the invoices received by debtors of the business, and where it completely takes over the administration of the sales ledger.

The **features** of this scheme are:

- the finance house manages the sales ledger, deals with credit control and collects the debts
- the finance house will normally lend up to 90% of outstanding invoice amounts as soon as the invoice is issued and will pay the balance (less charges) when the debtor pays up
- the customer will pay a finance charge for the amounts borrowed plus a percentage charge on turnover for the sales ledger management services; as it is a comprehensive scheme, it is far from cheap
- finance houses also provide an optional bad debt protection scheme – ie insurance against bad debts – known as **non-recourse factoring**, for which a further charge is payable
- factoring without bad debt protection is known as **recourse factoring** – ie if a debt goes bad, recourse has to be made to the customer who will have to stand the loss and write off the bad debt

The **advantages** of this type of scheme are:

- as it takes over sales ledger management a factoring company can save a business considerable time and money spent in chasing debts

- factoring companies have wide experience of credit management and are expert in the credit rating of businesses; this in turn will reduce the incidence of bad debt (applicable to recourse factoring only)

- it can protect a business against any bad debts (non-recourse factoring only)

Case Study

OLLY HARDY: SHORT-TERM FINANCING

situation

Stan L'Orelle is an accountant. During the week he has a meeting with a client, Olly Hardy, who is looking for guidance about improving the liquidity of the business he runs. Olly's business is an electrical appliance and repair company 'Bright Spark'. Most of his customers are businesses which he invoices on 60 days terms. He obtains the majority of his materials from an electrical wholesaler 'Blue Ridge Supplies' from whom he obtains 30 days credit on account. Sometimes, however, he has to buy one-off items from other suppliers and has to pay cash.

During his meeting with Stan, Olly mentions that some of his customers are very slow to pay, and following a recent cash purchase of electric heaters, his bank account is overdrawn, although he does not have an agreed overdraft facility. The bank manager has phoned him on a number of occasions asking him to call in to sort it out.

solution

the overdraft

Stan recommends to Olly that he meets with the bank manager to discuss the possibility of an overdraft facility. He will need to prepare a number of documents, with Stan's help, to help with his application to the bank:

- a cash flow forecast

- recent sets of accounts for the business

Once he has an agreed overdraft set up, Olly will be able to deal with short-term cash shortages, as long as he keeps the situation under control. Stan points out that the current account should normally swing from credit to debit in the course of trading.

the sales ledger

Stan points out that part of Olly's liquidity problem is caused by the fact that a number of his customers are not paying up on time, if at all. Stan recommends that Olly approaches a factoring company for invoice finance. He will probably need the more expensive 'without recourse' factoring service, as it will not only lend him money against invoices and insure against bad debts, it will also take over the running of his sales ledger, leaving him more time in which to run his business.

LONGER-TERM FINANCING SOLUTIONS

It is important when raising finance to **match the finance to the need**. We have already seen that an overdraft is ideal for a short-term borrowing requirement: it is flexible, you borrow what you need when you need it and repay when you can. Then, after twelve months and armed with your cash flow forecast, you can review the facility with the bank and renegotiate the facility for a further twelve months.

Occasionally, a business may build up an overdraft which never goes into credit. This is known as a 'hardcore' overdraft which has become a permanent source of working capital. This borrowing is usually paid off by the business over a period of years, the debt having been transferred into a loan account and transformed into a structured loan.

fixed asset finance

If you are purchasing assets which you will keep in the business for a year or more, you will have to make a choice from different types of **fixed asset finance**.

Businesses will need to acquire new fixed assets as part of expansion plans, or as replacements for existing items. Typical longer-term (fixed) assets include computers, equipment, vehicles, buildings and land.

The basic practice is to pay back the cost of the assets over the period for which they are retained. For example, computer and vehicle finance may be repaid over one to three years whereas if a business is buying land and property a commercial mortgage loan over twenty-five years would be fairly common.

Financing can be in the form of:

- repayment loans from the bank
- hire purchase from a finance company
- leasing from a finance company

bank loans

Bank loans are a long-term solution to the financing needs of a business. They are ideal for purchasing fixed assets such as equipment, land and buildings. As mentioned above, they can also be used for permanent financing of working capital.

The **features** of bank loans are:

- the period of the loan can be tailored to the expected life of the asset
- repayments can be made monthly, quarterly or annually

- sometimes a 'repayment holiday' can be arranged if the loan is for an asset from which the income generated will be subject to a delay, for example a major capital project which will take time to get into operation

- security will invariably be required to cover the loan (see pages 132-133 for details); in the case of land and buildings the security may be the land and buildings themselves

- interest rates can be

  - fixed for the period of the loan (normally up to ten years), which helps the financial planning processes of the business

  - variable, at a fixed percentage over the bank base lending rate (these loans are normally cheaper than fixed rate loans)

  - 'capped' – ie the bank will guarantee a maximum rate and will carry the risk if the market rates rise above the upper 'capped' limit

- an arrangement fee is charged at the beginning of the loan – it is typically around 1% of the amount borrowed

The **advantages** of bank loans are:

- repayments can be scheduled to suit the life of the asset

- repayment may be delayed if required

- the regularity of repayments helps the business in its financial planning processes

other ways of financing assets – hire purchase

Hire purchase allows a business to acquire assets and to pay for them by instalments over a period of time. There are two parties in the arrangement – a hire purchase company (finance company) and the customer. The assets provided in a hire purchase agreement – typically computer equipment – remain the property of the hire purchase company until the end of the agreement (after a couple of years, for example) when ownership then passes to the business, which can then carry on using the assets.

The business is responsible for the servicing and insurance of the assets during the period of the agreement.

Hire purchase is also a common way for individuals to acquire consumer goods; here there is the well-known risk of having the goods taken back if repayments fall behind!

other ways of financing assets – leasing

Leasing also involves two parties: the finance company which buys and owns the assets and the customer who pays for using the assets.

Leasing is therefore more appropriate when the business does not necessarily want to own the assets at the end of the period. Company car fleets, for example, are often leased, which is why you can often pick up a second-hand car bargain from a leasing company when the car is no longer being used in the car fleet.

There are two main types of lease: a finance lease and an operating lease.

A **finance lease** is where the repayments paid by the customer are calculated to cover the whole cost of the asset. At the end of the lease period the asset is sold by the leasing company and some of the money is passed as a rebate back to the customer. Alternatively the customer may want to keep the asset, in which case the lease is extended with lower payments made by the customer.

An **operating lease** is where the repayments paid by the customer are calculated to cover the fall in value of the asset during the period of the agreement. There is no rebate for the customer when the asset is sold at the end of the lease period – the leasing company retains all the sale proceeds. This is useful for assets such as cars for which there is an established second-hand market.

As with hire purchase, the business is responsible for the servicing and insurance of leased assets during the period of the agreement.

advantages of hire purchase and leasing

These two schemes in their various forms are flexible – as long as the asset will be required for the period of the agreement – and have many advantages for the business:

- the fixed repayment amounts help the business to plan its finances accurately
- a cash flow advantage of being able to match the payments to the finance company with income generated by the asset where appropriate
- it allows the business to enjoy the benefits of asset ownership without experiencing some of the problems, eg how to dispose of the asset when it is no longer needed

COMPARING OVERDRAFTS AND LOANS

Your assessments may ask you to compare the features, advantages and disadvantages of bank overdrafts and loans, often in the form of a memorandum relating to a specific situation. The Case Study which follows is a variant on this theme in that it explores how both forms of finance can (and indeed should) be used together. You should note that it is important to become familiar in your revision with all the forms of short-term and longer-term financing covered in the last few pages.

Case Study

FAWLTY CATERING: FINANCING EXPANSION

situation

The Board of Directors of Fawlty Catering Limited has approved an investment of £500,000 in a new fully fitted canteen which is to be built as an extension to the company's existing premises. You have been asked to draw up a memorandum to the Board explaining the advantages and disadvantages of using a bank overdraft and a bank loan for funding. You have been asked to provide firm recommendations for financing the project. Your answer is set out in the memorandum below.

MEMORANDUM

to	The Board of Directors	**date**	today
from	Ali McStudent	**subject**	Financing of canteen project

Set out below is a proposal for financing the new canteen.

bank overdraft

A bank overdraft is used for financing short-term needs such as working capital. It has the advantage of flexibility – the company will only need to borrow when it needs to and interest will only be payable on amounts borrowed. This need will arise when the new canteen is up and running.

Unless it is 'committed', the overdraft is repayable on demand, but in view of the liquidity and profitability of the company, it is unlikely that the bank will demand immediate repayment of its funds.

bank loan

A bank loan is used to finance the acquisition of fixed assets such as equipment, land and buildings, and so will be most appropriate for the new canteen project. We will need to negotiate with the bank features such as:

- the period of the loan
- the repayment schedule
- the interest rate (whether fixed, variable or capped)
- security required

As the project is a long-term one, a loan period of ten years would most closely match our earnings potential from the canteen. It may well be worth negotiating a 'repayment holiday' of at least one year to see us over the building period when we will not be receiving any income from the project.

As interest rates are currently low and are not likely to rise significantly, a variable rate loan would be the cheapest option. Interest would be paid monthly or quarterly and an arrangement fee paid.

Security will be needed by the bank. We may need to charge the company assets, or the Directors may need to provide guarantees supported by security. This will need to be discussed with the bank.

recommendations

A long-term bank loan will certainly be needed for the new canteen. Our projections propose a figure of £500,000 with repayments over ten years and a repayment holiday of twelve months.

Our cash flow projections show that an overdraft will eventually be needed to provide extra working capital for the operation of the new canteen. This will need to be negotiated with the bank.

Ali McStudent

BANK AND CUSTOMER RELATIONSHIP

Your studies require you to be familiar with the legal relationship between bank and customer, and as an extension to that, the arrangements made by a business to provide security for borrowing from a bank.

banker customer legal relationship

The important legal relationship between a bank and a customer is based on contract, ie a legal agreement. Both bank and customer have contractual obligations to each other. If they fail in these obligations and serious loss occurs, legal proceedings may follow. Both parties should therefore know where they stand. Examples of these rights and duties include:

- a **bank** has to comply with its customers' payment requests and pay the cheques that its customers write out

- a **bank** has to exercise care in dealing with its customers' affairs

- a **bank** has to provide regular statements of account

- a **bank** must keep its customers' dealings confidential, unless the law or the customer requires otherwise

A bank is also said to have a **fiduciary duty** to its customers, ie it must advise them in a responsible way if they rely on the bank to advise them and act in their best interests. This duty also exists, for example, between doctor and patient. The patient is said to take what the doctor says 'on trust' and so the doctor (or the banker in a similar position) must not take advantage of this situation.

If the bank fails in any of these obligations and the customer suffers loss as a result, the customer can take legal action against the bank. The situation is not all one-sided, however, as the customer has duties to the bank. For example, a customer must take care when writing cheques to prevent forgery occurring at a later date if the cheque is stolen.

There are various other legal relationships affecting the bank and the customer, for example:

- if a customer has deposited money with a bank, the bank is a **debtor** (it owes money to the customer) and the customer is a **creditor**; if, on the other hand, the customer is borrowing, the bank is the **creditor** (it is owed money) and the customer is the **debtor**

- a customer signing over property as security for a loan using a mortgage form is said to be a **mortgagor** and the bank a **mortgagee**

- a **bailor** is a customer passing something to the bank for safekeeping (eg a deed box); in this case the bank becomes a **bailee**

LOAN DOCUMENTATION AND LEGAL RIGHTS AND DUTIES

facility letters

Legal rights and duties are also set out in the formal documentation which is signed by the bank and its customer when the bank grants overdrafts and loans. These legal agreements are commonly known as **facility letters**, ie they are 'letters' which provide borrowing 'facilities'.

The extracts below are taken from a business loan facility letter for a partnership. Study them and read the notes that follow. Osborne Books is grateful to the Royal Bank of Scotland for kindly giving permission for the reproduction of these extracts from its loan documentation.

THIS IS AN IMPORTANT DOCUMENT. YOU SHOULD TAKE INDEPENDENT LEGAL ADVICE BEFORE SIGNING AND SIGN ONLY IF YOU WANT TO BE LEGALLY BOUND.

THIS AGREEMENT is made between:-

(1)   **The Royal Bank of Scotland plc** (the **"Bank"**); and

(2)   ******* and ******* (the **"Customer"**) being the partners of ****** (the **"Partnership"**)

to set out the terms and conditions on which the Bank is pleased to make available to the Customer a loan of £****** (the **"Loan"**).

1   **Purpose**

The Loan shall be utilised to ********.

2   **Preconditions**

2.1   The Bank shall not be obliged to provide the Loan unless the following conditions are satisfied on the date on which the Loan is drawn:-

(a)   the Bank has received the duplicate of this Agreement signed by the Customer;

(b)   any security to be granted in terms of Clause 8 is valued and completed to the satisfaction of the Bank;

(c)   the availability as security for the Loan of any existing security is confirmed to the satisfaction of the Bank; and

(d)   the Bank is satisfied that no default event as outlined in Clause 11 (an **"Event of Default"**) (or event which may result in an Event of Default) has occurred or may occur as a consequence of the Loan being drawn.

3   **Drawdown**

3.1   The Loan will require to be drawn down in one amount within 3 months from the date this Agreement is signed on behalf of the Bank.

This introductory part sets out basic details such as the name of the borrower, the amount and purpose of the loan and when it has to be taken ('drawdown').

10   **Undertakings**

10.1   The Undertakings in this clause shall remain in force until the Loan has been repaid in full.

10.2   The Customer shall immediately notify the Bank in the event of an Event of Default occurring.

10.3   The Customer shall not:-

    (a)   grant any security to any third party;

    (b)   other than in the ordinary course of business, sell, transfer, lease or otherwise dispose of any assets;

    (c)   enter into any obligation, whether by way of borrowing from another source, leasing commitments, factoring of debts, granting of guarantees or by any other means;

    (d)   make any change in the nature of business conducted by the Partnership;

    without the prior written consent of the Bank.

10.4   The Customer shall:-

    (a)   comply with all applicable environmental laws, regulations or practices;

    (b)   obtain, renew and comply with all environmental licences, permits or authorisations required for the purposes of its business; and

    (c)   conduct its business in a manner which will ensure that no environmental claim is made against it.

Here the customer agrees to certain **undertakings** or **covenants** such as not giving security to any other person without the consent of the bank and complying with all laws, regulations and environmental requirements.

The final extract shows how a customer might **default** on the loan, which would then immediately make the loan repayable on demand to the bank.

11.1   If any Event of Default occurs, then the Bank may by written notice to the Customer declare the Loan, all interest accrued and all other sums payable by the Customer under this Agreement to be immediately due and payable and/or terminate the obligations of the Bank under this Agreement. Each of the following events is an Event of Default:-

    (a)   the Customer fails to pay any amount payable under this Agreement on the due date;

    (b)   the Customer fails to comply with any provision of this Agreement and, where capable of remedy, such failure is not remedied to the reasonable satisfaction of the Bank within 7 days of the Bank giving notice to the Customer requiring the Customer to remedy the same;

    (c)   the Customer or any other grantor of the Security fails to comply with any provision of the Security and, where capable of remedy, such failure is not remedied to the reasonable satisfaction of the Bank within 7 days of the Bank giving notice to the Customer/other grantor requiring the Customer/other grantor to remedy the same;

    (d)   any information given or warranty or representation made by, or on behalf of, the Customer to the Bank proves inaccurate;

    (e)   any procedure is used against the Customer to attach or take possession of any property for payment of a debt;

    (f)   any insolvency proceedings are commenced against the Customer or the Partnership in any jurisdiction or the Customer makes arrangements with its creditors;

SECURITY FOR FINANCING

We have mentioned earlier in the chapter that banks require business customers to pledge security to cover borrowing. The basic principle involved is that banks quite rightly view lending to business customers as risky. They need to have the reassurance that if the business becomes insolvent and the customer defaults on the loan, they will have some form of property that they can sell or some form of guarantee that they can rely on in order to get some or all of their money back.

We will investigate this area of insolvency again in Chapter 11 when we describe how businesses implement a credit control policy and have to deal with customers who become bad debts.

The main types of **security** that a bank will accept are as follows:

mortgage

A mortgage is a legal document signed by a borrower pledging his/her property to a lender, eg a bank) to secure the borrowing. If the borrower fails to repay, the lender (eg the bank) is given the the power to sell the property in order to get the money back.

Note that the term 'mortgage' is often used to describe a house loan. Strictly speaking, however, the 'mortgage' is not the money but the security document signed by the borrower which enables the lender to sell the property if necessary.

guarantee

A guarantee is a document signed by Person A which states that if Person B (or Company B) does not pay up, Person A will have to do so instead. A bank will often take the guarantees of company directors to secure their company borrowing, and then back up the guarantees with mortgages over the directors' houses or other investments. This means that if the company defaults on its borrowing, the bank can demand that the directors pay up instead, and will be able to sell the directors' property to repay the loan.

fixed charge

A fixed charge is a document signed by a company borrower which states that if it defaults on a loan, the bank can sell company property specified in the document (eg property or investments) to repay the debt.

floating charge   A floating charge is a document signed by a company which states that if the company does not pay up to the bank on demand, the bank can sell or claim from the company's 'floating assets' (eg its stock, its cash balances, its debtors) which happen to be in the company's possession when the claim is made. These assets are 'floating' because they are changing from day-to-day.

As you can see, a fixed charge can enable the bank to sell off a company's fixed assets if the bank puts in its claim, and a floating charge will enable the bank to sell off what are basically the current assets of the company. Most banks when lending to companies will take a combined charge which is both fixed and floating, ie it is a charge over all of the company's assets.

credit assessment by banks

A bank will look very critically at the creditworthiness of a customer when deciding whether or not to lend. The factors a bank will bear in mind in this assessment process can be remembered through the mnemonic **PARIS**:

P   **Personality** of the borrower – the financial standing and track record of the borrower (supported where possible with financial statements and projections) and the experience and commitment of the borrower

A   **Amount** needed – is it the right amount for the requirement? Is it too much compared with the borrower's capital (ie gearing)? Has the borrower provided a cash flow forecast?

R   **Repayment** – can the customer afford the repayments? Will the schedule of repayments work? Again, has the borrower provided a cash flow forecast showing that the borrowing can be repaid?

I   **Interest and fees** – is the bank receiving the right return for the risk? Generally speaking, the higher the risk, the higher the interest rate charged.

S   **Security** – is there sufficient security available to cover the bank if the customer becomes insolvent, ie 'goes bust'?

One of the golden rules of banking is 'never lend on security' – in other words, a bank should not lend just because security is available. It is important that the customer is creditworthy and can afford to repay the borrowing. Security is there to enable the bank manager to sleep at night.

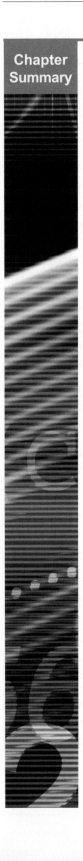

Chapter Summary

■ An organisation may need to raise finance to provide the necessary liquidity for its day-to-day operations and also for its longer-term survival.

■ The finance raised should be for the appropriate purpose and time period (short-term or long-term) and it should be for the right amount.

■ Short-term financing includes bank overdraft and invoice discounting and factoring from a finance company.

■ A bank overdraft allows an organisation to borrow on its current account up to a defined limit, paying interest only on what is borrowed. The facility provides a flexible source of liquidity. The organisation will be able to predict the likely level of borrowing by drawing up a cash flow forecast.

■ Invoice discounting provided by a finance company also helps liquidity by lending money against selected invoices issued by the organisation. Customers of the organisation do not know that this process is taking place because the normal debt collection processes will be carried out to obtain payment of the invoices.

■ Factoring provided by a finance company also provides short-term finance by lending money against invoices issued. In this process the customers of the organisation know that the process is taking place because they have to settle the invoices by paying the factoring company. In some schemes the factoring company also takes on the risk of bad debts.

■ Long-term finance is used to finance fixed asset purchase and also to fund long-term working capital requirements. 'Long-term' can mean anything from twelve months to twenty five years.

■ Bank loans are a common form of long-term finance for assets such as equipment, land and buildings. Loans are normally tailored to suit the expected life of the asset. Repayments are made on a regular basis but may be postponed at the start of the loan to allow for delays in receipt of income. Banks will normally require security for loans.

■ Hire purchase and leasing are further ways of acquiring the use of assets over a fixed time period. These facilities are made available not from banks but from their finance house subsidiary companies. In the case of these schemes, ownership of the assets will remain with the finance house during the initial and main period of the financing.

■ Organisations dealing with banks need to understand that a contractual legal relationship exists between bank and customer which implies a duty of care to the customer. In addition, a number of specific legal relationships also exist: debtor/creditor, mortgagor/mortgagee, bailor/bailee.

■ Banks require borrowers to sign facility letters which set out in detail the legal position between lender and borrower.

■ Businesses borrowing from the bank will invariably be asked to provide security to cover the borrowing. If the business fails, the bank will be able to recover all or part of its money from the realisation of its security. Security provided by a business might include a combination of supported guarantees (eg from directors) and a fixed and floating charge over assets.

■ A bank assessing the creditworthiness of a customer will assess critically a number of factors before making the lending decision (PARIS):

> **p**ersonality of the borrower
>
> **a**mount needed
>
> **r**epayment ability
>
> **i**nterest and fees
>
> **s**ecurity available to cover the borrowing

Key Terms		
	liquidity	the availability of cash or assets which can easily be turned into cash
	overtrading	a business which is expanding so quickly that its liquidity runs out because it has to acquire new stock and pay its creditors before it can collect sufficient funds from debtors
	overdraft	an arrangement ('facility') between a bank and a customer which allows the customer to borrow money on a current account up to a specified amount ('limit')
	invoice discounting	the borrowing of money from a finance company against unpaid invoices from selected debtors; the business that is borrowing continues to operate its own credit management system
	recourse factoring	the borrowing of money by a business from a finance company against unpaid invoices from debtors; the finance company operates the credit management system on behalf of the business, but the business stands the loss from any bad debts
	non-recourse factoring	the borrowing of money by a business from a finance company against unpaid invoices from debtors; the finance company operates the credit management system on behalf of the business and stands the loss from any bad debts incurred
	bank loan	borrowing from the bank for a period between one and twenty five years, with regular repayments, interest payments, an initial arrangement fee and (in the case of businesses) security taken to cover the bank in case of default
	hire purchase	an arrangement between a finance company and a business whereby assets are purchased by the finance company and used by the business, which makes regular payments; ownership of the assets passes to the business at the end of the repayment period

finance lease
an arrangement between a finance company and a business whereby assets are purchased by the finance company and used by the business, which makes regular payments to cover the cost of the assets, which remain the property of the finance company; at the end of the repayment period the business is normally given a rebate (refund) of some of the money paid and the finance company sells the asset to a third party – alternatively the business may retain the asset and continue the lease at a reduced rate

operating lease
an arrangement between a finance company and a business whereby assets are purchased by the finance company and used by the business, which makes regular payments to cover the fall in value of the assets, which remain the property of the finance company

fiduciary duty
the duty of an organisation or person (eg bank or doctor) to advise in a responsible way a person (customer or patient) who will take the advice 'on trust'

mortgage
a document signed by a borrower pledging property as security for the borrowing from the lender; the document allows the lender to sell the property if the borrower defaults on the loan

guarantee
a document signed by person A which states that person A undertakes to repay the debt of person B if person B fails to pay up on demand

fixed charge
a document signed by a company which states that if it fails to pay up on demand to the bank, the bank can sell specified assets owned by the company to recover the debt

floating charge
a document signed by a borrowing company which states that if it defaults on the borrowing, the bank can sell 'floating' assets (basically current assets) owned by the company at that particular time in order to recover the debt

Student Activities

answers to the asterisked (*) questions are to be found at the back of this book

6.1* (a) Describe the main features of a bank overdraft.

(b) Outline two advantages to a business of having a bank overdraft as short-term financing.

6.2* (a) Describe the features of invoice discounting and explain how it helps to improve the cash flow of a business.

(b) What is the difference, as far as the business is concerned, between the use of invoice discounting and factoring as a means of obtaining short-term finance?

(c) What is the difference to a business between recourse factoring and non-recourse factoring?

6.3* Describe the main features and advantages to a borrower of a bank fixed loan.

6.4* (a) What is the main difference between hire purchase and leasing?

(b) Explain the difference between a finance lease and an operating lease.

(c) Give an example of an asset which would be suitable for acquiring through hire purchase. Explain the reasons why this is an advantageous form of financing for the asset you have chosen.

(d) A company you are advising wishes to provide company cars for ten of its sales representatives. Suggest – with reasons – a financing scheme which would enable the company to retain the cars for two years and then exchange them for brand-new cars.

6.5* Draw up a table comparing a bank overdraft and a bank loan in terms of
- the period of the financing
- the types of asset which can most usefully be financed
- repayment arrangements
- the cost of the finance in terms of interest and fees
- any security required

6.6* (a) Explain why a bank would wish to take security over business borrowing.

(b) Describe the main features of a fixed charge and a floating charge over company assets.

(c) Someone you know who is a director of a limited company has been asked by the bank to give a guarantee over the company borrowing. Explain to him in simple terms what this means and what its implication might be for his personal assets.

6.7*   What are the legal terms used to describe a bank and its customer in the following situations?

(a)   The customer signs a mortgage over her property.

(b)   The bank looks after a customer's valuables in a deed box in its safe.

(c)   A customer deposits money in his bank account, bringing the balance to a positive figure of £5,000.

6.8*   Facility letters are issued by banks to customers who borrow by means of overdrafts and loans.

(a)   Who signs a facility letter?

(b)   Give three examples of an 'undertaking' or 'covenant' given by a customer.

(c)   Give three examples of an event which will place the customer in a 'default' situation.

6.9*   List and explain the considerations a bank should bear in mind when assessing the creditworthiness of a business customer who wants to borrow £10,000 over ten years.

6.10   A company, Swing Limited, has a £25,000 secured overdraft limit with ABC Bank PLC. The overdraft is up for its six monthly review and renewal next month. The bottom line of the cash flow forecast (the forecast bank account balance) for the next six months shows the following fluctuations:

Month 1	£3,450 (positive balance)
Month 2	£35,000 (positive balance)
Month 3	£12,500 (negative balance)
Month 4	£29,500 (negative balance)
Month 5	£25,500 (negative balance)
Month 6	£15,750 (positive balance)

You are to write a memo to the Finance Manager, Gordon Black, stating

- the nature of the financing requirement

- a recommendation of how the financing requirement can be met

6.11   Gordon Black, Finance Manager of Swing Limited, has been told by the Board of Directors that they want to renew some of the machinery in the production line so that the company can become more productive and competitive. Their enquiries show that the cost of renewal will be £250,000 and that the machinery should last for at least ten years. The company needs financing of £200,000 for this investment.

Gordon Black knows that you are studying for an AAT qualification and asks you to suggest a form of bank borrowing. Would you recommend a bank fixed loan or would you ask for an extended overdraft? He asks you to prepare a memo for him comparing the two types of finance and giving your own recommendation.

this chapter covers . . .

Organisations may from time-to-time have money to invest over the short-term. The word 'organisation' refers not only to businesses but also to public sector bodies such as local authorities and NHS trusts.

Organisations will try to obtain the best return – often measured by the interest rate – on their investments, but need to exercise caution when it comes to risk (higher risk investments normally offer a better return). Organisations in both the public and private sectors will therefore be subject to strict internal controls which will ensure that:

• investments are made only by employees who are authorised to do so

• investments are 'safe', ie reasonably risk-free

Typical investments include: government securities ('gilts'), local authority bonds, bills, and certificates of deposit.

This chapter also describes how the handling of cash and investment certificates is strictly controlled and how they are handled and stored securely.

PERFORMANCE CRITERIA COVERED

unit 15 OPERATING A CASH MANAGEMENT AND CREDIT CONTROL SYSTEM

element 15.2

Manage cash balances

B   Invest surplus funds in marketable securities within defined financial authorisation limits.

C   Ensure the organisation's financial regulations and security procedures are observed.

D   Ensure account is taken of trends in the economic and financial environment in managing cash balances.

E   Maintain an adequate level of liquidity in line with cash forecasts.

KNOWLEDGE AND UNDERSTANDING COVERAGE

4   Types of marketable security (Bills of exchange, certificates of deposit, government securities, local authority short term loans); terms and conditions; risks.

16   Managing risk and exposure.

28   An understanding that practice in this area will be determined by an organisation's specific financial regulations, guidelines and security procedures.

29   An understanding that in public sector organisations there are statutory and other regulations relating to the management of cash balances.

MANAGING LIQUIDITY SURPLUSES

cash surpluses

We saw in the last chapter that liquidity management involves anticipating liquidity shortages by arranging short-term finance in the form of a bank **overdraft**. This type of shortage will be indicated on the cash flow forecast. Financial planning by the organisation will also indicate the need for longer-term financing by way of bank **loans** or other asset finance.

If the balance at the bottom of a cash flow forecast is positive, however, it indicates that the organisation has a **cash** surplus which it may be in a position to invest. Note here that 'cash' has two meanings:

- 'cash' in the form of notes and coins (a shop, for example) – we will deal with the management of this type of cash at the end of this chapter (see page 149)
- 'cash' meaning money, perhaps sitting in a bank current account, which is available for investment

risk, return and exposure

The organisation will want to invest its cash surpluses so that they earn a return, normally in the form of interest. Certain rules apply to the level of return (or interest rate) available on investments.

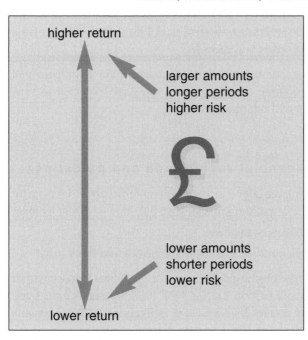

Generally speaking the rate of return will be higher:

- for larger amounts
- for less liquid amounts, ie for amounts invested for longer fixed periods or with longer notice requirements
- if there is more risk attached to the investment (many institutions are 'credit rated' for security of investment)

For example, £10 deposited for one day on a current account with a reputable bank will probably earn nothing at all: it is a small amount, it is there for a very short period of time and there is little or no risk attached. On the other hand, £1 million invested for a fixed six month period with a less well-known bank will earn a higher rate.

This is not to say, however, that all organisations will try and invest as much as possible for as long as possible in the least reputable banks. Organisations will have clear guidelines indicating the level of **risk** they are allowed to take (normally minimal!) and the level of **exposure** to which they can commit themselves. Exposure is a term normally applied to lending, but it can also apply to the amount invested with any one institution or type of investment.

the effect of economic and financial trends

Organisations which are investing over the longer term will need to be aware of the effect of trends in the economy, and particularly of the dangers of rising inflation and interest rates. We saw in Chapter 5 that rising inflation will also often prompt rises in interest rates as the Government's monetary policy moves to control the supply of money.

As far as an organisation's liquidity management is concerned, lower interest rates mean cheaper borrowing and lower costs, which is good news. But they also mean a lower return on investment, which is not such good news for an organisation which is very liquid. There is also a danger when investing long-term when interest rates are low. Suppose an organisation invests £50,000 at 3.5% p.a. for a twelve month term. If interest rates start to rise, the return on that investment will effectively start to fall. The organisation will be stuck with a 3.5% investment when market rates might give the same deposit a return of 4.25%.

This principle also works the opposite way. If interest rates are high (they have historically been as high as 15%) and you invest long-term at a high rate, eg 14%, you will do well when interest rates fall, as you will receive a higher return than market rates will provide.

It should, of course, be pointed out that the markets are intelligent and discount these trends to some extent, ie when rates are expected to rise, longer term investments will return a higher rate.

complying with financial regulations and guidelines

So far in this chapter we have talked in very general terms about investment by 'organisations'. These organisations with cash balances to invest include:

- **private sector** businesses of all sizes
- **public sector** organisations such as local authorities and NHS trusts

In the **private sector,** large businesses will have an Accounts Department or Treasury which will have a section dealing with liquidity management and investment of funds. In smaller businesses, it is likely to be the Accounts

Manager/Supervisor or, in the case of a sole trader business, the proprietor. Larger businesses will have a set of regulations setting out, for example

- the various authorities and responsibilities given to employees in day-to-day liquidity management, ie who can invest in what, and up to what limit
- the types of investment that are permissible and advisable
- a minimum requirement for highly liquid funds (eg overnight bank deposits)

In this way, sufficient liquidity will be maintained and risk minimised. This risk limitation forms part of the duties required by 'corporate governance' set out in The Turnbull Report published by the Institute of Chartered Accountants in England & Wales (www.icaew.co.uk). This report states that 'a company's system of internal control has a key role in the management of risks that are significant to the fulfilment of its business objectives'.

In the **public sector**, large organisations such as County Councils operate a Treasury function under the control of a County Treasurer. The Treasury will have a section dealing with day-to-day investment along the same lines as the corporate treasury in the private sector. The public sector body (eg the County Council) will have a set of Standing Orders (regulations) which will similarly set out the authorities and responsibilities vested in its employees and will dictate the types of investment which are permissible. These regulations should be covered in a 'Statement on Internal Control' drawn up by the local authority in order to comply with the requirements of The Accounts and Audit Regulations (England) 2003. Guidance on this subject is provided by the Chartered Institute of Public Finance and Accountancy – CIPFA (www.cipfa.org.uk).

TYPES OF INVESTMENT

We will now describe in detail some of the liquid funds in which private or public sector Treasuries may invest on a day-to-day basis. Your assessments may require you to give details of these funds and also explain how economic trends may affect your investment decision. This issue is covered in the Case Study which follows on page 148.

The types of investment include:

- money market deposits
- local authority deposits
- bills of exchange
- certificates of deposit
- Government stock ('gilts')
- corporate bonds

We have already explained and defined many of these investments in Chapter 5 (see pages 110 - 111). In this chapter we take a more practical view and explain the decisions that have to be made by a senior employee working in a private or public sector Treasury. We will first deal with short-term investments and then with longer-term securities.

SHORT-TERM INVESTMENTS

The treasurer will normally have on-line access to market rates. The data below has been adapted from rates shown in the Financial Times. The time periods range from overnight to one year. Study the variations in the rates and then read the notes that follow.

UK interest rates (short-term money markets)						
	overnight	7 days notice	one month	three months	six months	one year
	%	%	%	%	%	%
Interbank	3.41	3.66	3.91	4.20	4.22	4.47
CDs			3.81	4.00	4.13	4.38
Treasury Bills			3.75	3.88		
Bank Bills			3.81	3.94		
Local Authority deposits		3.75	3.81	3.88	4.06	4.38

- The **interbank** market is made up of short-term deposits placed by banks with each other. Company and local authority treasurers placing deposits with banks on 'money market' accounts – often overnight – are providing funds for this market. These deposits are usually referred to as **money market deposits** and earn good interest. For example, £1 million deposited overnight at 3.41% would earn over £94 interest a day.

- **CDs (Certificates of Deposit)** are tradeable certificates issued by banks, certifying that a sum of money, normally a minimum of £50,000, has been deposited and will be repaid on a set date, often six months later. They can be bought and sold on the market (at a discount) and whoever holds the CD on the repayment date will receive the amount stated on the certificate.

- **Treasury Bills** are three month tradeable certificates issued by the Bank of England and backed by the Government. They are sold to banks and other dealing institutions at a discount and the eventual holder will be repaid in full on the due date. As you will see from the table of rates on the previous page, the Treasury Bill offers the lowest rate. This is because it is backed by the Government and is seen to be a very low risk.

- **Bank Bills** are bills of exchange (see page 111) which are issued and payable by a bank. They are sold to banks and other dealing institutions at a discount and the eventual holder, (as with other tradeable securities) will be repaid in full on the due date. Like interbank deposits they offer a higher return, reflecting the greater risk of the investment (compared with the Government, at least).

- **Local Authority deposits** are short-term loans made to local authorities, and, like other Governmental low risk investments, generally provide a lower return than interbank deposits and bank bills, where the risk is higher.

fluctuation of rates

We have already commented on the difference in the rates quoted for the individual markets and securities. If you look carefully at the table on the previous page you will notice that:

- the rates increase as the period of the deposit increases – the return on the investment increases as it becomes less liquid (ie less available to the investor)

- the rates also increase as the risk increases – the lowest rate is the Treasury Bill where the borrower is the Government (low risk) and the highest is the interbank market where the money is lent to commercial banks (higher risk)

other short-term investments

The investments shown in the table on the previous page are the normal secure short-term investments which fulfil the 'safety' requirement of a company of local authority Treasurer. There are other investments which may be more risky, but which nevertheless sometimes feature in investment portfolios. **Commercial paper**, for example, represents short-term lending to first class quoted commercial companies. The securities issued by the companies through a bank take the form of loan notes (value £100,000 and above) with maturities between seven days and three months.

LIQUIDITY MANAGEMENT IN PRACTICE

Each working day the company or local authority Treasurer (or delegated authorised staff) will have to perform complex calculations and take decisions to ensure that there will be sufficient liquidity not just for that day or week, but for months ahead. The following data will need to be collected and analysed:

- the final cleared balance of the bank account the previous day
- details of maturing deposits and investments
- daily cash flow projections of sales receipts and payments

Any surplus funds can then either be placed on a money market account with the bank overnight (if it will be needed the next working day) or alternatively be placed in other short-term markets for periods such as one month, three months, six months or a year to meet longer-term requirements. This will all be done in accordance with the organisation's guidelines for risk and exposure management.

LONGER-TERM INVESTMENTS – GOVERNMENT STOCK

One of the safest ways of investing for the longer term is to lend money to fund Government debt. Investors can purchase '**Government stock**', also known as 'gilt-edged' stock or '**gilts**' for short, on account of its prestige and security. The various stock issues are often given the title 'Treasury' or 'Exchequer' stock to link them to the Government Department they are funding.

Gilts are popular longer-term investments for businesses and public sector organisations. They are more or less risk-free, they provide a regular income and they can always be sold 'second hand' in the stock markets. Their prices are reported daily in the financial press.

features of gilts

Gilts are mostly at a **fixed interest** rate, for example Treasury <u>5%</u> 2008, although some are index-linked, ie the return is linked to the Retail Price Index. The interest rate is often referred to as the 'coupon'.

Gilts are also mostly for a **fixed period**, for example the Treasury 5% <u>2008</u> mentioned above, although some are undated. War Loan 3.5%, for example, was issued during the Second World War in the hope that people would buy them as a patriotic gesture, perhaps never to have them repaid!

The maturity periods of gilts are classified as follows:

shorts	up to 5 years
mediums	5 to 15 years
longs	more than 15 years

As mentioned above, **gilts** can be traded, and the price will reflect market conditions at the time. Gilts are normally quoted in terms of £100, but can be traded in any amount. £1 of stock will be worth £1 on the maturity date. In the interim, however, gilts with an interest rate ('coupon') higher than prevailing rates will trade for more than £1, and gilts with a low coupon will trade at a lower price. For example, if you wanted to buy (at the time of writing) Treasury 8.5% 2007, you would have to pay £1.12 per £1 of stock. If you held the stock until the 'redemption' (repayment) date in 2007, you would receive just £1 per £1 of stock. £1 is known as the stock's 'par value'.

gilts and yields

An investor wanting to know the return on gilts should examine and compare the **yield** each stock provides. Yield means the same as 'return', but measuring it is not straightforward because

* the price of each stock fluctuates
* the length of time before the redemption date (when the stock is repaid) will vary

There are two main yields which an investor should look at:

* The **interest yield** is the annual return for the investor based on the price of the stock and the interest rate stated on the gilt (the coupon rate). Using the Treasury 8.5% 2007 mentioned above, the calculation is as follows:

$$\frac{\text{interest rate}}{\text{market price}} = \frac{8.5\%}{£1.12} = 7.6\%$$

In other words, because the market price of £1.12 is higher than the nominal value of £1, the effective interest rate reduces from 8.5% to 7.6%

* The **redemption yield** (the 'yield to maturity') takes into account the change in price of the stock to redemption (maturity). It involves:
  – the price paid for the stock
  – the interest rate stated on the gilt (the coupon rate)
  – the period of time which has to run before the stock is repaid (remember that the price returns to £1 per £1 of stock at the redemption date, affecting the yield)

The redemption yield is very useful because it allows stock with differing redemption dates to be meaningfully compared. It also enables the yield to be compared with the percentage rates offered by other investments.

For more information about the gilts market, visit www.dmo.gov.uk

RIVENDALE COUNTY COUNCIL: SHORT-TERM AND LONG-TERM INVESTMENTS

situation

Your name is Ron Raga and you work as a trainee in the the the Treasury Department of Rivendale County Council. You report to Assistant Treasurer Leo Glass. Your section deals with the investment of short-term funds on the money markets and also with long-term investments for the County Council Pension Fund, largely in gilt-edged stock.

On Tuesday Leo shows you two investment opportunities:

1   A quote for depositing £500,000 for one month on a money market account with the bank at an interest rate of 4.00% p.a.

2   Purchasing £500,000 Treasury 9% 2012 at £1.29 per £1 of stock. Interest (flat) yield 7%, redemption yield 4.77%.

Leo asks you to provide some notes:

*   describing the two investments and the markets for which they provide funds

*   explaining what type of investment they are best used for

*   explaining the difference between interest yield and redemption yield for the gilt-edged stock

*   providing information about the cost of dealing

*   explaining what effect a rise in interest rates would have on the return from the investments

solution

1   **Money market account**

The **money market account** deposit is placed with the bank and is repayable after one month. The investment will help to fund the interbank market.

It is a useful investment for short-term surpluses of cash, yielding 4% p.a. (in this case £500,000 x 4% ÷ 12 = £1,667).

There will be no costs attached to the deal, which can be transacted on-line or over the telephone.

A rise in interest rates before the end of the month in which the deposit is made might mean a very short-term reduction in potential earnings from interest, but it is likely that the 4% rate given on the deposit will have discounted any interest rate rise.

2   Treasury 9% 2012

The **gilt-edged stock** is purchased through a broker and obtained from the stockmarket.

As gilt-edged stock is issued on behalf of the Government, the money will be used to fund Government borrowing.

Gilts are useful for longer-term investments such as the County Council Pension Fund, and are not normally used for the short term. The stock may be sold before its maturity date in 2012, but dealing commission will have to be paid to the brokers on both the purchase and sale transactions, making it more expensive to deal with than the money market deposit.

The interest (flat) yield relates the price paid for the stock with its stated interest rate. It provides a good return at 7%. The redemption yield at 4.77% is a more useful point of comparison with other investment schemes as it takes into account the fall in value of the stock as it reaches the redemption (repayment) date.

A rise in interest rates will effectively reduce the rate of return on gilts because the market price of the stock will fall, pulling down both the flat yield and the redemption yield.

LOOKING AFTER CASH AND INVESTMENTS

Another function of the Treasury or Accounts Department in an organisation is one of simple housekeeping – looking after valuables such as:

- cash in the form of notes and coins
- investment certificates

cash handling

Cash in the form of notes and coins is a security risk and most organisations will have written procedures for dealing with it.

These range from the petty cash procedures for small balances held in an office to procedures laid down for the security of the large amounts of cash handled, for example, by the supermarkets. Whatever the extent of the risk, the procedures must be strictly adhered to at all times. Adequate insurance must also be maintained.

There is obviously a significant risk when a business has to deal with cash received from sales to the public. The procedures listed on the next page are fairly typical.

---

security procedures for cash sales

1 Cash from sales should be kept in a till, or under lock and key in a strong box or drawer.

2 Cash sales should be listed and reconciled with the amount of cash held at the end of each day. The listing may be a tally roll till listing, or a printout from an electronic till.

3 The cash and listings should be checked and verified by an employee at supervisory level.

4 If cash is stored on the premises overnight it should be placed in a safe or strongroom, under the supervision of a senior employee.

5 Cash receipts should be listed promptly on a paying-in slip and paid into the bank as soon as possible. Large volumes of cash may be taken to the bank by a security firm. Some businesses may use a bank night safe facility whereby the paying-in slip and cash are placed in a locked wallet and 'posted' through a letterbox into a chute in the bank wall after working hours.

---

looking after investment certificates

The use of certificates for investments is nowadays on the decline as electronic records are becoming more common. Nevertheless, investments in the form of paper certificates are still used and need to be recorded and stored carefully.

This is particularly important in the case of what are known as 'bearer' certificates such as Certificates of Deposit where the name of the owner is not recorded on the certificate; the certificate belongs to whoever is holding it at the time – just like a bank note. It belongs to the 'bearer'. The security risk is clearly high in this case.

Other investment certificates such as share certificates and gilts are more secure because the name of the owner is printed on the certificate.

If an organisation holds investment certificates it should therefore:

• keep an accurate internal 'register' of certificates held, recording details such as the issuer, the date, any reference number and the amount

• restrict handling of the certificates to authorised employees

• store the certificates safely, either in a safe or strongroom on the premises, or alternatively, at the bank

• maintain adequate insurance

Chapter Summary

- Risk and return have to be weighed up carefully when making an investment decision. Organisations generally have to minimise risk when investing liquid and longer-term balances.

- Organisations must be aware of external economic and financial considerations when making investment decisions. Care must be taken when investing at fixed rates when interest rates and inflation are rising, as the return on the investment will fall.

- Both public sector and private sector organisations normally have internal regulations which set down guidelines for maintaining liquidity of investments. They are also bound by external recommendations and regulations in the areas of risk management and internal control.

- The range of 'safe' investments for short-term liquidity surpluses includes: money market deposits, local authority deposits, bills and certificates of deposit (see Key Terms for explanations of these securities).

- The rate of return on investments generally increases in line with the amount deposited, the period of the deposit and the risk involved. Sensible liquidity management involves obtaining the best rate of return possible on a 'safe' range of investments.

- Liquidity management by a private or public sector Treasury takes place on a daily basis. Data used will include the previous day's bank balance, deposits and investments maturing and daily cash flow projections of sales receipts and payments.

- Government stock – 'gilts' – are longer-term investments which provide funds for Government borrowing. They are very low risk and normally pay a fixed rate of interest over a fixed period. They can be bought or sold 'second-hand' any time until they are due for repayment, and so are ideal investments for private or public sector Treasuries looking for longer-term safe return on their money.

- Organisations which deal with notes and coins on a regular basis – shops for example – need to establish procedures for the secure handling and storage of cash. These include the need to lock up cash, to reconcile cash received with listings of sales and to pay the cash into the bank as soon as possible.

- Organisations that deal with investment certificates – particularly bearer certificates – must ensure that they are accurately recorded and stored securely, either on the organisation's premises or at a bank.

Key Terms		
exposure		the amount of money invested by an organisation in any one institution or type of investment; it is a term which suggests the level of risk
interbank market		short-term deposits made by banks with each other
money market accounts		accounts for short-term deposits made by customers with banks; the surplus money is then used by the banks to place deposits in the interbank market
certificates of deposit		tradeable certificates issued by banks, certifying that a sum of money, normally a minimum of £50,000, has been deposited and will be repaid on a set date
treasury bills		three month tradeable certificates issued by the Bank of England and backed by the Government, sold to banks and other institutions at a discount and repayable at the full price on maturity
bank bills		bills of exchange (see below) issued and payable by a bank, sold to banks and other institutions at a discount and repayable at the full price on maturity
bill of exchange		a tradeable document issued by a company or local authority to provide evidence that an amount is owing to that company or local authority and has to be repaid on a certain date to the holder of the document
local authority deposits		short-term low-risk loans to local authorities
commercial paper		loan notes issued by first class commercial companies and available through banks, with maturities between seven days and three months

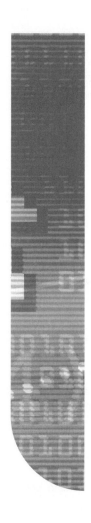

gilts

also known as 'Government stock' or 'gilt-edged stock' are investments which provide funds for Government borrowing and are tradeable 'second hand' at a price determined by the market; they represent a secure longer-term form of investment

redemption date

the date on which dated gilts are repayable at the price stated on the gilt (eg £1 for each £1 of stock)

interest (flat) yield

the yield on gilts which represents the annual return for the investor; it is based on the market price of the stock and the interest rate stated on the gilt

redemption yield

the yield on gilts which takes into account the fact that gilts change in value in the period up to the redemption date; it usefully compares the yield of the gilt with the yields offered by other investments

bearer certificates

investment certificates which do not have the name of the investor written on them, but which belong to the person holding them – the 'bearer'

Student Activities

answers to the asterisked (*) questions are to be found at the back of this book

7.1* How will the following factors affect the rate of return received on an investment?

(a)   the amount to be invested

(b)   the period of the investment

(c)   the risk attached to the investment

7.2* Economic trends can often affect investment decisions. What are the main dangers for an investor in fixed interest rate funds at a time when the rate of inflation is rising? How can this risk be avoided?

7.3* You work in the Treasury Department of your local authority. A new employee, Ken Toil, who is working in the investment section says to you one day over coffee:

'These money market deposits and gilts are really boring investments; if I wanted to make some money for the authority I would put the whole lot into shares in a supermarket or an airline; they are much more interesting investments – they gain in value and give a good return, unlike gilts some of which even seem to go *down* in value towards the redemption date.'

Is this a good idea? What would you say in reply?

7.4* The table below shows the rates for a number of short-term funds in which a private sector company or a local authority might invest.

Study the table and answer the questions that follow.

	overnight	7 days notice	one month	three months	six months	one year
	%	%	%	%	%	%
Interbank	3.41	3.66	3.91	4.20	4.22	4.47
CDs			3.81	4.00	4.13	4.38
Treasury Bills			3.75	3.88		
Local Authority deposits		3.75	3.81	3.88	4.06	4.38

(a)   Describe the interbank and local authority deposit markets and explain why there is a difference in the rates between the two.

(b)   How does a CD differ from an interbank deposit?

(c)   Explain what treasury bills are, and give reasons why a private sector company or a local authority would want to invest in them when the return is lower than that obtained on the interbank market.

7.5* The table below displays the type of data which investors in Government stock (gilts) will need when making investment decisions. Study the table and answer the questions that follow.

stock	price £1 of stock (pence)	interest yield %	redemption yield %
Treasury 7.25% 2007	109.37	6.63	4.57
Treasury 8% 2009	116.49	6.87	4.65
Treasury 5% 2012	101.89	4.91	4.72
Treasury 4.25% 2036	94.14	4.51	4.60

(a) For what type of investment are gilts most suitable?

(b) Explain what an interest yield and a redemption yield indicate, and why they can be numerically so different?

(c) Why should it cost £1.17 for £1 of Treasury 8% 2009 and only 94p for £1 of Treasury 4.25% 2036?

7.6* You work for Mullgo Sports, a company which manufactures sportsgear. The company has recently taken the decision to open a factory shop. This will involve dealing with quantities of notes and coin for the three tills which are being installed. The management realises that this will increase the security risks to the business.

The company has also recently invested in some gilts and has received the certificates from the broker.

(a) You are to write a checklist of the procedures which could be adopted in the handling of the cash and the records of cash receipts to minimise these risks.

(b) State what procedures the company might carry out on receipt of the gilts certificates.

7.7 You work for Rodof Insurance (UK) Ltd. The company has recently decided to move out of the West End of London, where it owns freehold premises, and relocate its offices to Slough, where property is cheaper. The company will receive £1m from the deal and is looking to invest it. You have been asked to prepare notes comparing bank money market deposits and gilt-edged securities as investments.

Granting credit – assessing the customers

Credit control is the process of managing customers who pay on credit so that settlement of debt is made on time.

Efficient credit control is essential for maintaining the liquidity of an organisation; money not received may mean that money will have to be borrowed.

This chapter takes an overview of the whole credit control process – from credit application to debt collection, and then concentrates on the ways in which an organisation assesses applications from customers to trade on credit terms. This assessment process involves:

- *examining the external sources of information – banks, credit rating agencies, other suppliers – which enable the organisation to evaluate the customer*

- *examining the internal sources of information available to help with the assessment decision – reports from colleagues (eg sales records, notes on visits) and analysis of financial accounts*

The next chapter describes how an account is set up, or, if the customer fails the assessment test, is refused.

PERFORMANCE CRITERIA COVERED

unit 15 OPERATING A CASH MANAGEMENT AND CREDIT CONTROL SYSTEM

element 15.3

Grant credit

A   *Agree credit terms with customers in accordance with the organisation's policies.*

B   *Identify and use internal and external sources of information to evaluate the current credit status of customers and potential customers.*

KNOWLEDGE AND UNDERSTANDING COVERAGE

6   *Legal issues: basic contract; terms and conditions of contracts relating to the granting of credit; Data Protection legislation and credit control information.*

7   *Sources of credit status information.*

8   *External sources of information: banks, credit agencies and official publications.*

18   *Interpretation and use of credit control information.*

30   *Understanding that practice in this area will be determined by an organisation's credit control policies and procedures.*

31   *An understanding of the organisation's relevant policies and procedures.*

AN OVERVIEW OF CREDIT CONTROL

importance of credit control

Credit control is the process of managing customers who pay on credit so that settlement of debt is made on time.

As we saw in the last two chapters, liquidity management in an organisation involves the timing of cash inflows and outflows – including financing and investing – so that the organisation has sufficient working capital and remains solvent. An important element of liquidity management is therefore the efficient functioning of the sales ledger – or in basic terms, customers paying up on time. If customers do not pay up on time, or – worse still – become insolvent, this can be the result of:

- credit terms being granted to customers who are not creditworthy (a failure in the system when the customer applied for credit), or

- the payments of the customer not being monitored effectively and warning signs of customer financial problems not being picked up (a failure of the sales ledger management system)

The result is likely to be the same: a bad debt and a consequent loss of profit.

the credit control function

Credit control is part of the accounting and finance function of an organisation. The number of people employed in credit control will depend on the size of the organisation. It may be a whole department, a section, or in the case of a small business, the accounts assistant or even the proprietor. The credit control activities carried out are summarised in the diagram on the next page, which you should study carefully. They include:

- assessing new applications for credit (either from new customers or from existing customers looking for an increased credit limit)

- monitoring sales ledger accounts by using reports such as the aged debtors summary

- chasing overdue debts and dealing with bad debts

Larger organisations are likely to have a **credit control policy**, a written set of procedures detailing issues such as assessment methods, credit terms granted, chasing of debts, and dealing with bad debts. An example is shown on page 172. It will normally be accompanied by documentation such as credit application forms, sales contracts and chaser letters.

People who work in credit control need to be highly experienced in communication skills: they are negotiators and persuaders, but should also be able to take on the role of rotweilers.

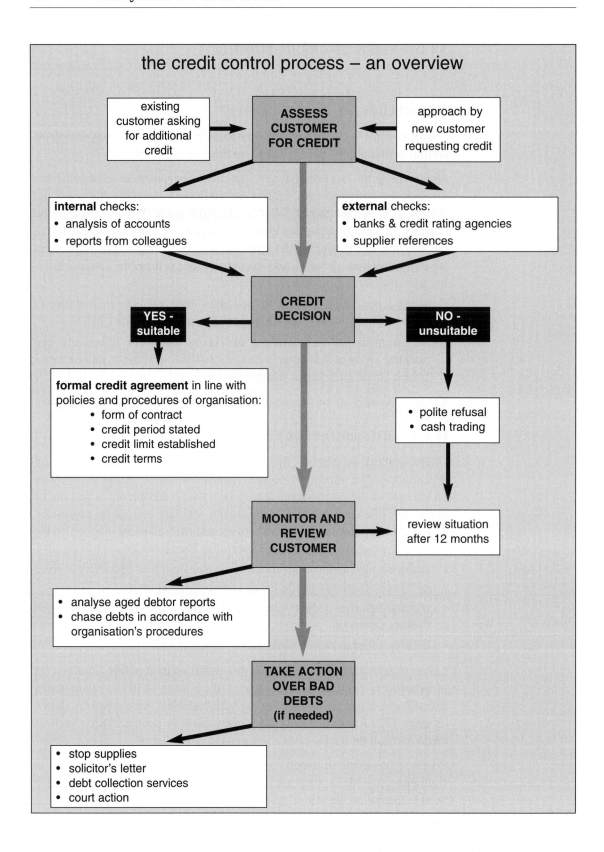

the credit control process – an overview

existing customer asking for additional credit

ASSESS CUSTOMER FOR CREDIT

approach by new customer requesting credit

internal checks:
• analysis of accounts
• reports from colleagues

external checks:
• banks & credit rating agencies
• supplier references

CREDIT DECISION

YES - suitable

NO - unsuitable

formal credit agreement in line with policies and procedures of organisation:
• form of contract
• credit period stated
• credit limit established
• credit terms

• polite refusal
• cash trading

MONITOR AND REVIEW CUSTOMER

review situation after 12 months

• analyse aged debtor reports
• chase debts in accordance with organisation's procedures

TAKE ACTION OVER BAD DEBTS (if needed)

• stop supplies
• solicitor's letter
• debt collection services
• court action

the credit control process

The diagram on the previous page illustrates the stages involved in the credit control process. These processes will be explained in detail in this and the following three chapters.

In this chapter we examine in detail the credit checks and analyses that are made when assessing the creditworthiness of a new or an existing customer. The sources of information are either external or internal.

EXTERNAL SOURCES OF INFORMATION ABOUT CUSTOMERS

Organisations can consult a variety of sources of external information:

• bank references

• supplier (trade) references

• credit rating agencies

The credit control policy document of the organisation (see page 172) is likely to provide guidance about establishing the creditworthiness of a new customer and indicate what external sources should be approached. It is common practice for an organisation to send out a letter to a new customer along the lines of the following:

Dear Sirs

Ref : Application to Open a Credit Account

Thank you for your request to open a credit account in our books.

So that I can consider your request I shall be grateful if you will supply me with:

- details of your bank account - bank, bank branch address and account name, plus your written authority to your bank to release information

- details (contact names, addresses, telephone numbers) of two trade references

Thank you.

Yours faithfully

S Gerrard

S Gerrard
Credit Control

Alternatively the organisation may have a credit application form which it sends to customers who are applying for a credit limit. This would request details such as:

- the registered name and address of a limited company, or
- the names, business and home addresses of partners, or
- the name, business and home address of a sole proprietor
- any trading name used
- at least two trade references
- bank details, plus an authorisation to obtain a bank reference
- credit requirement
- signature of the applicant(s)

An example is shown below.

APPLICATION FOR CREDIT

Please open a credit account in the name of ....

Address ....

....

Telephone.. Email...

Trading name(s) where applicable ....

Amount of credit required £ .... monthly, in total £ ....

Please accept this as authority to release information to the parties below for reference purposes.

signed .... capacity .... date..........................

signed .... capacity .... date..........................

Bank name..

Bank address...

Trade reference 1	Trade reference 2
Name..	Name..
Address	Address ....
....	....
....	....
Tel..	Tel..

bank references

Banks have traditionally been a valuable source of information about the credit standing of prospective customers.

One problem with bank references is the language in which they are written. Banks are masters of understatement. Just as school reports need interpretation – eg 'she is a quiet student' means 'she is asleep most of the time' or 'she is lively in class' means 'she talks incessantly' – so bank reports also need interpretation.

A request for a bank reference is normally worded along the lines of

'Do you consider Dodge E Builders Limited to be good for the figure of £10,000 trade credit per month?'

The replies that might be received are shown below, both in bank language and also in plain ordinary English. The replies are listed from top to bottom in order of creditworthiness.

bank reply	plain ordinary English
'Undoubted.'	'A good risk for the figure quoted.'
'Good for your figure and purpose.'	'A reasonable risk and most probably OK.'
'Should prove good for your figures and purpose.'	'Not so sure about this one - well worth investigating further before making a decision.'
'Although their capital is fully employed we do not consider the directors would enter into a commitment they could not see their way to fulfil.'	'This business has cash flow problems and should not be allowed any credit.'

When translated into plain English, bank references are limited but useful indicators of the prospective customer's creditworthiness.

trade references

It is common practice for organisations to ask for two trade references when assessing a customer's credit risk. These are not always reliable because the prospective customer might give as references suppliers who are not strict about credit control, and avoid quoting the suppliers who are red hot in chasing debts.

A standard letter asking for information from a trade referee is shown below.

Fine Dowt Limited

88 Station Road

Newtown NT6 9GH

Tel 01707 767188 Fax 01707 767022 www.finedowt.co.uk

Credit Control Manager
Esloy Engineering
Unit 16 Forest Estate
Bath BA2 4JP

We have received a request for credit from our customer Parsons Printers. They have quoted you as referee. We shall be grateful if you could answer the following questions.

How long have you been trading with the customer? ....years .... months

Terms granted   amount per month £....................

Total limit   £.....................................

Period of credit granted   ....

Payment record (please indicate as appropriate)   prompt / occasionally late / often late

Have you ever suspended credit?   Yes / No   When?...............................

Other relevant information ....

....

Thank you for your assistance. We will be happy to reciprocate at any time.

Yours faithfully

N Igmer

Nigel Igmer
Credit Controller

A reply to a trade reference may take a long time to process. The enquiring organisation can avoid delay by telephoning the enquiry to the 'sales ledger' staff after sending off the credit enquiry letter.

A dubious alternative adopted by some businesses is not to make the enquiry through the quoted referees but to telephone one of their own competitors (who are likely to deal with the customer) and speak to the sales ledger staff directly and informally – often receiving a very honest appraisal. This could result in a breach of the Data Protection Act (see page 165) by the replying organisation, however, and so is not to be recommended!

credit reference agencies

Organisations which frequently process new applications for credit often subscribe to **credit reference agencies**. These are commercial organisations which offer an on-line service for checking the credit rating of companies and individuals. They have extensive databases which provide a wealth of material which can be provided on demand, enabling an instant credit decision to be made. They do, of course, charge for the service, and there is the risk that some of the information may be out of date. Examples include:

- **Dun & Bradstreet** (www.dnb.com)
- **Experian** (www.experian.co.uk)
- **Equifax** (www.equifax.co.uk)

Reference enquiries can be made either on limited companies or on individuals. Reports from credit reference agencies on **limited companies** will provide details such as:

- three years' accounts
- payment history
- directors details
- any insolvency proceedings

Credit reference agencies are widely used for providing reports on **individuals** for organisations such as banks, credit card and hire purchase companies. Sole trader and partnership businesses are enterprises run by individuals. These reports will not produce much in the way of financial data (only limited companies have to file their accounts) but will provide information such as:

- names and addresses
- credit risk – based on any default on credit (including not paying credit card bills on time)
- county court judgements for non-payment of debt
- bankruptcy orders

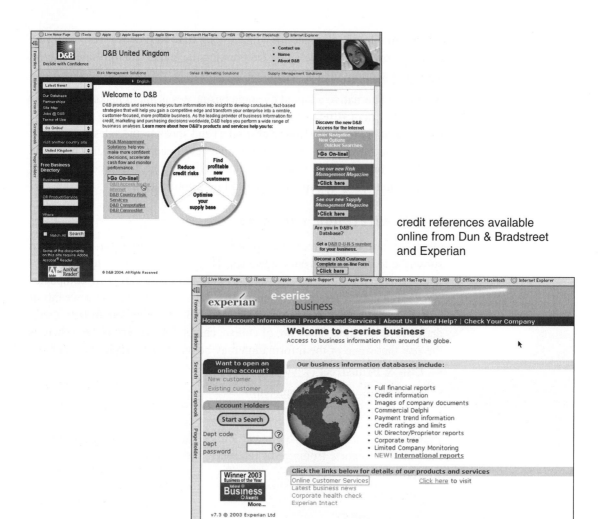

credit references available
online from Dun & Bradstreet
and Experian

Reports on individuals are sometimes requested to check up on the credit rating of directors of limited company customers. A director with a bad credit record can often be found to be running a company which is a poor credit risk.

The handling of personal data by credit reference agencies is governed by the Data Protection Act (see next page).

Companies House

Another source of information about limited companies is Companies House, the Government agency to which all larger limited companies are obliged by law to send their annual accounts and to which all companies send information of directors (www.companieshouse.gov.uk). This data is publicly available (at a cost), but financial data may not be completely up-to-date, as many companies file accounts well after the balance sheet date.

other published sources

If a credit control department wishes to find out about the creditworthiness of a large organisation it may find references and articles in the press, trade journals and online. The internet is a powerful tool here. Try doing a search on a well-known company name in www.google.co.uk, for example, and see what information and up-to-date news articles are produced.

a note on the Data Protection Act, 1998

When an organisation asks for a reference from a company, bank or credit reference agency, it is asking that organisation to disclose data it holds which relates to a third party (someone else). The law is very strict on this point as there is a real danger that the information may be incorrect or the person or organisation to which it relates does not want it to be released.

The current legislation covering this area is the Data Protection Act 1998, which has reinforced existing rules for the processing of personal data. It follows the guidelines of a European Directive and brings the UK in line with European legal principles. The Act applies to:

- data about individuals (eg sole traders, partners) but not about companies
- records held on computer – eg a computer database of names, addresses, telephone numbers, sales details of each customer ('data subject')
- manual records – eg a card index file system of customers details

All organisations which process personal data should register with the Data Protection Commission and should follow the eight guiding principles set out in the Data Protection Act. These principles require that personal data is handled properly. They state that personal data must be:

1 fairly and lawfully processed

2 processed for limited purposes

3 adequate, relevant and not excessive

4 accurate

5 not kept for longer than is necessary

6 processed in line with the data subject's rights

7 kept securely

8 not transferred to countries outside the European Union unless it is adequately protected in those countries

Individuals have the legal right to know what personal details about them is held by an organisation such as a credit reference agency. They should apply in writing to that organisation for a copy of the personal data held on file; they are likely to have to pay a small fee (£2, for example).

INTERNAL SOURCES OF INFORMATION ABOUT CUSTOMERS

External sources of information are often used when the individual or organisation applying for credit is not known to the enquirer. If an organisation needs to assess the credit risk of an existing customer – eg when an increase in credit limit is requested – much of the information needed may already be available within the organisation. This **internal** information includes:

- internal conversations, records of meetings and visits by employees of the organisation – eg by sales ledger and sales teams
- ratio analysis of the financial accounts of the customer

internal records

Suppose two existing company customers (A and B), each with a credit limit of £10,000 ask for an increase to £15,000 because of increased trading. The credit control staff could make enquiries within the organisation . . .

Company A:
Go-A-Head Limited

feedback from sales ledger team

'Yes, they always pay on time. Never go over their limit. No problems there.'

feedback from the sales team

'Yes, we went to see them last month. They seem well-organised and there is a good market for their product. They are well positioned for expansion. They find our prices very competitive. They are good to do business with.'

conclusion of credit control team

'On the face of it a good credit risk, but we will need to see their accounts.'

Company B:
Going-to-the-Wall Limited

feedback from sales ledger team

'Not sure. They always seem to be up to their limit or slightly over. The money comes in, but it is often late, and we have had to send out chasers.'

feedback from the sales team

'We asked to visit them, but they didn't seem keen. They have a high turnover of staff – we always seem to be dealing with someone different. I personally think that they have been over-ordering from us as I am not sure that their sales are up to target. I wonder if they need the higher limit to help fund their liquidity?'

conclusion of credit control team

'There appear to be problems here, so we will need to see their accounts. We may struggle to recover what is owed!'

analysing customer accounts

As we have seen on the previous page, feedback from within the organisation is a valuable source of information for credit assessment. It is essential that it is backed up wherever possible by an analysis of past and up-to-date financial statements of the customer. If up-to-date financial statements are not available, draft accounts or internal management reports should be requested for analysis. Ideally, at least three years' accounts should be analysed in order to show the trends in three key areas:

- **liquidity** – the ability of the business to repay debts as they fall due
- **profitability** – the ability of the business to maintain its capital and to provide funds for repayment of debts in the future
- **gearing** – the financial risk taken on by the business shown by comparing interest bearing liabilities and total capital employed

You should be familiar with ratio analysis from your other studies, so for the purposes of this book we will list the basic performance indicators which you should be able to apply. If you are unsure about this subject, you are recommended to study Osborne Books' *Limited Company Accounts Tutorial*, Chapter 7, 'Interpretation of Financial Statements'.

what is a good indicator?

The question is often asked: what is a 'good' current ratio or a 'good' liquid capital ratio? The answer is that it is impossible to give a fail safe answer. Businesses vary widely in the way their assets and liabilities are structured – compare a TV manufacturer and a supermarket, for example. There are some guidelines, however. These are shown below as notes, and should be used for guidance purposes only.

liquidity indicators

These indicators show the ability of the business to repay short-term debt from liquid or semi-liquid assets, and also to turn over its current assets such as stock and debtors.

INDICATOR	FORMULA	WHAT IT SHOWS
current ratio	$\dfrac{\text{current assets}}{\text{current liabilities}}$	working capital expressed as a ratio *ideally 2 : 1 or higher*
liquid capital ratio	$\dfrac{\text{current assets} - \text{stock}}{\text{current liabilities}}$	a ratio comparing liquidity with short-term debts *ideally 1 : 1 or higher*

stock turnover	$\dfrac{\text{stock x 365}}{\text{cost of sales}}$	the number of days on average that stock is held *– this will depend entirely on the nature of the stock; the figure should not increase over time*
debtor turnover	$\dfrac{\text{debtors x 365}}{\text{sales}}$	the number of days on average that it takes for a debtor to pay up *– this will depend on the nature of the business; 30 to 60 days is common*
creditor turnover	$\dfrac{\text{creditors x 365}}{\text{purchases}}$	the number of days on average that it takes to pay a creditor *– this will usefully show how promptly the business pays its debtors*

profitability indicators

These indicators show the ability of the business to generate profit which will enable it to repay its debts in the longer term.

INDICATOR	FORMULA	WHAT IT SHOWS
operating profit %	$\dfrac{\text{operating profit x 100}}{\text{sales}}$	profit made before deduction of tax and interest *– this should remain steady and in line with the industry average*
net profit %	$\dfrac{\text{net profit x 100}}{\text{sales}}$	profit made after deduction of all expenses *– this should ideally increase over the years, and not fall*
return on capital employed (ROCE)	$\dfrac{\text{operating profit x 100}}{\text{capital employed*}}$ * ordinary share capital + reserves + interest bearing capital + long-term loans	profit made related to the capital employed by the company *– this should also remain steady over the years*

financial position

Financial position measures the strength and long-term financing of a company. Two ratios are calculated: interest cover and gearing.

Interest cover measures the ability of a business to pay interest on borrowing from its profits.

interest cover	$\dfrac{\text{operating profit}}{\text{interest}}$	the safety margin of profit over interest payable *– the higher the figure the better*

The proportion of long-term debt to capital is known as **gearing**. This shows the extent to which the company is financed by debt. Gearing can be calculated in a number of ways. The formula below is commonly used.

gearing %	$\dfrac{\text{long-term debt* x 100}}{\text{capital employed**}}$	relationship between long-term debt and capital *– this should ideally be less than 50%, the higher the figure, the less secure the company*

*   interest bearing capital + long-term loans
** ordinary share capital + reserves + interest bearing capital + long-term loans

The Case Study which follows shows the credit assessment process in action.

Case Study

FIRTH ELECTRONICS: CREDIT ASSESSMENT PROCEDURES

situation

You work in the credit control section of Firth Electronics. You have been approached by a new customer, Bridge Trading Limited for credit of £10,000 a month. You have sent out your normal enquiries – a bank credit status request and two trade credit reference requests. Bridge Trading have also sent you their last three years' accounts for you to analyse.

The replies and accounts summary are shown below.

You have been asked to prepare notes summarising your assessment of this company.

National Bank PLC

status report: Bridge Trading Limited

Request: £10,000 trade credit per month

Report: Good for your figure and purpose

Response to trade credit enquiry, received from A Jones & Co

Re: Bridge Trading Limited: £10,000 trade credit per month

We have been trading with this company for five years and allow £15,000 credit per month on 30 day terms. The company can sometimes take longer to pay than allowed by these terms.

Response to trade credit enquiry, received from A Patel

Bridge Trading Limited £10,000 credit per month

We allow this customer £5,000 credit per month on 60 day terms. The account is usually paid on time, although sometimes payment can be late. The figure you quote is higher than the credit given by us but we know of no reasons why this customer should not be able to fulfil its liabilities.

SUMMARY OF FINANCIAL ACCOUNTS: BRIDGE TRADING LIMITED

	Year 1 £000	Year 2 £000	Year 3* £000
Sales	1,000	1,200	1,400
Cost of sales	600	800	1,000
Current assets	880	1,040	1,200
Current liabilities	620	710	750
Stock	200	220	280
Debtors	102	115	127
Creditors	150	161	195
Operating profit	80	94	112
Interest paid	20	34	32
Net profit	60	60	80
Long-term debt + interest bearing capital	200	200	250
Capital & reserves	400	460	520

*Year 3 was last year and the accounts were made up to 31 December.

solution

You process the data from the bank report, the two trade references and the three years' accounts, and set out the results in a table:

ANALYSIS OF FINANCIAL ACCOUNTS: BRIDGE TRADING LIMITED			
	Year 1	Year 2	Year 3
Current Ratio	1.42 : 1	1.46 : 1	1.60 : 1
Liquid Capital Ratio	1.10 : 1	1.15 : 1	1.23 : 1
Stock turnover	122 days	100 days	102 days
Debtor days	37 days	35 days	33 days
Creditor days	91 days	73 days	71 days
Net profit %	6%	5%	6%
Return on capital employed %	13.3%	14.2%	14.5%
Interest cover	4.0 times	2.8 times	3.5 times
Gearing	33%	30%	32%

You draw the following conclusions:

bank report

This indicates that the bank considers Bridge Trading Limited to be a reasonable credit risk, which, as far as bank reports go, is a positive response.

trade references

Both references draw attention to the fact that Bridge Trading Limited does pay up, but is often late in doing so. The analysis of the three years' accounts will therefore need to concentrate on the liquidity ratios. Late payment can either result from inefficiency or from illiquidity.

analysis of three years' financial accounts

The profitability ratios (net profit and return on capital employed) and gearing percentage all suggest a company with manageable debt and a consistently sound profit record. The interest cover shows an ability to cover interest costs from profit.

The current ratio and liquid capital ratio have both improved over the three years, although the current ratio does reflect the high level of creditors (see below). Debtor days at around 35 shows that the business is collecting its trade debts efficiently. It is the payment period (creditor days) that gives cause for concern, although there has been some improvement. The reason is not a lack of liquidity, but is either a conscious policy of delaying payment to help with short-term financing, or just a lack of efficiency. Whatever, the reason, Firth Electronics should not accept similar treatment.

recommendation

Bridge Trading Limited should be allowed the credit requested, as there is sufficient liquidity in the company, but on strict 30 days' terms. Payments should be carefully monitored and the company advised that any late payments could result in withdrawal of credit and an insistence on trading on cash terms only.

THE ORGANISATION'S CREDIT CONTROL PROCEDURES

It is important to appreciate that the credit assessments carried out in the Case Study and explained in the text of this chapter are likely to form part of the organisation's credit control procedures, often set down in a formal written policy document.

Where there is such a document, there will be operational requirements, set terms, standard documents, all of which will ensure that the administration of credit control runs smoothly and in line with the organisation's 'standard' procedures.

Another reason that standard procedures have to be followed is a legal one. The relationship between seller and buyer is one of contract, ie legal agreement. If that contract is broken – eg the buyer does not pay up – the seller may need to take the buyer to court. The law is very particular and if the seller is to be successful, it is very important that all the procedures have been carried out 'to the letter'. This is particularly important in relation to terms of payment. This issue will be dealt with in full on pages 181 to 186.

Set out below is an example of a typical Credit Control Policy Document. Note that Sales Department – who will be dealing with the customer on a day-to-day basis – will need to be notified of any default procedures.

CREDIT POLICY & PROCEDURES

New Accounts	1	One bank reference and two trade references required.
	2	Analysis of minimum of three years' accounts for limited company customers.
Credit Terms	3	Standard terms 30 days from invoice. Any extension to be authorised by Credit Controller.
	4	2.5% settlement discount at Credit Controller's discretion.
Debt Collection	5	Invoices despatched on day of issue.
	6	Statements despatched first week of the month.
	7	Aged debtors analysis produced and analysed first week of the month.
	8	Reminder letter sent first week of the month for accounts 30 days overdue (Letter 1).
	9	Telephone chaser for accounts 45 days overdue. Meeting arranged if required.
	10	Customer on stop list if no payment received within 15 days of telephone chaser (unless meeting arranged). Sales Department notified.
	11	Letter threatening legal action and stop list notification sent if payment not received within 30 days of first letter (Letter 2).
	12	Legal proceedings set in motion if payment not received within 30 days of Letter 2 – subject to authorisation by Finance Director and notification of Sales Manager.

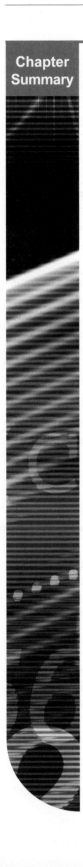

Chapter Summary

- An effective credit control policy is essential in an organisation if bad debts are to be avoided.

- The extent of the credit control function depends on the size of the organisation. The same basic functions will be carried out:
  - assessing applications for new credit from new customers
  - assessing applications for increased credit from existing customers
  - monitoring the sales ledger
  - chasing overdue debts
  - dealing with bad debts

- Organisations use a variety of external sources and internal sources to provide information when assessing credit risks. External sources are likely to be used more for new customers and internal sources for existing customers.

- External sources include bank references, trade references, credit rating agency reports and other publications. Some organisations ask the customer to complete a credit application form which will provide the data it needs.

- When using external sources of information the organisation will need to be aware of the restrictions of the Data Protection Act 1998 which regulates the disclosure of information about individuals (not companies) to third parties.

- Internal sources of information include records of meetings, conversations and visits by a variety of employees of the organisation, including the sales ledger staff and sales force.

- Another valuable exercise in credit assessment is the ratio analysis of financial accounts – preferably from three consecutive years. This is an important exercise for new customers and also useful for existing customers. Ratio analysis will provide information about the trends in:
  - liquidity
  - profitability
  - the financial position

  All of these will provide information about the customer's ability to re invoices when they fall due.

- An organisation's credit control policy will often be form
  Credit Policy document which ensures that all proce
  correctly.

<table>
<tr><td></td><td>**credit control**</td><td>the process of managing customers who pay on credit so that settlement of debt is made on time</td></tr>
<tr><td></td><td>**bank reference**</td><td>a credit report given by the customer's bank to supplier; the information is reliable but requires some interpretation</td></tr>
<tr><td></td><td>**trade reference**</td><td>a credit report authorised by the customer and given by an organisation which already provides the customer with credit facilities; this information may not be as reliable as a bank reference</td></tr>
<tr><td></td><td>**credit reference agency**</td><td>an organisation which provides a wide variety of credit data about companies and individuals on a commercial basis – often online – including financial accounts, payment histories, details of court proceedings and insolvencies; this information is very full but can be costly</td></tr>
<tr><td></td><td>**Companies House**</td><td>the Government agency which holds details of all limited companies and directors; larger companies file their annual accounts at Companies House</td></tr>
<tr><td></td><td>**Data Protection Act**</td><td>the legislation which regulates the disclosure of information held by individuals and organisations about third parties; it covers data held on computer and in paper-based records</td></tr>
<tr><td></td><td>**liquidity indicators**</td><td>performance indicators which show the extent of the liquidity of a business; for example the current and liquid capital ratios, stock turnover, debtor days and creditor days (see page 167 for formulas)</td></tr>
<tr><td></td><td>**profitability indicators**</td><td>performance indicators which show the ability of the business to generate the profit needed to provide liquidity; for example operating profit percentage, net profit percentage and ROCE (see page 168)</td></tr>
<tr><td></td><td>**financial position**</td><td>the extent of the reliance of the business on long-term debt; interest cover shows how well interest payments can be met from profit and gearing shows the reliance on long-term loans and interest bearing capital</td></tr>
</table>

Student Activities

answers to the asterisked (*) questions are to be found at the back of this book

8.1* You work for GML Importers Limited, an importer of toys from the Far East. The Credit Control Manager has received a letter from Toppo Toys Limited which operates a chain of 20 shops in the London area. Toppo Toys wishes to purchase stock from GML Importers Limited and is requesting credit facilities. You are to draft a reply using today's date and your own name. The company Credit Policy Manual states that to assess any new proposition you will initially need a banker's reference and two trade references.

Toppo Toys Limited

71 Clerkenwell Avenue

London EC1R 5BC

Tel 0207 8371199 Fax 0207 8371192 Email sales@toppotoys.co.uk

D Brinkwell, Credit Control Manager
GML Importers Limited
29 The Greenway
Slough SL2 7GH

Dear Mr Brinkwell,

Request for credit facilities

We have purchased stock from you over the last six months and would now be grateful if you could consider providing us with credit facilities. We would initially be looking for a facility of £10,000 on thirty days terms.

As we have been trading with you on a cash terms basis for six months we hope that this can be arranged with the minimum of formality.

We look forward to hearing from you.

Yours sincerely

B Attman

Bart Attman
Director

8.2* Your company, GML Importers Limited, is processing a new credit application for S Low Limited. Steve Low, the customer's MD, is anxious that the facility be set up as soon as possible. You find, however, that one of the trade references has not yet been received. You telephone the company concerned, but the manager who normally provides the references is away on holiday in Spain for the next two weeks. Your colleague suggests using a credit reference agency to obtain a back-up reference. Describe:

(a) the data that a credit reference agency will be able to provide about a limited company

(b) one major advantage and one major disadvantage of using a credit reference agency

8.3* A sales ledger assistant at your company, GML Importers Limited, receives a telephone call from a competitor business, Pronto Importers, who ask if the sales ledger assistant can provide some information about a mutual customer, Hal Johnson. They would like to know if you provide Hal Johnson with a credit limit, and if so, how much it is and whether the customer pays up on time. The sales ledger assistant is unsure how to deal with this request and asks you for advice. What would you advise? Give reasons for your recommendations.

8.4 You are assessing an application for a credit limit for £15,000 from a new customer, Stylo Limited. You have received a bank reference and two trade references. Stylo Limited has also provided you with a summary of its accounts for the last three years (see data below and on the next page).

Your company Credit Policy Manual requires that credit terms should initially be offered for a maximum of 30 days.

You are to:

(a) write comments on the bank reference

(b) write comments on the trade references

(c) analyse the accounts summary and draw up a table showing for the three years the following performance indicators:

- the current ratio and the liquid capital ratio
- debtor days and creditor days
- net profit percentage
- interest cover and gearing

(d) write comments on the performance indicators

(e) write a conclusion, stating your recommendations for the granting of the requested credit of £15,000 a month

---

Centro Bank PLC

status report: Stylo Limited

Request: £15,000 trade credit per month

Report: Should prove good for your figure and purpose.

Response to trade credit enquiry, received from B Ruckner Ltd

Re: Stylo Limited: £15,000 trade credit per month

We have been trading with this company for five years and allow £10,000 credit per month on 60 day terms. The company normally meets its commitments on time.

Response to trade credit enquiry, received from V Williams

Stylo Limited £15,000 credit per month

We allow this customer £5,000 credit per month on 60 day terms. The account is usually paid on time.

EXTRACT FROM FINANCIAL ACCOUNTS: STYLO LIMITED

	Year 1 £000	Year 2 £000	Year 3 £000
Sales	750	781	720
Cost of sales	350	363	348
Current assets	720	705	684
Current liabilities	680	656	663
Stock	200	220	280
Debtors	88	93	95
Creditors	58	63	62
Operating profit	80	86	94
Interest paid	60	71	80
Net profit	20	15	14
Long-term debt	121	150	175
Capital & reserves	125	145	160

Granting credit – setting up the account

The last chapter described the credit assessment process which collects internal and external information about a customer that is asking for credit terms. This chapter describes the next stage of the process:

- making the decision whether or not to grant credit
- advising an unsuccessful applicant in a tactful way so that business is not lost
- setting up an account for a successful applicant customer requiring credit terms

Setting up an account is a formal process establishing a legal relationship of contract between the supplier and the customer. This chapter describes:

- general terms of supply and payment
- discounts – including settlement discounts
- payment of interest on late payment

This chapter concludes with details of the legal implications of a trading relationship.

The next chapter describes how an account is monitored, with the overall aim of reducing the incidence of bad debts.

PERFORMANCE CRITERIA COVERED

unit 15 OPERATING A CASH MANAGEMENT AND CREDIT CONTROL SYSTEM

element 15.3

Grant credit

A   Agree credit terms with customers in accordance with the organisation's policies.

C   Open new accounts for those customers with an established credit status.

D   Ensure the reasons for refusing credit are discussed with customers in a tactful manner.

KNOWLEDGE AND UNDERSTANDING COVERAGE

6   Legal issues: basic contract; terms and conditions of contracts relating to the granting of credit; Data Protection legislation and credit control information.

17   Discounts for prompt payment.

18   Interpretation and use of credit control information.

30   Understanding that practice in this area will be determined by an organisation's credit control policies and procedures.

31   An understanding of the organisation's relevant policies and procedures.

GRANTING CREDIT – FACTORS AFFECTING THE DECISION

The last chapter concentrated on gathering sufficient information about a prospective customer so that a decision to grant credit can be made. It is important to appreciate that the decision will involve more than just the reading of references and the application of accounting ratios. Other factors to consider are

- ownership of the customer
- overseas customers
- amount of information available
- sales policy

ownership

Ownership of the customer will often determine the level of risk involved in granting credit. An organisation that has 'state' backing (eg the BBC or a local authority) will have a low risk status – ie it is very unlikely that the customer will fail to pay up on time. The same should be true of large companies and their subsidiary companies (which have their backing). It is the smaller organisations, eg start-up businesses, that are seen as being more risky, because failure rate in this sector is higher and bad debts more likely.

overseas companies

Overseas companies are a higher risk because of the possible problems the customer may have in obtaining and sending currency payments. Also, there will be complications with legal systems should it become necessary to take court action to recover debt. Consequently, trading with overseas customers may be on a 'cash up front' basis, at least to start with.

It must be stressed that overseas customers are not seen as being less creditworthy, it is just that the logistics of obtaining payment are more complex. Banks can be very helpful in this area in advising on country risk and setting up payment guarantee schemes.

insufficient information

It is possible that the amount of available information about a prospective customer is limited. This is particularly the case with a start-up business, which may be an excellently run company with good prospects, but the lack of any form of track record will make a credit decision hard to make. This situation may call for an initial refusal of credit with a promise of a review in, say, six months time when more information will have become available.

sales policy

There can be a tension within a commercial organisation between the sales function and the credit control function. Sales staff will want to obtain as many sales leads and new customers as possible in order to meet targets, even if the credit risks involved are higher than the credit control function would normally tolerate. The decision of whether or not to grant credit may therefore be swayed by current management policy, whether it be to 'play it safe' or to 'go all out for new sales'.

REFUSING CREDIT

The decision not to grant credit is a difficult one for all concerned. The organisation taking the decision is in danger of losing business because the potential customer may well go to another supplier; the potential customer will in turn lose both a supplier and a source of liquidity (remember that credit granted by a supplier = short-term financing).

The supplier is likely to suggest to the customer that cash trading (ie immediate 'on the nail' payment) would be an alternative until the credit status of the customer is reviewed in, say, six months time.

The supplier will have to treat the matter with great tact and diplomacy. A letter should be sent to the customer explaining the situation. The letter could incorporate some of the sentences shown below and should be written to relate to the circumstances of the case.

Dear Customer

Application for trade credit

'Thank you for your letter/application form of .... requesting credit of ....'

'We have assessed your application for credit using our usual criteria and have taken up references, but very much regret that we are unable to offer credit facilities to you at present.'

'We will be happy to review the situation again in six months time, when we have seen your latest financial accounts.'

'We very much value your custom and would be very pleased to trade with you on a cash basis for the time being. Our Sales Manager, Guy Weston, would be very interested in talking to you. His email address is gweston@gmlimporters.co.uk'

We look forward to hearing from you.'

---

half-way house credit

Some organisations, anxious not to lose a customer, might compromise and agree credit terms that are 'half-way' to what the customer requested. Examples of this are:

- shorter credit periods, eg 7 days rather than 30 days

- part payment, eg pay 25% cash terms and 75% after 30 days

This will not remove the risk of the customer not paying, but it reduces it, and may help to retain a good customer who would otherwise have gone to another supplier.

OPENING THE ACCOUNT

When the decision to grant credit has been taken, the account should be set up without delay. This will be advised in writing to the customer, normally in a formal letter. This will set out:

- the period for which credit will be made available (eg 12 months)

- the limit on the account, eg £20,000

- the credit terms, eg 30 days from date of invoice

- discounts (including any settlement discount available)

- payment details (optional)

- interest penalties for late payment

This document is an important one for legal reasons. It can be referred to in later documentation, eg conditions of sale printed on the back of an order acknowledgement or invoice, and will be binding on the purchaser in the contract of sale which is set up each time a supply is made. We will explain in more detail about contracts of sale and legislation relating to selling at the end of this chapter (see pages 184-187). We will first explain the terms which will be set out in the letter to the customer when the account is opened.

credit period and limit

This limit is the upper limit which will be set on the sales ledger account of the new customer for a set period of time. A rule of thumb calculation is that the limit should be twice the average monthly sales expected to be made to the customer. The period of the limit is normally twelve months.

credit terms

A number of credit payment terms need explanation. Note the distinction between 'net' – which refers to the timing of the supply of goods or services – and the use of the invoice date to calculate the payment date.

cash terms	immediate payment, ie zero credit
30 days from date of invoice	payment is due 30 days after the invoice date, eg payment of an invoice dated 10 March is due by 10 April
net monthly	payment of one month's supplies of goods or services is due at the end of the following month, eg payment of a delivery dated 10 March is due by 30 April
net 30 days	payment of a supply of goods/services is due 30 days after the delivery (the same principle is applicable to 'net 60 days' etc)

discounts

A discount is a percentage reduction in the selling price.

Trade discount is traditionally given to established customers who buy on a regular basis, although a new customer may be given it straightaway, particularly if it has been requested as part of a 'deal' to open the account. The amount will vary according to the product. For example, a textbook like this one will sell to a bookshop at a trade discount of around 30%.

Settlement discount (also known as cash discount) is a percentage reduction in selling price allowed when settlement is made earlier than normal, eg '2.5% discount for settlement within 7 days'. For example, a purchaser receiving an invoice for £100 (ignoring VAT) with these terms will only have to pay £97.50 (ie £100 less £2.50 discount).

Settlement discount is attractive **when interest rates are high**. This is because money that may otherwise have been borrowed on overdraft by the seller to finance working capital – at a high interest rate – will be paid into the bank earlier and the interest cost will be reduced accordingly. **If interest rates are low**, the cost to the seller of offering settlement discount (ie the reduction in the selling price) can be comparatively high, which makes it less attractive. The **annual equivalent** of the cost can be worked out by the formula shown below. The cost is worked out on an annual equivalent basis so that it can be compared with interest rates (also quoted per annum):

$$\left[\frac{d}{100-d}\right] \times \left[\frac{365}{N-D}\right] \times 100\% = \text{annual cost of discount}$$

Where d = settlement discount percentage

N = normal settlement period in days

D = settlement period for early payment in days

worked example – the cost of offering settlement discount

Your business is considering offering 1.5% settlement discount for payment of invoices within seven days rather than the thirty days normally offered. How much is it going to cost your business on an annual basis? How does it compare with the 14% it would cost you to finance the invoice on a bank overdraft?

solution

The formula is

$$\left[\frac{d}{100-d}\right] \times \left[\frac{365}{N-D}\right] \times 100\% = \text{annual cost of discount}$$

d	= settlement discount percentage	= 1.5%
N	= normal settlement period in days	= 30
D	= settlement period for early payment	= 7

The calculation is

$$\left[\frac{1.5}{98.5}\right] \times \left[\frac{365}{23}\right] \times 100\% = \text{annual cost of discount} = 24.17\%$$

This shows that the annual cost to the business will be 24.17% which is more expensive than financing the extra 23 days (ie 30 less 7 days) on overdraft at 14% per annum. Cash discount therefore does not look like a good idea.

Another disadvantage of offering settlement discount is that customers will take it and then pay the reduced amount later than the specified date! There is very little that can be done about this practice. With all these factors in mind, it is no surprise that settlement discounts are comparatively rare.

payment details

Payment can be made in a number of different ways, and these can have a cost implication. Generally speaking, payment by cheque and cash is more expensive both for the customer and the supplier in terms of handling costs and bank charges.

Many organisations actively encourage computer payments through the BACS system which transfers money from one account to another by computer. When setting up an account, the seller may request BACS payments instead of cheque payment.

interest penalties for late payment

It is common practice for organisations to include in their terms and conditions the right to charge interest on late payments. Not many organisations will necessarily enforce this right, because they then run the risk of alienating and losing the customer. The terms are normally included as an incentive to pay.

The first extract below is taken from the terms and conditions on account opening documentation. The second extract is taken from the terms printed on the back of an acknowledgment of an order.

Our terms are strictly 30 days net monthly. Interest will be charged at 2% per month (or part thereof) on all amounts unpaid after the due date.

If payment is not made when due the Company may cancel this contract and any other contract between the Customer and the Company, suspend any further deliveries and/or charge interest accruing on a daily basis on any amount unpaid by the Customer at a rate of 2 per cent per calendar month or part thereof that payment remains outstanding.

Interest on late payment is also enforceable in law, although, as mentioned above, organisations are only likely to take this action as a last resort. The statute is the **Late Payment of Commercial Debts (Interest) Act 1998** and the interest rate that can be charged is the Bank of England official dealing (base) rate plus 8%. It should be noted that there does not need to be a mention of this law in the 'terms and conditions' issued by the seller – it is an automatic legal right.

CUSTOMERS AND CONTRACTS

a contract is a legally binding agreement enforceable in a court of law

Contracts, which may be in writing, or by word of mouth (oral), are agreements between two parties. Examples include:

- a written contract which you sign if you buy a house
- an oral contract if you buy goods in a shop
- an oral contract if you order goods over the telephone

In each case somebody does something for which some kind of payment is made. A contract is **an agreement with legal consequences** because if the work done is not satisfactory, or if the payment is not made, the wronged party can take the other person to court for **breach of contract.**

So how does this affect buyer and seller?

Firstly, a contract is entered into each time an order is placed and goods or services are supplied. A contract must have these three essential elements:

1   an **agreement** – an offer and acceptance

     In the case of an order for goods or services the offer might be the written quotation from the supplier and the acceptance the placing of an order by the customer.

2   a **bargain** – value passes between the two parties

     The goods or services are supplied by the seller and payment is made by the customer. 'Bargain' here does not refer to any form of 'cheap deal', it means a 'sale'. The legal term for the value which passes is 'consideration'.

3   **intention to create legal relations** – the agreement is commercial

     This means that the seller and buyer are serious about what they are doing and know that if anything goes wrong solicitors could eventually be called in and the matter taken to the courts.

It is up to the supplier to make sure that when goods or services are sold that the terms and conditions of sale – ie the price and payment terms – are clearly set out. If there is then any problem, late payment or non-payment for example, the supplier can hold the customer to the stated terms, in a court of law if necessary. These terms are often printed on the back of the order acknowledgement or invoice issued by the supplier, as in the example extract shown below.

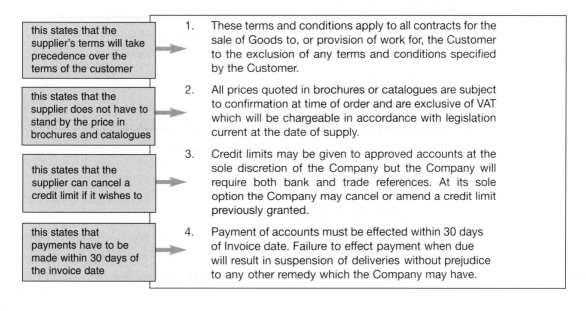

this states that the supplier's terms will take precedence over the terms of the customer

1.   These terms and conditions apply to all contracts for the sale of Goods to, or provision of work for, the Customer to the exclusion of any terms and conditions specified by the Customer.

this states that the supplier does not have to stand by the price in brochures and catalogues

2.   All prices quoted in brochures or catalogues are subject to confirmation at time of order and are exclusive of VAT which will be chargeable in accordance with legislation current at the date of supply.

this states that the supplier can cancel a credit limit if it wishes to

3.   Credit limits may be given to approved accounts at the sole discretion of the Company but the Company will require both bank and trade references. At its sole option the Company may cancel or amend a credit limit previously granted.

this states that payments have to be made within 30 days of the invoice date

4.   Payment of accounts must be effected within 30 days of Invoice date. Failure to effect payment when due will result in suspension of deliveries without prejudice to any other remedy which the Company may have.

retention of title

Another term which sometimes appears on the front of invoices and in the small print on the back of sales documents is that ownership of the goods sold does not pass to the buyer until payment has been made. This is known as a **retention of title** clause.

This may sound an odd arrangement, but it is included so that in the unlikely event of the buyer becoming bankrupt/insolvent, the seller may attempt to reclaim the goods and so get some money back. This is workable when the goods are easily identifiable, such as books or packets of crisps, but causes problems when the goods are raw materials, eg blank paper or potatoes.

An example of a retention of title clause is shown below.

---

5. Title in all Goods supplied by the Company shall vest in the Company until the Company has received full payment in respect thereof.

SELLING AND STATUTE LAW

There are a number of statutes (Acts of Parliament) which govern the way in which goods and services are sold, and these obviously affect the way in which businesses operate.

Note that a credit control department cannot exclude these statutes through clever wording of terms and conditions. They are part of English statute law and are binding on all relevant business dealings.

The principal statutes are the Trade Descriptions Act, the Sale of Goods Act (as amended) and the Unfair Contract Terms Act.

Trade Descriptions Act

The Trade Descriptions Act makes it a criminal offence:

• to make false statements about goods offered for sale

• to make misleading statements about services

Examples of offences therefore include:

• stating that a car for sale has clocked up 15,000 miles, when in fact the figure is 25,000 miles

• making a misleading statement about the price of goods, eg saying 'Now only £49.95, was £99.95' when it has only ever sold for £69.95

• making a misleading statement about a service, eg 'our dry cleaning is guaranteed to remove every stain' when it does not, or 'our apartments are within easy reach of the sea' when they are fifteen miles away

Sale of Goods Act 1979

This Act and subsequent amendments (including the Supply of Goods and Services Act 1982) state that you are entitled to expect any goods that you buy from a shop to be:

of 'satisfactory quality'

This means they must meet the standard that a 'reasonable' person would expect given the description and the price.

'fit for the purpose'

The goods must do what they are supposed to do, or what the shop claims they can do: an umbrella should keep the rain out, a watch should keep accurate time.

'as described'

The goods must be what they are claimed to be: a 'leather coat' must be made of leather, a 'surround sound cinema system' must provide surround sound.

If any of these three conditions is not met, the purchaser is entitled to a full or a part refund, depending on how soon the fault appears, how serious it is and how quickly the matter is taken up. Note also the following practical points:

- the buyer can accept a replacement, but can also insist on a refund if a replacement is not wanted
- the buyer does not have to accept a credit note for spending on other purchases
- a shop is not entitled to put up a notice saying "No Refunds!"

Unfair Contract Terms Act

Any organisation that tries to insist on *unfair* terms (eg in small print on the back of a sales contract) may be in breach of the Unfair Contract Terms Act. This would protect, for example, holidaymakers who are not put up in the hotel they booked because the small print stated that the holiday company had the right to move them to another resort. This would be seen as an 'unfair term' and would enable the holidaymaker to seek compensation. In short, a business cannot 'contract out' through the small print.

It must be stressed that the terms must be 'unfair' in order to break the law. Terms and conditions on sales documentation are normally carefully worded so that they will stand up to examination in a court of law. Generally speaking, the supplier has the upper hand in dictating terms.

We will describe the processes of taking court action for the recovery of debt in Chapter 11.

Chapter Summary

- The decision to grant credit involves a variety of different factors involving levels of risk: internal and external credit information, the nature of the ownership of the organisation, its location, the amount of information available and the level of risk attached to the sales policy.

- If credit is to be refused, the communication of the refusal to the potential customer should be carried out in a tactful and diplomatic way.

- Some organisations may be willing to compromise and offer limited credit terms to a partially risky customer; these terms might include a shorter credit period or acceptance of part payment of invoices.

- When the decision to grant credit has been made, the supplier should set out the credit terms in writing for the customer. This should include:
  - the credit period
  - the credit limit
  - the payment terms
  - details of discounts
  - payment instructions
  - interest penalties on late payment

- The granting of settlement discount is normally more cost effective when interest rates are high. The annual cost of granting the discount can be calculated by formula and compared with the current cost of borrowing.

- Penalties on late payment can be written into the credit terms as required. There is also a statutory right to claim interest on late payments under the Late Payment of Commercial Debts (Interest) Act 1998.

- Every time an organisation sells goods or services it enters into a contract – a legally binding agreement – with its customer. If the customer defaults on these terms, a breach of contract occurs which could be grounds for court action if the case is seen as being sufficiently serious.

- The terms and conditions of the contract of sale are often set out on the back of sales documentation and may refer back to the original credit terms communicated to the customer when the account was opened.

- Sales of goods and services are also regulated by statute law, including the Trade Descriptions Act, the Sale of Goods Act (as amended) and the Unfair Contract Terms Act. An organisation is bound by this law and cannot contract out of its terms.

Key Terms		
	credit terms	the terms on which credit is made available to a customer; they will involve the credit period, amount, discounts, payment details, late payment penalties
	trade discount	discount given to customers who trade on a regular basis
	settlement discount	discount given for early settlement of invoices (also known as 'cash' discount)
	interest penalties	penalties charged on amounts outstanding after the due date of payment, charged at a fixed rate of interest
	contract	a legally binding agreement enforceable in a court of law; it has three elements: 1 an agreement, comprising an offer and an acceptance 2 a bargain, ie value passing between the two parties (also known as 'consideration') 3 an intention to create legal relations, ie a commercial agreement which could be taken to a court of law if the need arose
	breach of contract	breaking of the terms of a contract and grounds for taking legal action
	retention of title	the right of a seller of goods to retain ownership of the goods until payment is made
	Late Payment of Commercial Debts (Interest) Act	allows suppliers to charge interest on overdue amounts owing
	Trade Descriptions Act	makes it a criminal offence for a seller to make false and misleading statements about goods and services
	Sale of Goods Act	goods sold should be of satisfactory quality, fit for the purpose and as described by the seller
	Unfair Contract Terms Act	regulates against unfair terms ('small print clauses') in contracts

Student Activities

answers to the asterisked (*) questions are to be found at the back of this book

9.1* (a) A supplier has written a letter advising the granting of a credit limit to a new customer. List the main terms of credit that you would expect to see included in the letter.

(b) Do these terms constitute a contract between the supplier and the customer? Give reasons for your answer.

9.2* An invoice for goods supplied is dated 27 April. The goods are delivered on 2 May.

When is the invoice due for payment if the terms are

(a) 30 days of date of invoice?

(b) net monthly?

(c) net 30 days?

9.3* (a) What is the annual cost to an organisation of granting settlement discount of 1.5% for settlement within 30 days? The normal payment period granted is 60 days.

(b) Would granting settlement discount be an attractive option for the seller if the cost of borrowing on overdraft was

(i) 15% p.a.

(ii) 25% p.a.

Give reasons for your answers.

9.4* A supplier has not included a late payment interest penalty clause in the terms and conditions of supply issued to a customer.

The customer is consistently late in settling invoices. Can the supplier charge interest without having this clause in the terms and conditions of supply? If the supplier did decide to charge interest, what authority would the supplier have for doing so?

9.5* Which of the following arrangements are not contracts in terms of the three elements of contract?

State the reasons for your decision in each of the four situations and suggest what you could do to rectify each situation.

(a) A friend paints your kitchen as a favour, but makes a right mess of it.

(b) You buy a newspaper for 50p in a local shop, having picked it up off the rack, but when you get home you find that you have got the wrong paper.

(c) A company sends off for a free sample of a promotional pen. When it arrives it does not work.

(d) A business writes out an order for stationery worth £150, but omits to post it. It then complains to the supplier when the goods do not arrive.

9.6* A supplier quotes the following conditions on the back of an order acknowledgement (extract only). Explain in plain English what each of the terms means. (Note: the supplier is referred to as the 'Company').

---

2. All prices quoted in brochures or catalogues are subject to confirmation at time of order and are exclusive of VAT which will be chargeable in accordance with legislation current at the date of supply.

3. Credit limits may be given to approved accounts at the sole discretion of the Company but the Company will require both bank and trade references. At its sole option the Company may cancel or amend a credit limit previously granted.

4. Payment of accounts must be effected within 30 days of Invoice date. Failure to effect payment when due will result in suspension of deliveries without prejudice to any other remedy which the Company may have.

5. Title in all Goods supplied by the Company shall vest in the Company until the Company has received full payment in respect thereof.

9.7 You receive the following memo from the Credit Control Department.

Carry out the stated instructions, using the Credit Controller's name and today's date.

MEMO

to   A Student

from   Jon E Wrotton

subject   Credit refusal: Duff Enterprises

Please draft the text of a letter for my signature to D Brent, Finance Manager, Duph Enterprises, Unit 1 Belleview Estate, Station Road, Slough, SL2 7GD.

We have turned down an application for £10,000 a month for this customer. The trade references were OK, but the bank reference was guarded and we were working from final accounts that were 15 months out of date. Liquidity looked a bit thin and we would need to see the latest figures (due in about four months).

We are keen to trade on a cash basis straightaway and should review the situation in six months time when the latest accounts have been analysed. The sales rep who would deal with them is Helen Didmore.

Thanks.

J. W.

10 Monitoring and controlling the sales ledger

this chapter covers . . .

In the last two chapters we described the credit assessment of customers and the opening of sales ledger accounts. In this chapter we explain how sales ledger accounts are monitored using an aged debtors summary which shows:

- the extent to which individual accounts have debts outstanding
- average periods of credit given to sales ledger accounts as a whole
- the warning signs of accounts turning into doubtful and bad debts

This chapter describes how debts are chased and customers are persuaded to pay on time, so helping the liquidity of the organisation. These procedures are carried out in line with an organisation's credit policy document.

This chapter also looks at alternative methods of collecting debts, including:

- credit insurance (insuring against bad debts)
- factoring and invoice discounting (lending money against invoices issued)

In the next and final chapter we describe how an organisation deals with customers that will not or cannot pay invoices, either because they are short of cash, or because they are insolvent.

PERFORMANCE CRITERIA COVERED

unit 15 OPERATING A CASH MANAGEMENT AND CREDIT CONTROL SYSTEM

element 15.4

Monitor and control the collection of debts

A   Monitor information relating to the current state of debtors' accounts regularly and take appropriate action.

B   Send information regarding significant outstanding accounts and potential bad debts promptly to relevant individuals within the organisation.

C   Ensure discussions and negotiations with debtors are conducted courteously and achieve the desired outcome.

KNOWLEDGE AND UNDERSTANDING COVERAGE

18   Interpretation and use of credit control information.

19   Methods of collection.

20   Factoring arrangements.

21   *Debt insurance.*

22   *Methods of analysing information on debtors: age analysis of debtors; average periods of credit given and received; incidence of bad and doubtful debts.*

23   *Evaluation of different collection methods.*

25   *Liquidity management.*

26   *Understanding that the accounting systems of an organisation are affected by its organisational structure, its administrative systems and procedures and the nature of its business transactions.*

31   *An understanding of the organisation's relevant policies and procedures.*

AGED DEBTORS ANALYSIS

aged debtors analysis and liquidity

An **aged debtors analysis** is a summary of amounts owed by customers, analysed into time period columns showing how long the amounts have been outstanding. It shows an organisation which of its customers are slow in settling invoices and which customers may become bad debts.

An aged debtors analysis is an essential report which pinpoints the cause of potential **liquidity** problems and is critical in the process of liquidity management. Funds not received from debtors are funds which will need to be financed from elsewhere and will increase the costs of the organisation.

format of an aged debtors analysis

An aged debtors analysis can either be drawn up **manually**, or it can be printed out as a report from a **computer accounting package**. There is no 'set' format for the aged debtors analysis, but the report normally follows the same columnar pattern.

An example of a computer printed aged debtors analysis from a Sage™ computer accounting package is shown and explained at the top of the next page. An alternative spreadsheet version, showing percentages of the periods for which amounts have been outstanding, is shown at the bottom of the next page.

The **credit control policy** of the organisation will normally state when the aged debtor analysis should be produced. This is normally after the end of each month after the statements have been sent out. From the analysis the organisation decides which customers it is going to chase up, and how. It may send a letter or an email, or it may telephone the customer. Again, the credit control policy will set out guidelines for how and when communications should be sent.

The illustration below shows an aged debtors analysis produced as a report from the Sales Ledger in a Sage™ computer accounting program.

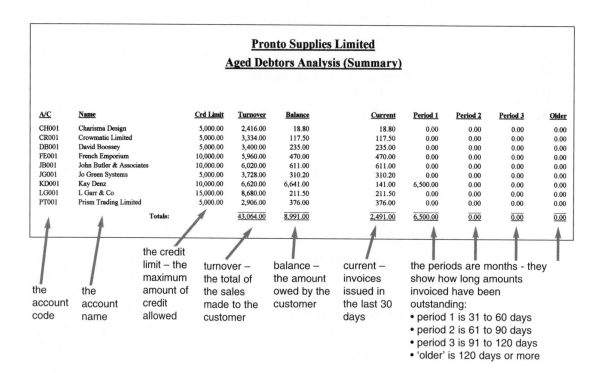

A/C	Name	Crd Limit	Turnover	Balance	Current	Period 1	Period 2	Period 3	Older
CH001	Charisma Design	5,000.00	2,416.00	18.80	18.80	0.00	0.00	0.00	0.00
CR001	Crowmatic Limited	5,000.00	3,334.00	117.50	117.50	0.00	0.00	0.00	0.00
DB001	David Boossey	5,000.00	3,400.00	235.00	235.00	0.00	0.00	0.00	0.00
FE001	French Emporium	10,000.00	5,960.00	470.00	470.00	0.00	0.00	0.00	0.00
JB001	John Butler & Associates	10,000.00	6,020.00	611.00	611.00	0.00	0.00	0.00	0.00
JG001	Jo Green Systems	5,000.00	3,728.00	310.20	310.20	0.00	0.00	0.00	0.00
KD001	Kay Denz	10,000.00	6,620.00	6,641.00	141.00	6,500.00	0.00	0.00	0.00
LG001	L Garr & Co	15,000.00	8,680.00	211.50	211.50	0.00	0.00	0.00	0.00
PT001	Prism Trading Limited	5,000.00	2,906.00	376.00	376.00	0.00	0.00	0.00	0.00
	Totals:		43,064.00	8,991.00	2,491.00	6,500.00	0.00	0.00	0.00

Pronto Supplies Limited
Aged Debtors Analysis (Summary)

the account code

the account name

the credit limit – the maximum amount of credit allowed

turnover – the total of the sales made to the customer

balance – the amount owed by the customer

current – invoices issued in the last 30 days

the periods are months - they show how long amounts invoiced have been outstanding:
• period 1 is 31 to 60 days
• period 2 is 61 to 90 days
• period 3 is 91 to 120 days
• 'older' is 120 days or more

An aged debtors analysis can also be set out on a spreadsheet, as seen in the illustration below.

FAIRARM FOODS			AGED DEBTORS ANALYSIS		July 2005		
Account	Account number	Credit Limit	Balance	up to 30 days	31 - 60 days	61 - 90 days	91 days & over
Droof & Co	8721	1000.00	164.50	164.50	0.00	0.00	0.00
Flagand Ltd	8532	750.00	376.00	376.00	0.00	0.00	0.00
Granaro Supplies	8612	750.00	499.38	499.38	0.00	0.00	0.00
Les Gola Restaurant	7951	2000.00	1632.75	799.00	833.75	0.00	0.00
Romrod Designs	6025	2000.00	1926.88	380.00	0.00	1046.88	500.00
TOTALS			4599.51	2218.88	833.75	1046.88	500.00
Percentage			100%	48%	18%	23%	11%

how to use the aged debtors analysis

The columns of the aged debtors analyses on the previous page include:

- **account name and account number**

  Note that most aged debtors analyses will have more accounts than are shown here – possibly hundreds, shown in alphabetical order for ease of reference. This report is shortened for the purposes of illustration.

  The sales ledger account number is listed for reference purposes. In the case of the computer analysis, the account number is the computer account number allocated to the sales ledger account.

- **credit limit and balance columns**

  These two columns are compared to find out whether any customer is exceeding the allocated credit limit.

- **invoice 'age' columns**

  The remaining four columns here show how long the invoices which make up the total balance column have been outstanding.

Note that in the case of the second aged debtors analysis, the percentage outstanding for each period is shown in a row below the totals.

When analysing the report, the credit controller will look not only at individual accounts, but also at a number of relationships and trends by comparing this report with the previous month's analysis. For example, the percentages on the bottom row will indicate how quickly invoices are being settled. If percentages towards the right start to rise, there will be pressure on the company's liquidity, which will be seen in the company's bank balance.

Analysis of individual accounts is likely to start with a look at the far right-hand column. Are there any accounts with invoices which are well overdue? The £500 for Romrod Designs (second analysis), outstanding for over 91 days, could indicate a number of situations and will need to be investigated:

- the invoice (or invoices) might be subject to a dispute and remain unpaid
- extended credit may have been given on the invoice(s)
- Romrod Designs may be experiencing cash flow problems

This process will then continue as each column from right to left is scrutinised for 'out-of-order' amounts. Whatever the situation, action will need to be taken, in line with the Credit Control Policy.

Are there any accounts which are exceeding their credit limit? This will be picked up from a comparison of the credit limit and balance columns for each customer. Any excess of the limit will need to be investigated and action taken according to the guidelines in the Credit Control Policy.

It is normal practice for any action taken to be written on the report, eg 'send Letter 1 . . . telephone customer . . .threaten legal proceedings' and so on.

updating the aged debtors analysis

An organisation that uses a computer accounting program such as Sage™ can rely on the computer to update the ledgers regularly and produce an aged debtors analysis automatically, at the click of a mouse.

An organisation that uses a manual accounting system has more work to do in updating the aged debtors analysis each month, as each figure will have to be changed manually. A computer spreadsheet can help in producing totals and calculating percentages, but all the sales transactions will still have to be taken into account when completing the analysis.

Your assessments may give you an aged debtors analysis at the end of Month 1 and then ask you to update it from double-entry accounts or daybooks and cashbook to produce the aged debtors analysis for the end of Month 2.

This process, based on a sales ledger account, is illustrated below.

worked example – updating the aged debtors analysis from the ledger

situation

Samways Limited operates a manual accounting system and produces an aged debtors analysis at the end of each month. The sales ledger account for one of the customers is set out below. The terms for the account is 30 days credit (ie settlement within 30 days of invoice date).

Merryways Ltd					
Date	Details	Dr	Date	Details	Cr
2005			2005		
15 Feb	Invoice 4310	400.00	15 May	Cheque (Invoice 4420)	700.00
31 Mar	Invoice 4420	700.00	30 May	Cheque (Invoices 4525/4533)	750.00
19 Apr	Invoice 4525	300.00			
21 Apr	Invoice 4533	450.00			
13 May	Invoice 5102	550.00			
29 May	Invoice 5310	250.00			

The data from the ledger account is used to update the aged debtors analysis. This process will also be carried out with the other sales ledger accounts (not shown here). The Merryways account is used to illustrate the process.

The aged debtors analysis is set out in the following format:

Aged Debtors Analysis					
Customer	Total due	1 - 30 days	31 - 60 days	61 - 90 days	91 days and over

solution

The first step is to work out which debit entries from the account will need to be entered in the aged debtors analysis. This involves omitting the invoices for which payment has been received and entering the remainder in the appropriate column in the aged debtors summary, as shown below. Note that you would not cross through entries in the actual ledger – this is done here to show how you identify the current amounts outstanding.

Merryways Ltd					
Date	Details	Dr	Date	Details	Cr
2005			2005		
15 Feb	Invoice 4310	400.00	15 May	~~Cheque (Invoice 4420)~~	~~700.00~~
31 Mar	~~Invoice 4420~~	~~700.00~~	30 May	~~Cheque (Invoices 4525/4533)~~	~~750.00~~
19 Apr	~~Invoice 4525~~	~~300.00~~			
21 Apr	~~Invoice 4533~~	~~450.00~~			
13 May	Invoice 5102	550.00			
29 May	Invoice 5310	250.00			

Aged Debtors Analysis as at 31 May					
Customer	Total due	1 - 30 days	31 - 60 days	61 - 90 days	91 days and over
Merryways Ltd	1,200.00	800.00			400.00

It is clear from the analysis of this customer's account that on the whole invoices are being paid promptly (the £800 is not due until next month) but one invoice for £400 has been outstanding for over 90 days and will need urgent investigation. It may be a disputed invoice or it may have been overlooked and will need to be chased. The Credit Control Policy will give guidance on the correct procedure to be followed.

As mentioned on the previous page, if a manual book-keeping system is used, the figures for the updated aged debtors analysis may also be obtained from other accounting records, for example:

- sales day book (invoices issued)
- cash book (money received in settlement of invoices)

In conclusion, your assessment may require you to carry out a series of calculations from a variety of data related to a limited number of customers to produce the aged debtors summary. Your next task will then normally be to comment on the summary and recommend actions to other people in the organisation, in line with the Credit Control Policy.

AGED DEBTORS ANALYSIS – TAKING ACTION

Credit Control Policy

It is normally assumed in your assessments that a Credit Control Policy exists which sets out the procedures for chasing debts and guidelines for the timing of:

- invoices and statements of accounts sent to the customer
- production of the aged debtors analysis
- the making of telephone calls chasing overdue invoices
- the sending of emails or faxes chasing overdue invoices
- the sending of letters chasing overdue invoices
- setting up a meeting with the customer to discuss non-payment
- placing a customer on a 'stop' list, withdrawing further credit
- sending a letter threatening legal action
- taking legal action

The example policy shown below is taken from Chapter 8. Note the instructions set out in the 'Debt Collection' section.

CREDIT POLICY & PROCEDURES

New Accounts

1 One bank reference and two trade references required.

2 Analysis of minimum of three years' accounts for limited company customers.

Credit Terms

3 Standard terms 30 days from invoice. Any extension to be authorised by Credit Controller.

4 2.5% settlement discount at Credit Controller's discretion.

Debt Collection

5 Invoices despatched on day of issue.

6 Statements despatched first week of the month.

7 Aged debtors analysis produced and analysed first week of the month.

8 Reminder letter sent first week of the month for accounts 30 days overdue (Letter 1).

9 Telephone chaser for accounts 45 days overdue. Meeting arranged if required.

10 Customer on stop list if no payment received within 15 days of telephone chaser (unless meeting arranged). Sales Department notified.

11 Letter placing account on stop and threatening legal action if payment not received within seven days (Letter 2).

12 Legal proceedings set in motion if payment not received within 30 days of Letter 2 – subject to authorisation by Finance Director and notification of Sales Manager.

standard communications

The organisation is likely to have a set of standard **letters** which will vary in tone from the polite request for payment to the formal threatening of legal action. Even if the organisation does not have a written Policy, it is likely to have standard letters in its files. It is important that the standard letters are used as they will be designed to place the creditor (ie the issuer of the invoices) in a strong position should legal action become necessary. This is covered in full in the next chapter.

The **telephone** is a very efficient means of communicating a message and assessing reasons for non-payment. A letter can easily be put in a file and ignored, but a telephone call from a persistent creditor is difficult to ignore.

The chart below shows how an invoice can be chased. It is important to note that this is only an example and not a definitive method: different organisations will have different policies and processes.

We will explain the use of letters and the telephone in chasing debt in more detail in the pages that follow.

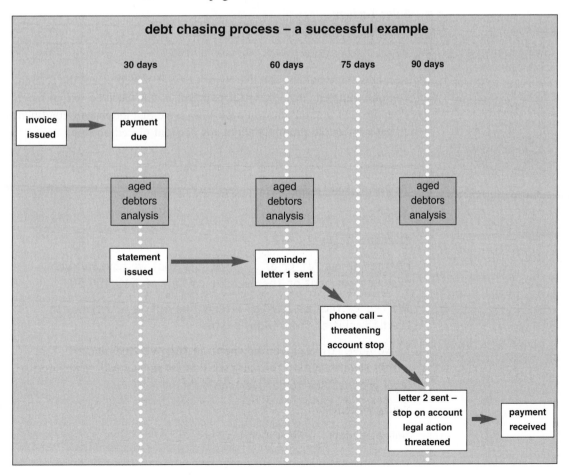

examples of letters

The first of the letter texts shown here is suitable for a 'Letter 1', ie the first chaser letter sent out (see item 8 in the Policy on page 198).

To Purchases Ledger

Dear Sir

Overdue Account 24122

We note from our records that your account balance of £10,456.50 is now overdue. The agreed payment terms are 30 days of invoice date.

Please settle this outstanding amount by return of post.

We attach an up-to-date statement.

Yours faithfully

Sales Ledger

The second letter would be suitable for a 'Letter 2' which places the account on stop and threatens legal action if payment is not received within seven days (see item 11 in the Policy on page 198). Note that the Sales Department would have to be told promptly about any account placed on stop.

To Purchases Ledger

Dear Sir

Overdue Account 24122

Further to our letter of . . . . we note that we have not yet received payment of the overdue amount of £10,456.50.

We regret that we have no alternative but to withdraw our credit facilities from today's date.

If we have not received payment of the overdue amount within seven days of the date of this letter we will commence legal proceedings to recover the debt.

Yours faithfully

Sales Ledger

---

using the telephone

The telephone is normally resorted to when statements and letters fail to have any effect. The telephone is a useful means of communication because it demands an immediate reply.

Organisations with a poor payment record will often come up with a variety of lame and blatantly untrue excuses on the telephone. It is the job of the person chasing the debts to have ready answers for all of these. A careful note should be made of all conversations. The table below provides some common examples of excuses and possible replies.

customer excuse	your response
'We have not received the invoice.'	'We will fax/email a copy today. Please let me know for whose attention it should be marked.'
	Comment: *A very common excuse. When sending a copy, ensure that it is addressed to the right person and is accompanied by a request for immediate payment.*
'There is nobody here to sign the cheque.'	'When will the authorised person be back? Are there any pre-signed cheques in the office?'
	Comment: *Do not accept the suggestion that there is unlikely to be anyone around to sign it for a while – there should always be someone who has been given suitable authority. If a signatory is going to be away for a long time, he/she will normally sign some blank cheques.*
'The cheque is in the post.'	'Please can you confirm to which address it was sent, and when?'
	Comment: *Oh yes? This excuse is so lame that it has become a standing joke. You will need to confirm the full details of the cheque and state a time limit for receipt before telephoning again and asking for a duplicate to be sent.*
'The computers are down.'	'Can you tell me when they are likely to be working again? Are you able to issue a hand-written cheque?'
	Comment: *A computer system that has failed will not be able to print out cheques. This is another lame excuse, although it is more likely to be true. You should insist that if the delay is an extended one (ie days rather than hours), the customer should write out a cheque by hand.*

aged debtors analysis – using discretion

It is important to appreciate that the debt-chasing actions carried out as a result of the monthly check through the aged debtors analysis should reflect the standing and payment record of each customer. Any Credit Control Policy cannot be relied upon to work 'by formula'.

For example, a **major customer** who accounts for a significant percentage of sales turnover and always pays up in the end will be treated with respect and will not necessarily be hounded for every overdue invoice. It is more likely that a diplomatic telephone call will achieve the desired result.

Conversely a relatively **small customer** with a poor payment record will be given less benefit of the doubt and will be pressed hard for overdue payments.

DOUBTFUL AND BAD DEBTS

Part of the job of the person working in credit control is to assess from the information to hand if a customer is going to default and not pay the balance due. The available information might include:

- **the aged debtors analysis** – the extent to which a customer's amounts owing are concentrated in the right-hand columns, ie to what extent they are overdue

- **internal information provided by the sales team** – they will know from visits and meetings if the customer bears the 'tell tale' signs of struggling financially, eg selling off assets, stockpiling, reducing the price of stock

- **internal information provided by the credit control staff** – the customer not responding to chasers, the customer providing poor excuses for non-payment, the customer's finance staff not taking telephone calls

- **comments from other organisations in the trade**, eg 'I know that ABC Limited is struggling' or 'I hear that ABC Limited staff wages are in arrears' or 'the ABC Limited MD has sold his Porsche'

doubtful debts

If a customer looks like he/she/it is going to default, the debt is said, for obvious reasons, to be '**doubtful**'. All this means is that the organisation, weighing up the probabilities, reckons that it is unlikely that it will get paid.

There is still a possibility that the money will come in, but it is 'doubtful'.

methods of making provision for doubtful debts

As you will know from your earlier studies, organisations adjust their accounting records by making **provision for doubtful debts** and setting the provision off against profits in a 'provision for doubtful debts account'. This provision is often **a set percentage**, eg 2%, of the total debtors, the percentage being based on experience within that type of organisation. If this method is adopted, the day-to-day running of credit control based on the aged debtors analysis will **not** be affected by the making of the provision.

Another method of making provisions for doubtful debts is to **carry out the process for individual debts** rather than relying on a percentage of total debtors. This means that each time the organisation assesses the aged debtor analysis, individual accounts which look unlikely to pay up are marked up for a doubtful debt provision, referred to management (eg the Credit Controller) and entered in a 'provision for doubtful debts account'. This is a less common method, largely because it is far more involved and time-consuming, but it is a method which features in assessments which require that you 'indicate accounts for which provision should be made.' This method is featured in the Case Study which follows.

dealing with bad debts

Bad debts are doubtful debts which have lost the element of doubt – it is considered by the organisation that they will definitely not be paid and will need to be written off in the accounts against profits in a 'bad debts written off account'. The treatment of bad debts and the situations which cause them are covered in detail in the next chapter.

Case Study

RENARD LIMITED: CREDIT CONTROL PROCEDURES

situation

You work as a credit control clerk for Renard Limited, a company that manufactures and sells brushes.

An extract from the company's Aged Debtors Analysis and its Credit Control Policy are set out below, together with notes on the individual customer accounts.

You are to asked to write a memo to Gordon White, Credit Controller, to

• analyse the situation of the four accounts in the aged debtors analysis

• recommend action that should be taken

• recommend whether any provision for doubtful debts should be made

Aged Debtors Analysis					
Customer	Total due	1 - 30 days	31 - 60 days	61 - 90 days	91 days and over
Bruin Ltd	10,200.00				10,200.00
Ottaway Trading	4,100.00	2,340.00	950.00		810.00
R C Ratz	1,500.00		500.00	1,000.00	
S Quirrel	15,570.00	9,654.00	3560.00	2356.00	

CREDIT CONTROL POLICY (extract)

Debt Collection

1 Invoices to be issued on day goods are despatched.

2 Statements despatched first week of the month.

3 Aged debtors analysis produced and analysed first week of each month.

4 Reminder letter sent when a debt is 30 days overdue.

5 Telephone chaser for accounts when a debt is 45 days overdue.

6 Second letter and customer on stop list when debt is 60 days overdue and a meeting arranged with customer as soon as possible.

7 Letter threatening legal action is sent when debt is 90 days overdue.

8 Legal proceedings set in motion when debt is 120 days overdue, subject to agreement of Finance Director.

CUSTOMER BACKGROUND NOTES

Bruin Limited   No orders have been received from this customer for some months. No responses have been made to chaser letters. Telephone calls have been answered by the switchboard operator but the finance staff have always been unavailable.

Ottaway Trading   This account has been trading normally, but occasionally invoices have been overlooked or lost because of inefficiency. Reminder letters have been sent and a telephone call made about the £810 invoice, when the response was 'We will look into it.'

R C Ratz   Roland Ratz has been trading with you for a number of years and generally takes 60 days rather than 30 days to pay. Invoices have never been known to be outstanding for longer than 90 days.

S Quirrel   Sam Quirrel has only been trading with you for six months. He has a new business which is expanding rapidly. Last week he asked for an increase in his limit. He has not responded to earlier chasers.

MEMO

to   Gordon White, Credit Controller

from   A Student

date   today

subject Credit control: problem customers

Bruin Limited

This account gives cause for concern. They have ceased trading with our company. An invoice for £10,200 remains unpaid and has been outstanding for over 90 days. Indications are that the company is in financial difficulties. We should send our letter threatening legal action and bring the matter to the attention of the Finance Director. It would be worthwhile making enquiries in the trade if anything is known of this company's financial state. It is recommended that a provision for doubtful debts should be made for this debt.

Ottaway Trading

This account has always paid eventually. A telephone chaser should be made about the £950 short-term overdue amount and a definite date for payment agreed. The £810 may either be a lost or a disputed invoice. This must also be chased on the telephone and the problem resolved promptly. No provision for doubtful debts need be made.

R C Ratz

This is a good account which has been with us for a number of years. A reminder letter should be sent about the overdue amounts (£1,500) but no further action should be taken. No provision for doubtful debts need be made.

S Quirrel

This situation gives considerable cause for concern. It is very likely that this new customer is overtrading and financing his liquidity at our expense – by not paying invoices. His request for an increased limit would confirm this. He has therefore become a substantial credit risk. Recommended actions are to place the account on stop and demand repayment of the overdue £5916 by return. This should be set out in a formal letter. The due dates of the current invoices should be put in the diary and the amounts chased if not received on time. It is recommended that a provision for doubtful debts should be made for this debt. Sales Department should be notified of our action.

OTHER METHODS OF COLLECTING TRADE DEBTS

There are a number of financial services available to organisations which can help them with debt collection and the avoidance of bad debts. These services are provided by banks, insurance and other financial institutions. They will improve or safeguard the liquidity of the organisation, but at a cost. They include:

- **credit insurance** – insuring against the risk of non-payment, both in the UK and overseas
- **factoring** – employing a finance company to run the sales ledger and in some cases insure against bad debts
- **invoice discounting** – borrowing money against invoices

We will explain these in turn.

UK sales – credit insurance

Credit insurance replaces cash lost when a debt goes bad. Specialised companies such as Eulen Hermes and Coface UK offer tailor-made solutions for different types and sizes of organisation. Typical options include:

- **whole turnover insurance** – general (up to 90%) coverage in the case of debtor default (non-payment of debts)
- insurance limited to **key accounts** – up to 40 customers with up to 100% coverage
- **single account** insurance – 100% cover

Premiums will depend on the risk involved and the insurer will insist on credit analysis of larger customers.

overseas sales – export credit insurance

Businesses that sell goods and services abroad are often advised to set up **export credit insurance**. This covers:

- the **credit risk** of selling to an overseas buyer – inevitably it is more difficult to chase up overseas debts, and should the debt turn bad, it is likely to prove difficult to bring court action against the customer
- the **political risk** of selling to a country where the political situation is less stable and might produce a revolution, civil war or economic collapse, all of which would reduce the possibility of receiving payment

Export credit insurance cover is available from **private sector commercial companies** for the supply of consumer goods and services sold on credit.

The Government's **ECGD** (Export Credits Guarantee Department) offers up to 95% cover for capital goods and service provision.

factoring

A factoring company lends money against the invoices received from debtors of the business, providing liquidity before the invoice due dates. The factoring company takes over the administration of the sales ledger. It will normally lend up to 90% of outstanding invoice amounts as soon as the invoice is issued and will pay the balance (less charges) when the debtor settles.

Factoring companies also provide an optional bad debt protection scheme – ie insurance against bad debts – known as **'non-recourse' factoring**, for which a further charge is payable.

Factoring without bad debt protection is known as **'recourse' factoring** – ie if a debt goes bad, recourse has to be made to the customer who will have to write off the bad debt.

There is more information about factoring on page 123.

invoice discounting

Here a finance house lends money against invoices issued to selected customers of the organisation, but the organisation continues to operate its own sales ledger and credit management system. As a result, the customers do not realise that the financing is being carried out.

The finance house will normally only be prepared to set up invoice discounting for an organisation which has good credit management procedures in place. The finance house will generally lend between 60% to 90% of the invoice value.

There is more information about invoice discounting on pages 122-123.

effect on liquidity management

The first of the three schemes described above – **credit insurance** – safeguards liquidity and avoids the danger of a substantial customer default, an event which could have a catastrophic effect on liquidity and profitability.

The other two schemes – **factoring** and **invoice discounting** – will improve liquidity because income from sales will be received sooner rather than later. The organisation will have a reduced working capital financing cost, but will also incur charges for the services.

The organisation will need to consider carefully the cost/benefit situation. For example, in a time of high interest rates, the early receipt of money from invoices could reduce interest costs considerably. In a time of low interest rates, the benefit might only be marginal because borrowing by way of overdraft would be relatively cheap and a viable alternative.

Chapter Summary

■ The aged debtors analysis is the report used by the credit control function to provide information about how long amounts have been outstanding on each customer account. It can also show total amounts outstanding on the sales ledger by percentage over different time periods. There are normally columns in the analysis for:
  - customer name
  - customer account number
  - credit limit
  - the balance of the account
  - different time periods for amounts outstanding

■ The aged debtors analysis is regularly produced either as an automatic report from a computer accounting program or as a manual calculation from the accounting records.

■ Most organisations will have a Credit Control Policy which gives guidelines for the actions to be taken with customer accounts which have become overdue.

■ Letters are useful in the formal process of debt collection, although they can easily be ignored by the customer. Letters are normally standardised and graded according to the seriousness of the situation.

■ Telephone calls, when used with skill, cannot be ignored and are a persuasive means of chasing overdue amounts. The person telephoning should have replies ready for the usual excuses for non-payment.

■ The standing and payment record of each customer should also be borne in mind when chasing debts. The aged debtors analysis cannot be relied upon as the sole source of information about the customer.

■ Credit insurance is available for UK sales, either for the whole of the sales ledger, or for a group of key accounts, or for single accounts.

■ Credit insurance is also available for overseas sales. Commercial insurance covers consumer goods and services and ECGD (a Government Department) offers cover for capital goods and for services.

■ Factoring companies lend money against debtors' invoices, either with bad debt cover (non-recourse factoring) or without bad debt cover (recourse factoring). The factoring company manages the sales ledger.

■ Invoice discounting involves lending money against invoices, but the organisation keeps control of its sales ledger.

Key Terms		
	aged debtors analysis	a summary of amounts owed by sales ledger customers, analysed into columns, showing how long the amounts have been outstanding
	invoice age	the period of time for which an invoice has been outstanding
	credit control policy	a document drawn up by an organisation which sets out procedures for managing the sales ledger, including actions to be taken in order to chase outstanding debts, eg letters, telephone calls and legal proceedings
	account stop	withdrawal of credit facilities on a debtor's account
	doubtful debt	a sales ledger debt which is unlikely to be paid – but there is still the chance that it may be paid; a provision may be made in the accounts for the debt
	bad debt	a sales ledger account which is written off in the books against profit
	credit insurance	an insurance policy which covers the possible loss of money through a customer defaulting on payment, ie loss through a bad debt
	export credit insurance	special insurance to cover the risk of non-payment by overseas customers either through customer default or through some political event
	ECGD	Export Credits Guarantee Department, a Government department offering export credit insurance for UK exporters of capital goods and services
	factoring	a service managing the sales ledger of another organisation and lending money against the organisation's invoices
	non-recourse factoring	a factoring service which offers protection against bad debts, ie the factoring company stands the loss of a customer default
	recourse factoring	a factoring service which does not offer protection against bad debts, ie the factoring company does not stand the loss of a customer default, but has 'recourse' to the creditor organisation to cover the loss

Student Activities

answers to the asterisked (*) questions are to be found at the back of this book

10.1* The extract below from the aged debtors analysis of Dowzee Limited shows the total amount outstanding and the period totals.

Standard terms are payment 30 days after invoice date.

The company does not have a written Credit Control Policy.

The company does not have any standard chaser letters but instead relies on sending out statements every month and making telephone calls to slow payers.

DOWZEE LIMITED: AGED DEBTORS ANALYSIS

Account	Account number	Credit Limit	Balance	up to 30 days	31 - 60 days	61 - 90 days	91 days & over
TOTALS			52,129.50	18,982.00	15,786.50	10,891.00	6,500.00
Percentage			100%				

You are to:

(a) work out the percentages (to the nearest percentage) of each period total

(b) explain the effect of the situation on the liquidity of the company

(c) identify any problems with the credit control of the company

(d) suggest solutions to the problems

10.2* Explain the difference between a doubtful debt and a bad debt.

10.3* Explain what is meant by 'credit insurance' and give three examples of typical credit insurance schemes.

10.4* Describe the principal difference between

(a) invoice discounting and factoring

(b) recourse and non-recourse factoring

10.5   You are debt chasing at the beginning of the month and have a list of customers to telephone. Some of them are co-operative and agree to settle overdue amounts straightaway, but some are less helpful. How would you deal with the following situations which all relate to amounts that are over one month overdue? The Credit Control Policy states that a telephone chaser should be made in each case and payment by return of post requested.

(a)   The customer says 'I think the cheque was posted to you yesterday, so should be with you today or tomorrow.'

(b)   The customer says 'the cheque is waiting for signature, but the line manager who has to sign it is off sick with a bad back.'

(c)   The customer says 'Sorry, but we don't seem to have received this invoice.'

(d)   The customer says 'this is in hand but our cheque issuing is now computerised and the next payment run is in ten days time in the middle of the month.'

10.6*   Bechen Posche UK Ltd operates a manual accounting system and produces an aged debtors analysis at the end of each month. The sales ledger account for R Brooklyn is set out below. The terms for the account is 30 days credit (ie settlement within 30 days of invoice date).

R Brooklyn					
Date	Details	Dr	Date	Details	Cr
14 Apr	Invoice 1210	800.00	15 Jul	Cheque (Invoice 1298)	400.00
31 May	Invoice 1298	400.00	30 Jul	Cheque (Invoices 1328/1337)	1,100.00
15 Jun	Invoice 1328	600.00			
26 Jun	Invoice 1337	500.00			
15 Jul	Invoice 1409	650.00			
31 Jul	Invoice 1467	175.00			

The layout of the aged debtors analysis is as follows:

Aged Debtors Analysis as at 31 July					
Customer	Total due	1 - 30 days	31 - 60 days	61 - 90 days	91 days and over
R Brooklyn					

You are to:

(a)   Complete the entry for the R Brooklyn account in the aged debtors analysis.

(b)   Write comments on the account and identify any potential problems.

(c)   Suggest solutions to any problems identified in (b).

10.7 An extract from the aged debtors analysis for S Freud Limited as at 31 October is shown below, together with details of payments received from debtors and invoices issued during November.

An extract from the Credit Control Policy of S Freud Limited is also shown below.

S Freud Limited – Aged Debtors Analysis as at 31 October					
Customer	Total due	1 - 30 days	31 - 60 days	61 - 90 days	91 days and over
Karl Young & Co	7,500.00			7,500.00	
Fred Neesher	4,500.00	2,300.00	2,200.00		
J Bentham	799.00		399.00	400.00	

Payments received during November

Fred Neesher	£1,200.00	Payment of invoice dated 5 September
	£1,000.00	Payment of invoice dated 10 September
	£1,300.00	Payment of invoice dated 15 October
J Bentham	£400	Payment of invoice dated 20 August

Invoices issued during November

Fred Neesher	£1,750	Invoice dated 5 November
	£2,600	Invoice dated 15 November
	£745	Invoice dated 22 November
J Bentham	£100	Invoice issued 18 November

S FREUD LIMITED – CREDIT CONTROL POLICY (extract)

- One month's credit allowed from date of invoice.
- Statements despatched on first working day of the month.
- Aged debtors analysis produced at the beginning of each month.
- Reminder Letter 1 sent when account is 31 days overdue.
- Telephone chaser made when account is 45 days overdue.
- Reminder Letter 2 sent when account is 61 days overdue. This threatens legal action and account stop if payment not received within 7 days.
- Account stop and legal proceedings to be instigated and provision for doubtful debts to be made if payment not received as a result of Letter 2.

You are to:

(a)   Update the aged debtor analysis for S Freud Limited as at 30 November.

(b)   State how discussion should be conducted with overdue accounts.

(c)   Write a memo dated 30 November to Ivor Pound, Credit Controller, setting out the actions which should be taken with each of the three customers (in line with the Credit Control Policy), including any recommendations for doubtful debt provision. Use your own name.

Collecting debts and dealing with insolvency

In the last chapter we described the credit control process in action and explained the use of the aged debtors summary as the basis for taking action to recover money owing from debtors.

In this chapter we take the process a stage further and describe how organisations try to recover amounts which the debtor either will not or cannot repay. This involves a number of stages and options:

• ensuring that there is a valid debt and underlying contract on which to base any action

• using debt collection agencies to recover the debt

• using a solicitor to recover the debt

• taking the debtor to court to recover the debt on the basis of the contract of sale

• taking the debtor through the insolvency courts and dealing with debtors who are already insolvent

It must be stressed throughout that debt chasing and taking legal action can be expensive processes; they should only be resorted to if there is a reasonable chance of recovering the money.

PERFORMANCE CRITERIA COVERED

unit 15 OPERATING A CASH MANAGEMENT AND CREDIT CONTROL SYSTEM

element 15.4

Monitor and control the collection of debts

A   Monitor information relating to the current state of debtors' accounts regularly and take appropriate action.

B   Send information regarding significant outstanding accounts and potential bad debts

D   Use debt recovery methods appropriate to the circumstances of individual cases and in accordance with the organisation's procedures

E   Base recommendations to write off bad and doubtful debts on a realistic analysis of all known factors

KNOWLEDGE AND UNDERSTANDING COVERAGE

9   Legal issues: remedies for breach of contract.

10   Legal and administrative procedures for the collection of debts.

11   *The effect of bankruptcy and insolvency on organisations.*

22   *Methods of analysing information on debtors: age analysis of debtors; average periods of credit given and received; incidence of bad and doubtful debts.*

23   *Evaluation of different collection methods.*

26   *Understanding that the accounting systems of an organisation are affected by its organisational structure, its administrative systems and procedures and the nature of its business transactions.*

27   *Understanding that recording and accounting practices may vary in different parts of the organisation.*

31   *An understanding of the organisation's relevant policies and procedures.*

BAD DEBTS – THE FINAL FRONTIER

doubtful and bad debts

In the last chapter we saw that a **doubtful debt** is a debt that is **unlikely** to be paid and will have to be provided for in the accounts. A **bad debt**, on the other hand, is a debt that will **definitely not** be paid and will have to be written off in the accounts to profit and loss account as an expense to the business.

is it worth it?

A bad debt is the final stage in the credit control process. It occurs when the organisation gives up trying to recover the debt and decides to minimise its losses by writing it off through the profit and loss account.

As we will see in this chapter, as the debt recovery process moves to the stage where debt collection agencies, solicitors or court action are involved, the costs start to mount up. The question has to be asked 'is it worth it?' This can happen when

- the debt is relatively small when compared with the cost of recovery
- the debtor looks like becoming insolvent (unable to pay debts)
- the debtor is insolvent (a bankrupt individual or company in liquidation)

It must be remembered that an organisation is only likely to recover a debt – even through court action – if the debtor has the money or other realisable assets to enable the debt to be repaid. To use a common phrase, there is no point 'flogging a dead horse'!

If you are working in credit control you may have to recommend bad debts for writing off. The Credit Control Policy may allow you to write off small debts (say up to £100), but you will need to refer larger amounts to the Credit Controller.

is there a contract of sale?

A **contract** is the legal agreement which should underlly all sales transactions. This does not mean that there has to be a formal written document relating to every invoice – a contract can be oral (word of mouth), but there does have to be an agreement which involves:

- an offer for sale and an acceptance of the offer, eg when an order is placed by a customer
- money changing hands (eg at an agreed price)
- the realisation by seller and buyer that the agreement can have legal consequences

Please see Chapter 9 (pages 184-186) for further details of commercial contracts.

The important point here is that if a debt is to be pursued through legal channels including solicitors and the courts, there must be a valid contract relating to it.

If the debtor can show that there is no contract, the organisation has no hope of being able to recover the money. The following are examples of 'no hope' situations:

- the debtor has not signed an order form where the order form is the agreement to purchase
- the goods or services have been supplied, but have not been ordered
- an order has been cancelled by the debtor by email before goods were despatched

breach of contract

Legal action can be taken against a debtor when a contract is in existence because non-payment is a **breach of contract** – the debtor is not carrying out an agreed part of the bargain.

There are a number of **remedies** available for breach of contract in a wide variety of situations. The remedy chosen will depend on the type of contract. For example, a builder who is contracted to build a house and disappears off site before putting the roof on, can be ordered by the court to complete the work (the remedy of **specific performance**). If, however, the person having the house built refuses the builder access to the site, the builder could **terminate** the contract and demand payment for what had been done (the remedy of **quantum meruit**, which means 'what it deserves').

These situations do not have much in common with credit control in an organisation. Here the remedy of **action for the price** – ie taking legal action in the courts for recovery of an unpaid debt – is the normal remedy for breach of contract.

USING THIRD PARTIES FOR COLLECTING DEBT

When an organisation finds that its own credit control process is proving unsuccessful in getting debtors to pay up, it can employ third parties, such as debt collection agencies and solicitors, to try and recover debts.

debt collection agencies

Debt collection agencies are commercial organisations that collect debts on behalf of clients. They are normally paid by taking a percentage of the amount collected. In other words, the more successful they are, the more they receive – which is a major incentive for being successful. They tend to be effective at debt collecting because after a while debtors tend to ignore the credit control letters and telephone calls of the creditor, but when an independent body is called in to collect debt, they take more notice and are more likely to pay. Debt collection agencies have a distinct psychological advantage.

A typical debt collection schedule follows a number of steps in quick succession until payment is received:

Day 1	Send a chaser letter to the debtor.
Day 4	Telephone the debtor.
Day 12	Telephone the debtor again.
Day 20	Send a letter threatening legal action.
Day 28	Start legal proceedings – suing for the debt in the courts

Debt collection agencies may achieve a success rate of around 70%. The organisations that employ them should carefully monitor their success rates to ensure that they are operating efficiently.

solicitors

Debtors do not like receiving letters from solicitors chasing debts and threatening legal action in the courts. A solicitor's letter is therefore often an effective way of recovering a well-overdue invoice.

When employing a solicitor for this purpose it is important to use a firm that specialises in debt collection. Solicitors are not cheap, nor will the Small Claims Court (see page 218) reimburse solicitors' costs, so they should only be used when there is a reasonable chance of the debtor being able to repay the amount owing. It is also important to be precise when providing the solicitor with details of the debt and debtor, eg the exact amount owed, the name and address of the debtor. Any mistake might invalidate the claim.

TAKING THE DEBTOR TO COURT

There are two ways in which a debtor may be taken by a creditor to court:

• to **enforce repayment of the debt** – assuming that the debtor is solvent and can repay debts when they are due; this is the most common form of court action taken as part of the credit control process

• to bring about the **bankruptcy** (of an individual) or **liquidation** (of a company) – assuming that the debtor is insolvent and is unable to repay debts when they are due and hoping that some money will be realised from the debtor's assets; this is a last resort action and is not often taken as part of the credit control process

We will look first at the process of taking the debtor to court to enforce payment of the debt.

the court system – amounts of claim

If the claim for recovery of debt is £5,000 or less it can be dealt with in the **Small Claims Court**, which is part of the **County Court**. The Small Claims Court was introduced as a 'fast track' court for straightforward cases. It has the advantage that you do not necessarily have to use a solicitor or barrister – you can present the case yourself if you wish. In some cases the matter can be resolved by means of a telephone conference.

The main **County Court** deals with claims up to £50,000 and the **High Court** deals with claims over £25,000. Most claims for repayment of debt are dealt with in the main County Court and the Small Claims Court.

When completing the paperwork for the claim to the court it is vital that details such as identifying the debtor and the debt are correct, for example:

• the name of the individual or the company

• the address of the individual or the company

• the amount owing

• the date of the debt

When the paperwork has been lodged, the court will issue a 'default summons' to the debtor who can either agree to the claim (which is unlikely), ignore it (in which case judgement will go against the debtor) or go ahead with the court proceedings.

the court system – what happens if you win

If the County Court or Small Claims Court decision goes in the favour of the creditor, a County Court Judgement will be issued against the debtor.

The debtor will either pay up, in which case the debt is repaid and all is well, or the debtor will refuse to pay, either because he/she does not want to, or because he/she does not have sufficient assets to repay the debt.

One initial option to persuade the debtor to pay up is a court order for an **oral examination** of the debtor. The debtor is required to come to court to be questioned on details of income, capital and savings. This procedure is likely to put pressure on the cross-examined debtor to pay the creditor the money due; this is because the debtor should have revealed, under oath, the money or realisable assets that are available to repay the debt.

enforcement of the judgement

If the debtor does not pay up it will be necessary to apply to the court for enforcement of the judgement so that the debt can be repaid in full, or (more likely) in part.

There are a number of options open to the creditor who wishes to enforce judgement by court order:

garnishee order

This is a court order which the creditor can have sent to a third party who owes the debtor money, requiring the money to be paid direct to the creditor. A common example of the third party is a bank or building society which has an account for the debtor. The order will claim the due amount from the bank or building society account of the debtor on that day. This will only work if the money is in the account. If the account is low in funds or overdrawn, the creditor will get little or nothing. It is all a question of timing and knowing when money has been paid in.

warrant of execution

This order is a request for the court bailiffs to enter the debtor's home or business premises to seize belongings or assets to sell and pay off the debt. The restrictions here are that the bailiffs are not allowed to break down the door or to seize essential living items or 'tools of the trade'.

warrant of delivery

If the debtor has goods which belong to the creditor (for example goods sold and covered by a 'retention of title' clause (see page 186), the creditor can obtain a court order – a 'warrant of delivery' – which will give the court bailiffs authority to obtain and collect the goods.

attachment of earnings If the debtor is working and earning, an Attachment of Earnings Order may be granted by the court. This will require the debtor's employer to deduct a certain amount from the debtor's salary on a regular basis until the debt is repaid. The judge will decide on the proportion which can be deducted, as the debtor will clearly need to retain a proportion for living expenses.

charging order If the debtor owns property the creditor can apply to the court to 'register a charge' on the property to show that the creditor has an interest in the money received from the eventual sale of the property. This is more of a 'last ditch' defence and can run into major problems if the debtor has family and children who will be made homeless if the property is sold.

Of these court orders, the warrant of execution (sending in the bailiffs) and attachment of earnings (deduction from salary) are the most reliable and most common remedies.

If all else fails, the debtor can resort to the insolvency courts to bring about the sale of the debtor's assets and the distribution of the money realised to **all** of the creditors. This is described in detail on the next page.

'NO HOPE' DEBT OR BAD DEBT?

It is important to repeat at this point that it is only worth a trade creditor taking a debtor to court and enforcing a court order if the debtor has funds and other assets available to repay the debt. Note that the term 'trade creditor' refers to a commercial ('trade') organisation which sells goods or services on credit and does not take any security for the debt.

More often than not an overdue debt will be the result of a debtor running into serious financial difficulties, in which case no amount of costly court action will produce any results.

No available assets means no repayment.

The solution in this case is to write the amount off as a bad debt in the accounts, where at least the amount can be set off through profit and loss against the tax liability of the organisation.

We look further at this type of situation in the Case Study on page 223.

DEBTORS AND INSOLVENCY

the insolvency process in a nutshell

insolvency is being unable to pay debts as they fall due

A creditor such as a trading business owed money can take a debtor to court **to prove that the debtor is insolvent**. The result of this is that the court will then arrange for the debtor's assets to be sold off and **all** the creditors repaid as far as is possible with the money realised by the sale. It is unlikely that the creditors will get all their money back – in fact trade (unsecured) creditors are often at the back of the queue for repayment and may get little or nothing at all. The insolvency process for **trade creditors** is therefore a last resort and money owed very often ends up as a bad debt.

some legal terminology

The laws that cover insolvency and all its complexities are:

- **Insolvency Act 1986**, which has been amended to some extent by
- **Enterprise Act 2002**

The notes on insolvency in this book are not exhaustive, but do cover the Unit 15 requirements. Further information can be found at the very helpful official website www.insolvency.gov.uk

The law is never straightforward and so there are some terms to remember:

An individual (eg sole trader or partner in a partnership) who is proved by the court to be insolvent becomes a **bankrupt**. The individual normally remains a bankrupt for 12 months, after which he/she is discharged, although arrangements to repay debt from earnings may run for a further two years.

A limited company that is proved by the court to be insolvent is said to be **in liquidation**. A limited company cannot therefore be said to be 'bankrupt'.

the stages of the insolvency process

Suppose you run a business and a major debtor of yours – a sole trader – will not pay up. You wish to make them bankrupt. The stages are:

1   Ensure the debt is £750 or more (a lower amount is not sufficient for the bankruptcy process).

2   Make a 'statutory demand' to the debtor on an official form for the amount owing.

3   If payment is not received within three weeks, send in a 'creditors petition' to the court. A meeting of all creditors may be called by the

court. Creditors will be asked to send in a statement ('proof') of what they are owed by the debtor.

4   The court makes a bankruptcy order against the debtor and appoints an official (the 'trustee in bankruptcy') who arranges the sale of the debtor's assets (except domestic items and tools of the trade) and distributes the money to the creditors in the following order of priority:

- the costs of the bankruptcy proceedings (ie court costs and fees)

- preferential debts (items such as employee wages)

- any floating charge holder (ie the bank which has a secured overdraft - see page 133)

- unsecured creditors such as trade creditors (ie you)

You will see from this that trade creditors of a bankrupt individual are last in the list to be paid off. What little remains after court costs, employee wages and the secured bank overdraft have been paid off in full, has then to be shared proportionally between trade creditors. So if, for example, trade creditors are owed £50,000 and there is only £5,000 left, they will get a 'dividend' of 10p in the £. They may be lucky to get this!

Note also the following:

• Trade creditors who do not start the insolvency process themselves will be advised by the court when bankruptcy proceedings are under way and will be asked to send in a statement of what they are owed; they will be kept informed of the progress of the proceedings and will receive any 'dividend' in due course.

• The process for putting limited companies into liquidation follows very much the same pattern, except that the shareholders of the company will be the last in the queue for repayment of their investment from the proceeds of the sale of assets.

administration and administrative receivers

The law is not always helpful in its choice of terminology. The terms **administration** and **administrative receivers** are a case in point. They both relate to areas of insolvency where the interests of trade creditors are not looked after particularly well, but they relate to very different situations.

1   **Administration** is a state of affairs where an organisation which is running into solvency problems has an administrator appointed by the court to run its affairs. When an organisation is in administration – football clubs sometimes seem to fall into this category – no other creditor can petition for bankruptcy or liquidation. The organisation is protected from creditors, including the bank.

2   The other situation involves a bank which has the security of a floating charge over the assets of a company to secure its overdraft. The security document enables the bank to appoint an **administrative receiver** to sell the secured assets of the company. In this situation the unsecured creditors will again be practically last in the queue for repayment while the bank will be able to maximise the amount it receives.

In the Case Study that follows we look at a variety of situations which involve recommendations and decisions which have to be made within the Credit Control function relating to:

- debt collection
- court action
- insolvencies
- provision for doubtful debts and bad debt write offs

Case Study

WESSEX LIMITED: DEALING WITH PROBLEM ACCOUNTS

situation

You work as a credit control clerk for Wessex Limited, a company that manufactures high quality garden furniture.

At the end of the month you are asked to analyse the aged debtors analysis and deal with any queries relating to problem sales ledger accounts.

The main queries you have been presented with are set out below. You have been asked to:

- state what action you would take in each case
- suggest where provision for doubtful debts is to be made
- indicate if any debt is to be written off as a bad debt

You are to set out your recommendations in a memo to the Credit Controller, Tom Hardy.

1   **Slow paying accounts**

You note from the recent aged debtors analysis that five accounts are more than 90 days overdue (standard terms are payment at the end of the month following the invoice date). None of the accounts is responding to your letters and telephone calls. All of the accounts have just been sent a letter threatening legal action.

Tom Hardy, the Credit Controller, has commented to you "There's no point taking these accounts to court – we do a lot of business with them and they are basically sound. They just need a good kick to make them pay!"

2 Wildeve Limited – disputed transaction

Wildeve Limited has a history of being an awkward customer. There is currently £1,200 more than 90 days outstanding. Your investigations show that this amount relates to a shipment of chairs which Wildeve Limited claims was not ordered. You look through your copy sales invoice file and cannot trace a purchase order or any record of how the order was placed. The latest email from the customer says "You can come and collect the goods if you wish. They are still in their original packing. You will be liable for the carriage costs."

Tom Hardy asks "Shall we call in our solicitor?"

3 John Newson – County Court debtor

You have successfully obtained a County Court judgement against John Newson for non-payment of a debt for £6,000. John Newson is a salaried purchasing manager for a chain of garden centres and has also been running a sole trader business as a landscape designer 'on the side'. You believe he has substantial assets, but he is refusing to pay, even after the court judgement.

Tom Hardy asks "What can we do to get this man to pay?"

Suggest two suitable methods of enforcing the judgement.

4 Ken Everdene – bankruptcy order

Tom Hardy brings you an official letter which is notification of a bankruptcy order made against your customer Ken Everdene. You check the account balance and your aged debtors analysis and find that Ken owes a total of £4,500 represented by invoices spread over a 30 to 90 day period.

5 Stourminster Consultancy Limited – notice of Administration

You have been worried about the account of Stourminster Consultancy Limited which has been overdue to the extent of £1,750 for a couple of months. You have heard from local reports that the business has been having problems in meeting its commitments. You now receive notice that it has been placed in Administration.

solution

Please see memo on the next page.

MEMO

to   Tom Hardy, Credit Controller

from   A Student

date   today

subject Credit control: problem accounts

1   **Slow paying accounts**
I recommend the employment of a debt collection agency. The accounts are likely to be stirred into action and make payment when the pattern of debt chasing changes and accelerates. It would be too costly and inappropriate to employ a solictor at this stage when there is a reasonable likelihood of the money being paid. No provision for doubtful debts needs to be made yet.

2   **Wildeve Limited – disputed transaction**
Unfortunately in this case there is no evidence of an order, which is the acceptance of our offer for sale, and so there is no valid contract. Unless evidence can be found, we will be liable for collection of the goods and will have to cancel the invoice. We cannot sue where there is no contract.

3   **John Newson – County Court debtor**
Enforcement of the court judgement could be made either as an attachment of earnings (the debtor has a salary from his employer) or as a warrant of execution (sending the bailiffs in). Other remedies such as garnishee order, warrant of delivery or charging order will not be so effective. Provision for doubtful debts needs to be made at this stage.

4   **Ken Everdene – bankruptcy order**
The bankruptcy order indicates that bankruptcy proceedings have been commenced against this customer. We will have to complete a proof of debt form for the court, listing the invoices totalling £4,500. It is doubtful if we will receive much of a dividend, but provision for doubtful debts needs to be made at this stage. This may well become a bad debt at a later stage.

5   **Stourminster Consultancy Limited – notice of Administration**
The fact that this company has been placed in Administration means that creditors such as ourselves can do very little apart from carry out our usual debt chasing procedures. We are unable to take any legal action or consider insolvency proceedings. It would be wise to make provision for doubtful debts at this stage.

A Student

Chapter Summary

- The credit control function of an organisation may decide to use a third party such as a debt collection agency or a solicitor to chase up debts. These third parties can often exert more pressure on a debtor than the creditor.

- The credit control process of an organisation must assess whether the process of debt collection through legal action can be justified in terms of the size of the debt and the likelihood of recovering the debt.

- It is important that a valid contract underlies all sales transactions. If legal action is to be taken to recover a debt there must be a contract on which to sue the debtor.

- An organisation can take a debtor to court either to enforce repayment of debt or to bring about the bankruptcy of an individual or the liquidation of a company.

- A County Court judgement requiring the debtor to repay the debt owing is the most common outcome of legal action taken by the credit control function of an organisation.

- If the debtor does not repay the debt after judgement has been made in the creditor's favour, the creditor can obtain a court order to enforce repayment. The most common of these are warrant of execution (using bailiffs to seize assets) and attachment of earnings (deduction from salary).

- Taking court action to bring about the bankruptcy or liquidation of a debtor is another way of obtaining repayment of some element of the debt outstanding.

- Bringing about the bankruptcy or liquidation of a debtor in the courts will result in all the assets of the debtor being sold off and distributed (in principle) to all the creditors.

- The distribution of the sale proceeds of the assets in a bankruptcy or liquidation of a debtor is made in a strict order of priority: court costs and fees, preferential creditors, floating charge holders and then unsecured trade creditors. Creditors who are owed money on invoices are therefore last in the list and may receive little or no money.

- The credit control function of an organisation must know about the effect of alternatives to the normal insolvency route − for example administrations and the appointment by secured creditors (such as a bank) of administrative receivers. These alternatives significantly weaken the position of a trade creditor.

Key Terms		
	doubtful debt	a sales ledger debt which is unlikely to be paid
	bad debt	a sales ledger account which will not be paid and is written off in the books against profit
	contract	an agreement between two parties which must involve an offer and acceptance, the passing of value (eg a money payment) and the intention that it can be sued on if necessary
	breach of contract	breaking of a term (or terms) of the contract which can be remedied through taking legal action in the courts
	debtor	the individual or organisation who owes the money – against whom court action may be taken
	creditor	the individual or organisation who is owed the money – and who takes court action
	action for the price	taking legal action in the courts for the recovery of an unpaid debt
	debt collection agency	a commercial organisation which collects debts for third parties
	Small Claims Court	a 'fast track' court for less complex cases, including suing for recovery of debts under £5,000; the case does not need to involve a solicitor or barrister and can be brought by the creditor in person
	oral examination	a court order requiring the debtor to be cross examined in court to provide details of assets – used when the debtor refuses to pay up
	garnishee order	a court order claiming money from a third party (eg a bank account) which is owed to the debtor
	warrant of execution	a court order authorising the bailiffs to seize the assets of a debtor who refuses to pay up
	warrant of delivery	a court order authorising the bailiffs to seize assets belonging to the creditor but held by the debtor

attachment of earnings	a court order requiring an employer to deduct a proportion of the debtor's earnings and pay it to the creditor
charging order	registration of a charge (interest) in a property belonging to the debtor which entitles the creditor to be paid part of the money received for the property when it is sold
insolvency	being unable to pay debts as they fall due
bankruptcy	the situation where an individual (eg sole trader or partner) is taken to court and proved to be insolvent so that his/her assets can be sold and distributed to creditors
liquidation	the situation where a limited company is taken to court and proved to be insolvent so that its assets can be sold and distributed to creditors
statutory demand	a formal written demand to the debtor from the creditor demanding repayment of a debt (at least £750) within 21 days; a necessary condition for the bankruptcy/liquidation process
trade creditors	commercial organisations that supply goods and services on credit and on an unsecured basis – often the last to be paid off in insolvency proceedings
preferential creditors	creditors such as employees who are owed wages by the debtor and who will be paid off in priority to trade creditors
administrative receiver	an individual appointed under a floating charge (bank security) to sell the assets of the debtor when the security is called in; this ensures that the bank will be paid in priority to the trade creditors
administration	arrangement whereby a debtor running into solvency problems has an administrator appointed by the court to run its affairs; while an administrator is in place no creditor can take legal action to recover debts

Student Activities

answers to the asterisked (*) questions are to be found at the back of this book

11.1* Fastrak College operates distance learning courses in book-keeping and payroll. Students enrol by completing and signing an application form and sending it with a cheque to the Fastrak administration office who then issue a formal contract to the student.

Bob Ratchett applies to do a course in book-keeping which is due to start on 1 April. He telephones the Fastrak College office at the end of March to complain that his course materials -- tutorial texts, workbooks and CDs – have not been sent to him. The office say that they have not yet received his signed application form and cheque for £500. Bob says that they are in the post and so the office agree to send him all the course materials. They never hear from him again.

Fastrak College realises six months later that the signed application form and the £500 payment have not been received. The College writes chaser letters to Bob and telephones his work number, which they have on file. Bob does not reply to the letters which are returned 'Gone Away' and a workplace colleague says "Bob does not work here anymore. He got a job in Aberdeen, I think."

You are to explain, with reasons:

(a)   what action – including legal action – Fastrak College is able to take to recover the £500

(b)   what internal action the credit control function within Fastrak College should take if it is unable to recover this debt

11.2* Explain the advantages and disadvantages of employing a debt collection agency for the collection of debts from customers who do not reply to chaser letters and who are always unavailable when called on the telephone.

11.3* Brightman Importers Limited distributes sports equipment within the UK. The credit control function is very busy and incurs a number of bad debts every year.

It is 30 June and the year-end accounts are being prepared. You have printed out a list of problem accounts, together with notes on action taken.

It is standard company policy to write off doubtful debts under £250 at the financial year end.

Amounts over 90 days are normally first chased with a letter threatening legal action and stating that the account has been placed on stop.

customer	amount over 90 days (£)	doubtful debt provision made	action taken
R Bootle Limited	150	yes	legal action threatened, account on stop
Tessa Sims	2,500	yes	chased by telephone
R Patel	1,250	no	none
Ken Chang	175	yes	legal action threatened, account on stop
R Pumkiss	4,575	yes	County Court judgement made against customer. He still refuses to pay.

You are to write a memo to the Credit Controller, explaining what action you would recommend to be taken with the following:

(a) R Bootle Limited. The balance of this account is £150. Letters sent to the customer have been returned marked 'Gone Away'.

(b) Tessa Sims. You know that this customer is wealthy and is just using late payment as a means of financing her own liquidity. She just needs a stronger form of warning. To date she has just received chasers by telephone as she is a personal friend of one of the directors.

(c) R Patel. This account has just moved into the 90 days overdue category and as yet no action has been taken.

(d) Ken Chang. This account has been overdue for ten months. You notice in the local paper that a bankruptcy order has been made against him.

(e) You have taken Ron Pumkiss through the Small Claims Court and obtained judgment against him. He still refuses to pay. He is self-employed and lives in an expensive house in the town.

11.4* There are two main methods of taking legal action for the recovery of debt:

• taking a debtor to the County Court to obtain a judgement for the repayment of debt

• petitioning to the court for the bankruptcy of a debtor

Explain in the form of short notes

(a) the way in which the two processes work

(b) how the two processes differ in the way in which they affect the position of the debtor and the creditor

11.5 You work for Britney Imports which is owed £5,000 by Dodgee Trading Limited, which has recently been put into liquidation.

You receive a schedule from the court stating that £400,000 has been realised by the sale of the company's assets. The creditors that are paid out of this sum are :

• liquidation costs of £85,000

• preferential creditors of £127,000 (employee wages)

• Midwest Bank floating charge to cover the company's overdraft £150,000

• Unsecured trade creditors of £190,000 (including the £5,000 owed to Britney Imports)

You are to calculate

(a) the amount available for unsecured trade creditors

(b) the 'dividend' (pence in the £) which will be available for unsecured trade creditors

(c) the amount Britney Imports should receive

(d) the amount Britney Imports will have to write off as a bad debt

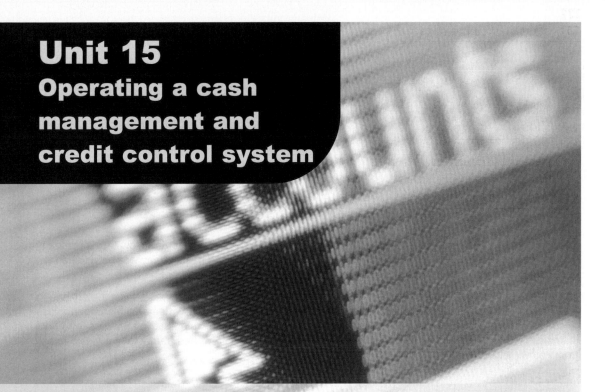

Unit 15
Operating a cash management and credit control system

Simulation 1: Sleepy Hollow Limited

Element coverage

15.1 monitor and control cash receipts and payments

15.2 manage cash balances

15.3 grant credit

15.4 monitor and control the collection of debts

Scenario and contents

This practice Simulation is based on Sleepy Hollow Limited, a business which manufactures and sells timber bed frames. The tasks include:

- the preparation of a cash flow forecast for the company
- an assessment of the impact on cash flow of a reduction in the selling price of bed frames and recommendations for action to be taken
- a description and analysis of investment opportunities for surplus funds
- recommendations for financing a £1 million capital investment requirement
- recommendations for implementation of secure cash handling procedures
- analysis of an application for credit facilities involving ratio analysis, interpretation of references and a draft reply to the request
- updating an aged debtors analysis and recommending actions to be taken

Suggested time allocation: four hours

SIMULATION 1
SLEEPY HOLLOW LIMITED

SITUATION

Your name is Jo Morphews and you work as an accounting technician at Sleepy Hollow Ltd, a company which manufactures and sells timber bed frames to the UK retail trade. The company was established ten years ago and it has consistently increased its turnover and profitability over that period.

Despite the fact that the industry remains very competitive, the company has a stated aim to continue to grow its position in the UK bed market both organically and by acquisition when suitable opportunities arise. As a consequence, the company is planning a major expansion of its production facilities in its next financial year. In addition, the company plans to commence the sale of bed frames direct to the public from its own factory shop.

Personnel

Accounting Technician	Yourself, Jo Morphews
Financial Controller	Steve Tranz
Production Director	John Leathy
Sales Director	Pat Illow

TASKS

Task 1

The latest balance sheet of Sleepy Hollow Ltd is set out on page 234. Refer to this and to the information provided in the memo from John Leathy on page 235, the memo from Pat Illow on page 236 and the memo from Steve Tranz on page 237.

Steve Tranz asks you to prepare a cash flow forecast for each of the four months ending 30 April 2004 based on the information provided and using the pro-forma on page 243. You should use the rough work space provided on page 244 to set out your workings for the quantities of wood to be purchased, the number of beds to be produced and the receipts from customers for each of the four months.

Steve Tranz asks you to calculate the impact on the forecast closing cash balance at 30 April 2004 if the sales price for a bed is only £95 in January, February and March. Use page 245.

Task 2

Steve Tranz asks you to identify those receipts and payments which require careful control and to suggest what action should be taken if receipts fall behind budget. Write a memo to Steve Tranz using page 246.

Task 3

On 31 December 2003 the company placed cash of £150,000 on a four month deposit account earning interest at the rate of 6% per annum. An extract from the Financial Times gilt prices show that Treasury Stock 9% 2009 may be purchased at a price of £112.50. The flat yield is 8.66% and the redemption yield is 6.2%. Steve Tranz asks you to prepare notes to brief the Directors on what is meant by "gilt edged securities" and the advantages and disadvantages of investing, at the price shown, in Treasury Stock 9% 2009. Use page 247 for your answer.

Task 4

The Board of Sleepy Hollow Ltd has approved an investment of £1 million for new cutting machinery which is planned to be made in July. Explain in a memo to the Board:

- the advantages and disadvantages of funding the purchase with either a bank overdraft or a bank loan

- your recommendation of which would be the preferred method of financing

Use page 248 for your answer.

Task 5

Sleepy Hollow Ltd plans to make cash sales from a factory shop with effect from April 2004. No procedures have yet been drafted for the control of cash resulting from these sales. Pat Illow has asked you to set out a draft note of the procedures to be followed for the handling of cash from these sales. You should set this out on page 249.

Task 6

A copy of a request for credit facilities from the Finance Director of Dreams Ltd, a retailer of furniture is set out on page 238. The company has also supplied its profit and loss account for the year ended 30 June 2003 (page 241). In addition, in accordance with the credit policy of Sleepy Hollow Ltd, two trade references have been obtained from Carpets Ltd and Wardrobes Ltd and these are set out on pages 239 and 240. Steve Tranz has asked you to:

- prepare a memo to Steve Tranz setting out any concerns you have in connection with the request – you should include an analysis of the profit and loss account of Dreams Ltd and refer to the trade references (use page 250 for your answer)

- draft a letter, for Steve Tranz' signature, to Mr D Jones in reply to the original request for credit facilities (use page 251 for your answer)

Task 7

The policy for the collection of debts is set out on page 241. Extracts from the cash book and sales day book for January are found on page 242 together with an extract from the aged debtors listing at 31 December 2003. Steve Tranz has asked you to:

- update the aged debtors list for the selected accounts at 31 January 2004, stating for each account what credit control action is required (use page 252)

- draft a note of the matters to be discussed by telephone with Owen Ltd (use page 252)

DATA

SLEEPY HOLLOW LIMITED

BALANCE SHEET AT 31 DECEMBER 2003

	£	£
Fixed assets		
Land and buildings		150,000
Plant and machinery	1,800,000	
Less depreciation	820,000	
		980,000
		1,130,000
Current assets		
Stock		
Wood	200,000	
Finished goods	120,000	
Debtors	800,000	
Cash on deposit	150,000	
	1,270,000	
Current liabilities		
Trade creditors	180,000	
Overdraft	520,000	
	700,000	
Net current assets		570,000
		1,700,000
Represented by		
Share capital		500,000
Retained profits		1,200,000
		1,700,000

MEMO

To: Jo Morphews, Accounting Technician

From: John Leathy, Production Director

Re: Budgetary Information

Date: 4 January 2004

I set out below the information you recently requested:

- The cost of a metre of wood is expected to remain at £5 per metre for the next twelve months.

- Each bed will continue to use 10 metres of wood.

- As you know our beds take 2 hours of labour time to manufacture and we currently pay our production staff £5 per hour. I expect to pay our production staff £5.25 per hour with effect from 1 April 2004.

- Our stock is valued at marginal production cost and our fixed production overheads are £105,000 per month. This includes depreciation of £15,000.

- At 31 December 2003 our wood stocks amount to 40,000 metres and our finished bed stocks totalled 2,000 in number.

- I plan to increase finished bed stocks by 200 beds each month but I shall reduce wood stocks to 30,000 metres at the end of March 2004 and then to 20,000 metres at the end of April 2004. They will remain at this level throughout the remainder of the year.

MEMO

To: Jo Morphews, Accounting Technician

From: Pat Illow, Sales Director

Re: Budgetary Information

Date: 29 December 2003

The sales information you requested is as follows:

- Sales to the retail trade are expected to be 5,000 beds in January 2004 and to then increase by 400 beds for each of the following months so that April 2004 sales will be 6,200 beds.

- I expect minimal sales from the factory shop this year. You should budget for sales of 100 beds per month with effect from April 2004.

- Beds will be sold to the retail trade at a price of £100 until 31 March 2004 and we will then implement a price increase of 5%. Sales made from the factory shop will be made at a price of £120.

- Sales department costs are expected to be fixed and amount to £20,000 per month including depreciation of £1,500 per month.

To: Jo Morphews, Accounting Technician

From: Steve Tranz, Financial Controller

Re: Budgetary Information

Date: 31 December 2003

In preparing the budgeted cash flow to April next year please incorporate the following:

- Although it is our policy for all trade customers to pay within 30 days, for budgetary purposes you should assume that 40% of retail trade customers pay 1 months after the date of sale and 60% pay 2 months after the date of sale.

- You should assume that the debtors at 31 December 2003 will pay as follows:

  In January 2004   £500,000
  In February 2004   £300,000
                      £800,000

- All purchases of wood will be paid for one month in arrears as at present. All other costs will be paid in the month in which they are incurred.

- All factory shop sales will be made for cash which will be banked daily.

- Administration overheads should be budgeted to be £25,000 each month.

- Overdraft interest is charged by the bank each month and should be budgeted at the rate of 1% per month on the overdrawn balance at the end of the previous month.

- The cash on deposit will mature on 30 April 2004 and will be credited together with interest to our current account on that date. The cash was placed on deposit today earning interest at the rate of 6% per annum.

DREAMS LTD
17 High Street
Newport
SA1 4FT

Mr S Tranz
Financial Controller
Sleepy Hollow Ltd
Tregarn Trading Estate
Cardiff
CF1 3EW

21 December 2003

Dear Mr Tranz

Request for credit facilities

We are a long-established company and trade as a retailer of furniture. We are keen to do business with your company. In order to facilitate this we would be grateful if you could confirm that you will be able to provide us with £20,000 of credit on 60-day terms. I enclose a copy of our latest audited profit and loss account. You may also wish to contact two of our existing suppliers for trade references. I would suggest the following two:

Carpets Ltd
Monnow Way
Bristol
BS7 6TY

Wardrobes Ltd
Gerrard Park
Liverpool
L4 1HQ

I look forward to hearing from you shortly.

Yours sincerely

D Jones

David Jones
Finance Director

CARPETS LTD

Monnow Way
Bristol
BS7 6TY

Jo Morphews
Accounting Technician
Sleepy Hollow Ltd
Tregarn Trading Estate
Cardiff
CF1 3EW

28 December 2003

Dear Ms Morphews

In response to your request for credit information on Dreams Ltd our response is as follows:

- We have traded with the company for four years.

- We allow the company £10,000 of credit on 30 day terms.

- We find that on average the company takes 60 days to settle their account with us.

We are not aware of any other information which you should consider.

Yours sincerely

A Evans

Anne Evans
Credit Controller

Wardrobes Ltd

Gerrard Park
Liverpool
L4 1HQ

Jo Morphews
Accounting Technician
Sleepy Hollow Ltd
Tregarn Trading Estate
Cardiff
CF1 3EW

28 December 2003

Dear Ms Morphews

In response to your request for credit information on Dreams Ltd our response is as follows:

- We have traded with the company for 3 months.
- We allow the company £2,500 of credit on 30-day terms.
- The company settles its account with us in accordance with our credit terms.

We are not aware of any other information which you should consider.

Yours sincerely

J Corkhill

J Corkhill
Credit Controller

DREAMS LTD

Profit and loss account for the year ended 30 June 2003

	2003	2002
	£000	£000
Turnover	1,800	1,750
Cost of sales	(1,250)	(1,190)
Gross profit	550	560
Net operating expenses	(500)	(550)
Operating profit	50	10
Interest payable and similar charges	(30)	(20)
Profit/(loss) before taxation	20	(10)
Taxation	-	3
Profit/(loss) after taxation	20	(7)
Dividends	(10)	-
Retained profit/(loss) for the year	10	(7)

SLEEPY HOLLOW LTD

DEBT COLLECTION POLICY

1 Invoices must be issued on the same day as goods are despatched.

2 An aged analysis of trade debtors is to be produced monthly.

3 Statements are to be despatched on the first working day of each month.

4 A reminder letter must be sent when a debt is 14 days overdue.

5 A telephone call to chase payment must be made when a debt is 21 days overdue.

6 The customer will be placed on the stop list when the debt is 30 days overdue and a meeting arranged with the customer to discuss the operation of the account.

7 A letter threatening legal action will be sent when the debt is 45 days overdue.

8 Legal proceedings to be commenced when a debt is 60 days overdue subject to agreement with the Financial Controller.

SLEEPY HOLLOW LTD

AGED DEBTOR ANALYSIS AT 31 DECEMBER 2003 (EXTRACT)					
		Days			
Customer	*Total*	*0 – 30*	*31 – 60*	*61 – 90*	*90+*
Adams Ltd	4,120.00	4,120.00			
Hoddle Ltd	1,200.00	800.00	400.00		
Owen Ltd	600.00	600.00			
Ince Ltd	3,500.00			3,500.00	

Note: the agreed credit period for each of these customers is 30 days from the invoice date.

SALES DAY BOOK FOR JANUARY 2004 (EXTRACT)

Customer	*Date*	*Gross*	*VAT*	*Beds*
Adams Ltd	4 Jan	352.50	52.50	300.00
Hoddle Ltd	6 Jan	587.50	87.50	500.00
Owen Ltd	7 Jan	235.00	35.00	200.00
Owen Ltd	14 Jan	235.00	35.00	200.00
Adams Ltd	28 Jan	587.50	87.50	500.00

CASH BOOK RECEIPTS FOR JANUARY 2004 (EXTRACT)

Receipt	*Date*	*Total*	*Sales*	*Sundry*
Adams Ltd	7 Jan	3,020.00	3,020.00	
Hoddle Ltd	10 Jan	100.00	100.00*	
Adams Ltd	14 Jan	1,100.00	1,100.00	

*payment of invoice dated 10.11.03

ANSWER PAGES

Task 1

SLEEPY HOLLOW LIMITED

CASH FLOW FORECAST FOR THE FOUR MONTHS ENDING 30 APRIL 2004

	Jan £	Feb £	Mar £	Apr £
Receipts				
Trade sales				
Factory sales				
From deposit				
Total Receipts				
Payments				
Wood suppliers				
Production wages				
Production overheads				
Sales department costs				
Administration costs				
Overdraft interest				
Total Payments				
Cash Flow for month				
Bank balance brought forward				
Bank balance carried forward				

Task 1: Workings for cash flow forecast

Task 1 (continued)

SENSITIVITY ANALYSIS

Task 2

MEMO

To:

From:

Re:

Date:

Task 3

> **NOTES ON GILT-EDGED SECURITIES**

Task 4

MEMO **To:** **From:** **Re:** **Date:**

Task 5

DRAFT PROCEDURES FOR CASH SALES

Task 6

MEMO

To:

From:

Re:

Date:

_____

Task 6 (continued)

SLEEPY HOLLOW LIMITED
Tregarn Trading Estate
Cardiff
CF1 3EW

Task 7

AGED DEBTOR ANALYSIS AT 31 DECEMBER 2003 (EXTRACT)					
		Days			
Customer	Total	0 – 30	31 – 60	61 – 90	90+
Adams Ltd					
Hoddle Ltd					
Owen Ltd					
Ince Ltd					

Task 7

Credit control actions needed

Adams Ltd:

Hoddle Ltd:

Owen Ltd:

Ince Ltd:

Matters to be discussed with the Purchase Ledger Controller of Owen Ltd:

Unit 15
Operating a cash management and credit control system

Simulation 2: Heski Components

Element coverage

15.1 monitor and control cash receipts and payments

15.2 manage cash balances

15.3 grant credit

15.4 monitor and control the collection of debts

Scenario and contents

This practice Simulation is based on Heski Components, a business which manufactures computer equipment. The tasks include:

- comparing a cash flow forecast for a past period and the actual figures achieved, explaining differences, analysing the cash flow forecast, carrying out sensitivity analysis and suggesting action to be taken

- the preparation of a cash flow forecast for the business

- analysis of an application for credit facilities from two customers involving ratio analysis and interpretation of references

- notes for a talk to business students about forms of bank lending and bank lending criteria

- updating an aged debtors analysis and recommending actions to be taken

Suggested time allocation: four hours

SIMULATION 2
HESKI COMPONENTS

SITUATION

Your name is Susan Belling and you are an accounting technician working as an assistant to the Financial Controller, Lee Bennett, at Heski Components. Today's date is 10 January.

Heski Components is a company that makes components to sell to manufacturers of equipment for educational institutions. It was established 10 years ago and is planning to expand. The company currently has three departments: Department 1 makes keyboards, Department 2 manufactures circuit boards and Department 3 makes screens.

Heski Components has a 31 December year end.

Personnel

Assistant Accountant	Susan Belling (yourself)
Financial Controller	Lee Bennett
Credit Control Manager	Angela Radstock
Factory Manager	Graham Bolt
Sales Manager	Jemma Daly

TASKS

Task 1

Refer to the memo from Lee Bennett (point 1) on page 256, the forecast and actual cash flows for Department 2 for the final three months of last year on pages 258 and 259, the forecast for Department 2 for January and February of this year on page 260, and the list of assumptions for the forecast for March, April and May on page 261, and the memos from Jemma Daly and Graham Bolt on pages 262 and 263.

(a)   In a memo to Lee Bennett:

- compare the cash flow forecast and actual cash flow for Department 2 for the final three months of last year, listing any differences and suggesting why they may have occurred, together with any corrective action

- explain one way in which Heski Components' cash flow could be affected by an increase in inflation higher than 4%

- explain one disadvantage of the method used to project cash flow for Department 2

(b)   Additionally:

- prepare a cash flow forecast for March, April and May for Department 2, based on the assumptions outlined

- explain the effect the cash flow forecast of purchasing the machine, if it were to be bought in March on the basis of monthly instalments

Use the proformas provided on pages 272 - 273 for 1(a) and pages 274 - 275 for 1 (b).

Task 2

Refer to the memo from Lee Bennett (point 2) on pages 256 - 257, the references for Lear Ltd on pages 264 - 265 and the references and the financial statement extracts for Brightlites Ltd on pages 266 - 268 and the extract from the procedures manual on page 269.

In a memo to Lee Bennett, make a recommendation as to whether Lear Ltd and Brightlites Ltd should have credit terms, extended to them by Heski Components based on the reference information for both companies, and the ratio analysis and profitability of Brightlites Ltd.

You should write your answer on page 276.

Task 3

Refer to the memo from Lee Bennett (point 3) on page 257.

Prepare notes, which should include:

- an introduction explaining what a bank loan and an overdraft are
- a recommendation of the type of borrowing Beanet Ltd and Amo Ltd should take
- a brief outline of three of a bank's lending criteria

You should write your answer on page 277.

Task 4

Refer to Lee Bennett's memo on page 257 (point 4), the extract from the aged debtors analysis for November on page 270, the extract from the list of transactions for December on page 270 and the memo from Angela Radstock on page 271.

(a)   Using page 278, update the extract from the aged debtors analysis.

(b)   Using pages 279-280, write a memo to Angela Radstock which:

- lists appropriate follow-up actions, together with any recommendations about the writing off of current outstanding debts

- suggests two alternative methods of making contact with non-paying debtors when they do not answer follow-up letters

- includes a draft debt collection policy for collecting outstanding debts – this should outline steps taken from the first month that a debt is overdue

DATA

MEMO

To:	Susan Belling
From:	Lee Bennett
Date:	10 January
Subject:	Work for this week

I have been unexpectedly invited to a conference in France for four days. As you already know there is a lot of urgent work on and I need you to prepare the following for me.

1.   I have left a copy of the cash flow forecast and actual cash flow for the final three months of last year for Department 2 on my desk. Please compare the two and write me a memo listing any differences and suggested corrective action.

     The bank has asked me to comment on how we would be affected by an increase in inflation higher than the 4% assumed in our forecasting. Could you give me some brief comments on this, relating them to the forecast for Department 2.

     We base our forecasts on past forecasts and any new assumptions. I wonder if there are any disadvantages in working this way? Again the bank has asked me why we do this – could you suggest any problems we may experience with this approach.

     Attached to this memo is the cash flow forecast for January and February, together with a list of assumptions and other information to be used in forecasting the cash flow for Department 2 for March, April and May. You should prepare a forecast for March, April and May; the forecast for these months should be based on the list of assumptions and the forecast information for January and February.

     There is a possibility that the machine to be bought in March may be paid for in interest free monthly instalments over a 12 month period. How would this impact on the cash flow forecast?

2.   We need to assess the creditworthiness of Lear Ltd. It is a very new company which has placed a large order and any problems it has paying would have an impact on our cash flow. I have asked them for financial statements but since they are in their first few months of trading they are unable to offer these. However I have left two references on your desk (I have not had time to read them). I need you to go through this information and recommend whether or not we extend credit to them.

We also need to assess the creditworthiness of Brightlites – a long established company – which has placed a smaller order and requested credit. I have left some financial statements for Brightlites on my desk, together with two references. Again I need a recommendation as to whether or not to extend credit to them.

3.   We will be having a visit from some business students next week. I have arranged a programme which includes a short talk on bank borrowing and lending criteria. I would like you to prepare and deliver this talk using the following scenarios:

Scenario 1

Beanet Ltd is a medium sized company which manufactures Christmas decorations. It needs more working capital to fund the development of the company. The pattern of cash flows is seasonal.

Scenario 2

Amo Ltd is a small family-run engineering company. It is seeking to finance an extension to its main factory. The industry it works in is not subject to seasonality.

A brief outline of a bank's lending criteria should also be covered.

4.   Please update the aged debtors analysis from November and write a memo to Angela Radstock listing any appropriate actions. Angel Radstock has written me a memo concerning debt collection. Please read this memo, which is on my desk, and work on the actions.

Many thanks.

Lee

CASH FLOW FORECAST FOR THE FINAL THREE MONTHS OF LAST YEAR

DEPARTMENT 2

	October £000	November £000	December £000
Receipts			
Sales:			
Cash	10	10	10
Credit	80	90	90
Sale of assets	0	0	10
Total Receipts	90	100	110
Payments			
Purchase of machine	25	0	5
Purchase of vehicles	10	0	0
Rent	12	12	12
Wages	15	16	16
Purchases	40	43	44
Selling/administration	10	10	10
Total Payments	112	81	87
Net cash flow	(22)	19	23
Brought forward cash/bank balance	5	(17)	2
Carried forward cash/bank balance	(17)	2	25

CASH FLOW ACTUALS FOR THE FINAL THREE MONTHS OF LAST YEAR

DEPARTMENT 2

	October *£000*	*November* *£000*	*December* *£000*
Receipts			
Sales:			
Cash	9	9	10
Credit	82	89	91
Sale of assets	0	0	10
Total Receipts	91	98	111
Payments			
Purchase of machine	28	0	5
Purchase of vehicles	10	0	0
Rent	12	12	12
Wages	17	17	18
Purchases	45	45	46
Selling/administration	10	10	10
Total Payments	122	84	91
Net cash flow	(31)	14	20
Brought forward cash/bank balance	5	(26)	(12)
Carried forward cash/bank balance	(26)	(12)	8

CASH FLOW FORECAST FOR THE FIRST TWO MONTHS OF THIS YEAR

DEPARTMENT 2

	January £000	February £000	
Receipts			
Sales:			
Cash	10	10	
Credit	91	92	
Total Receipts	101	102	
Payments			
Machine	35	0	
Vehicles	5	4	
Rent	12	12	
Wages	16	16	
Purchases	40	41	
Selling/administration	11	11	
Total Payments	119	84	
Net cash flow	(18)	18	
Brought forward cash/bank balance	15	(3)	
Carried forward cash/bank balance	(3)	15	

LIST OF ASSUMPTIONS TO BE USED IN THE PREPARATION OF THE CASH FLOW FORECAST FOR DEPARTMENT 2 FOR MARCH, APRIL AND MAY

1. You may round your figures to the nearest thousand.

2. The sales for March, April and May should be based on the attached memo from Jemma Daly.

3. A machine costing £24,000 and a vehicle costing £10,000 are to be bought in March. Both will be paid for in full in the month of purchase. A machine costing £10,000 is to be bought in May; a deposit of £2,000 will be paid on purchase and the balance will be spread over four equal monthly instalments starting in June.

4. There will be a rent review at the end of February and it is expected that rent will be increased by £1,000 per month. It will remain at £13,000 per month for the rest of the year.

5. The wages bill should be based on the attached memo from Graham Bolt.

6. The cash to be paid for purchases in March is expected to be the same as in February. It will increase by 2% in April and by a further £500 in May.

7. Selling and administrative costs are expected to remain the same in March and April, and rise by 10% in May.

MEMO

To: Lee Bennett

From: Jemma Daly

Date: 8 January

Subject: Sales Forecasts, March – May

Further to your recent request for sales forecasts for Department 2 for March to May, I have put together a table showing the following figures:

- Cash sales in March are expected to increase by 20% from February, April sales will increase by a further 10% and May sales will be the same as April sales.

- I have estimated the credit sales for February to May – payment will be received in the month following the month of sale.

Item	Price per item £	February	March	April	May
			Quantity Ordered		
Circuit board a1a	800	50	50	50	55
Circuit board a2b	600	80	90	100	100
Tailored circuit boards	1,000	5	5	10	10

Jemma

MEMO

To: Lee Bennett

From: Graham Bolt

Date: 7 January

Subject: Schedules for March – May

I have worked out the number of labour hours needed for March, April and May:

March	2,400 hours
April	2,500 hours
May	2,600 hours

In March and April there will be 2,000 hours available at the normal hourly rate of pay, any hours above 2,000 in each month will be paid at the hourly overtime rate. In May there will be 2,200 hours available at the normal hourly rate of pay, any further hours will be at the hourly overtime rate.

I can now confirm that the rates of pay have been agreed at £6.80 per hour normal time and £8.50 per hour overtime – these rates apply from the 1 March.

Graham

HESKI COMPONENTS
11 Trench Road
Litton
LN2 7AS
Tel: 01221 4455667

PRIVATE AND CONFIDENTIAL

Credit Manager
Driva and Co Ltd
Headley Park
Litton
LT6 9ZA   5 January

Dear Sir or Madam

We have recently received a request from a customer or ours, Lear Ltd, quoting you as a reference. We would be grateful if you would answer the following questions and return this letter in the enclosed stamped addressed envelope.

1.   For how long has Lear Ltd been trading with you?

   Three months

2.   Did you take up references for Lear Ltd when you began trading with them?

   Yes, one reference

3   How long a credit period do you normally extend to Lear Ltd?

   One month

4.   Does Lear Ltd make payments in accordance with credit terms?

   Yes

5.   Have you ever suspended credit being extended to Lear Ltd?

   No

   If YES please give date and period of suspension

6.   Please supply any other information which you consider relevant.

Thank you for your help.

Yours faithfully

Angela Radstock

Credit Control Manager

HESKI COMPONENTS
11 Trench Road
Litton
LN2 7AS
Tel: 01221 4455667

PRIVATE AND CONFIDENTIAL

Credit Manager
Tilton Ltd
Bruin Court
Litton
LT7 8WW   5 January

Dear Sir or Madam

We have recently received a request from a customer or ours, Lear Ltd, quoting you as a reference. We would be grateful if you would answer the following questions and return this letter in the enclosed stamped addressed envelope.

1.   For how long has Lear Ltd been trading with you?

      Four months

2.   Did you take up references for Lear Ltd when you began trading with them?

      Two references

3   How long a credit period do you normally extend to Lear Ltd?

      6 weeks

4.   Does Lear Ltd make payments in accordance with credit terms?

      Yes

5.   Have you ever suspended credit being extended to Lear Ltd?

      No

      If YES please give date and period of suspension

6.   Please supply any other information which you consider relevant.

Thank you for your help.

Yours faithfully

Angela Radstock

Credit Control Manager

HESKI COMPONENTS
11 Trench Road
Litton
LN2 7AS
Tel: 01221 4455667

PRIVATE AND CONFIDENTIAL

Credit Manager
Tolla Components Ltd
41 Anfield Street
Litton
LT6 8GV   5 January

Dear Sir or Madam

We have recently received a request from a customer or ours, Brightlites Ltd, quoting you as a reference. We would be grateful if you would answer the following questions and return this letter in the enclosed stamped addressed envelope.

1.   For how long has Brightlites Ltd been trading with you?

      Three years

2.   Did you take up references for Brightlites Ltd when you began trading with them?

      Two references

3   How long a credit period do you normally extend to Brightlites Ltd?

      6 weeks

4.   Does Brightlites Ltd make payments in accordance with credit terms?

      Yes

5.   Have you ever suspended credit being extended to Brightlites Ltd?

      No

      If YES please give date and period of suspension

6.   Please supply any other information which you consider relevant.

Thank you for your help.

Yours faithfully

Angela Radstock

Credit Control Manager

HESKI COMPONENTS
11 Trench Road
Litton
LN2 7AS
Tel: 01221 4455667

PRIVATE AND CONFIDENTIAL

Credit Manager
Kentech Ltd
St Andrews Road
Litton
LT6 6BB   5 January

Dear Sir or Madam

We have recently received a request from a customer or ours, Brightlites Ltd, quoting you as a reference. We would be grateful if you would answer the following questions and return this letter in the enclosed stamped addressed envelope.

1.   For how long has Brightlites Ltd been trading with you?

     Seven years

2.   Did you take up references for Brightlites Ltd when you began trading with them?

     Two references

3   How long a credit period do you normally extend to Brightlites Ltd?

     Two months

4.   Does Brightlites Ltd make payments in accordance with credit terms?

     Yes

5.   Have you ever suspended credit being extended to Brightlites Ltd?

     No

     If YES please give date and period of suspension

6.   Please supply any other information which you consider relevant.

Thank you for your help.

Yours faithfully

Angela Radstock

Credit Control Manager

EXTRACT FROM THE ANNUAL ACCOUNTS OF BRIGHTLITES LTD

BALANCE SHEET

	This year	Last Year
	£000	£000
Fixed assets		
Intangible fixed assets	500	400
Tangible fixed assets	800	700
Investments	600	580
	1,900	1,680
Current assets		
Stocks	300	290
Debtors	900	800
Cash	10	50
	1,210	1,140
Current liabilities		
Trade creditors	1,000	900
Other	10	30
	1,010	930
Total assets *less* current liabilities	2,100	1,890
less		
Long Term Liabilities	200	200
	1,900	1,690
Financed by		
Called up share capital	800	800
Profit and loss		
b/f	890	600
retained	210	290
c/f	1,100	890
	1,900	1,690
PROFIT AND LOSS ACCOUNT		
Profit after interest and taxation	400	490

EXTRACT FROM PROCEDURES MANUAL

Extending credit to new customers

The supply of goods/services on credit necessarily involves risk. To minimise that risk the following steps should be taken before extending credit to a new customer.

1. Two references from independent referees should be obtained. Any problems raised by the references should be followed up and further references should be taken if appropriate.

2. The latest set of accounts of a company should be obtained and ratio analysis undertaken.

   The ratio analysis should include the following ratios:

   • current ratio

   • acid test (quick) ratio

   • debt ratio (total short and long term creditors: net fixed assets plus current assets)

   Any problems raised by the analysis should be followed up.

3. Assuming points 1 and 2 are satisfactory, a credit limit should be set by the Credit Control Manager. This should initially be a very conservative limit which is closely monitored. The limit may be reviewed after six months.

4. Once a credit limit has been set the customer should be offered one month's credit from date of sale.

EXTRACT FROM AGED DEBTORS ANALYSIS 30 NOVEMBER

name	code	total owing £	<1 month £	1–2 months £	2–3 months £	>3 months £
Carpenter	A101	10,000	5,000 (inv 81a)	5,000 (inv 63a)		
Hopton & Son	F223	2,000	500 (inv 121f)	600 (inv 98f)	900 (inv 54f)	
Jojo & Co	A413	11,000	5,000 (inv 91a)	3,000 (inv 59a)	3,000 (inv 45a)	
Spokes Ltd	C190	6,500				6,500 (inv 111c)
TOTAL		29,500	10,500	8,600	3,900	6,500
Percentage		100%	36%	29%	13%	22%

Note: all the above customers have been given one month's credit.

CUSTOMER PROFILES

Carpenter   A large company which was set up five years ago. Carpenter is an important customer which has placed relatively large orders for the past four years. The company regularly pays a week or two after the payment date.

Hopton & Son   This is a medium sized family run company which places fairly small orders on a regular basis. It has a very poor record of payment and continually pays several months late.

Jojo & Co   Jojo & Co is quite a new customer which asked for three months credit but has only been granted the usual one month's credit. Jojo & Co seems to have tried to resolve this by taking the three months anyway. The orders placed are quite large so this is an important customer.

Spokes Ltd   Spokes Ltd is quite a new company. It has only ever placed the one order with Heski Components and this has not been paid despite two reminder letters having been sent. There are no pricing or delivery queries and no complaints about the actual goods. There are rumours of financial problems.

EXTRACT FROM LIST OF TRANSACTIONS FOR DECEMBER

Carpenter   Paid invoice 63a. Invoice 81a remains unpaid. Invoice 101a £6,000 issued.

Hopton & Son   Paid invoice 54f. Invoices 98f and 121f remain unpaid.

Jojo & Co   Paid invoices 45a and 59a. Invoice 91a remains unpaid. Invoice 103a £2,000 issued.

Spokes Ltd   No transactions.

MEMO

To: Lee Bennett

From: Angela Radstock

Date: 8 January

Subject: Re: our meeting of 7 January

Further to our recent conversation, I agree we do need to make a list of alternative ways of contacting non-paying debtors and also formulate a debt collection policy.

Thank you for offering to arrange for these to be drafted. I look forward to discussing them at our next meeting.

Angela

ANSWER PAGES

Task 1 (a)

MEMO

To:

From:

Date:

Subject:

Task 1 (b)

<table>
<thead>
<tr><th colspan="4">CASH FLOW FORECAST FOR MARCH, APRIL AND MAY

DEPARTMENT 2</th></tr>
<tr><th></th><th>March
£000</th><th>April
£000</th><th>May
£000</th></tr>
</thead>
<tbody>
<tr><td>**Receipts**

Sales:

  Cash</td><td></td><td></td><td></td></tr>
<tr><td> Credit</td><td></td><td></td><td></td></tr>
<tr><td>Total Receipts</td><td></td><td></td><td></td></tr>
<tr><td>**Payments**

Machine</td><td></td><td></td><td></td></tr>
<tr><td>Vehicles</td><td></td><td></td><td></td></tr>
<tr><td>Rent</td><td></td><td></td><td></td></tr>
<tr><td>Wages</td><td></td><td></td><td></td></tr>
<tr><td>Purchases</td><td></td><td></td><td></td></tr>
<tr><td>Selling/administration</td><td></td><td></td><td></td></tr>
<tr><td>Total Payments</td><td></td><td></td><td></td></tr>
<tr><td>Net cash flow</td><td></td><td></td><td></td></tr>
<tr><td>Brought forward cash/bank balance</td><td></td><td></td><td></td></tr>
<tr><td>Carried forward cash/bank balance</td><td></td><td></td><td></td></tr>
</tbody>
</table>

Task 1 (b) workings

Task 2

MEMO

To:

From:

Date:

Subject:

please continue on another sheet of paper if you need to

Task 3

NOTES ON BANK FINANCING

please continue on another sheet of paper if you need to

Task 4 (a)

AGED DEBTORS ANALYSIS

name	code	total owing £	<1 month £	1–2 months £	2–3 months £	>3 months £
Carpenter	A101					
Hopton & Son	F223					
Jojo & Co	A413					
Spokes Ltd	C190					
TOTAL						
Percentage						

Task 4 (b)

MEMO

To:

From:

Date:

Subject:

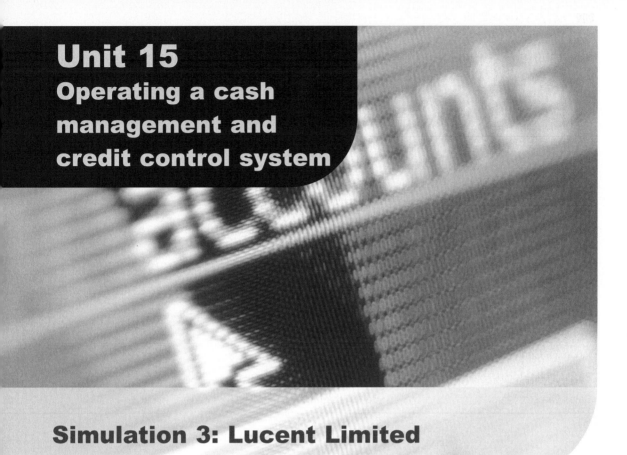

Unit 15
Operating a cash management and credit control system

Simulation 3: Lucent Limited

Element coverage

15.1 monitor and control cash receipts and payments

15.2 manage cash balances

15.3 grant credit

15.4 monitor and control the collection of debts

Scenario and contents

This practice Simulation is based on Lucent Limited, a business which manufactures and sells candles. The tasks include:

- the preparation of a cash flow forecast for the company
- an assessment of the impact on cash flow of a reduction in the selling price of candles and recommendations for further action to be taken
- assessment of the financing needs of the business and a comparison of a term loan and an overdraft
- a description and analysis of investment opportunities for surplus funds
- a written reply to an application for credit facilities from a customer
- a memo setting out reasons why a request for credit might be refused
- an analysis of an aged debtors analysis and recommendations for action to take with the various debtors

Suggested time allocation: four hours

SIMULATION 3
LUCENT LIMITED

SITUATION

Your name is Pat Smith and you work as an accounting technician at Lucent Ltd, a company which manufactures and sells candles. The company was established ten years ago.

The company sells candles from its own shop, and to other retailers throughout the UK.

Personnel

Assistant Accountant	Yourself, Pat Smith
Financial Controller	Amy Williams
Production Director	Ross Morris
Sales Director	Ben Mohammed

TASKS

Task 1

The latest balance sheet of Lucent Ltd is set out on page 284. Refer to this and the information provided in the memo from Ross Morris on page 285, the memo from Ben Mohammed on page 285 and the memo from Amy Williams on page 286.

- Amy Williams asks you to prepare a cash flow forecast for each of the three months ending 30 June 2001 based on the information provided and using the proforma cash flow forecast on page 289. You should use pages 290 and 291 to set out your workings for the number of candles to be produced, the raw materials to be purchased and the receipts from trade sales for each of the three months.

- Amy Williams asks you to calculate the impact on the forecast levels of cash and trade debtors at 30 June 2001 if sales to credit customers are made at a price of £1.50 and not £1.65 for each of the three months. Suggest two actions the company could take to reduce any adverse impact on cash flow that such a policy may create. Use pages 292 - 293.

Task 2

The company has an overdraft facility of £225,000 with its bank which is due for renewal in April 2001. Amy Williams has asked you to draft a memo to the Board setting out the size of facility required and whether an overdraft facility or term loan is more appropriate for the company's needs. You should date your memo 10 April 2001.

Use the memo on pages 294 - 295.

Task 3

An offer has been received to purchase the company's freehold retail site for £400,000. The company has accepted the offer and completion of the sale is expected to take place in July 2001. The Board of Directors has asked Amy Williams to consider how this money might be invested. In preparation for her meeting she has now asked you to prepare notes on the following matters.

- gilt-edged securities and bank deposits as investment opportunities appropriate for any surplus funds from the sale of the property.

- the security procedures which should be arranged for each type of investment

- the effect of any increase in base rate on both types of investment.

Use page 296 for your answer.

Task 4

A copy of a request for credit facilities from a director of Fancy Goods Ltd, a retailer of candles and other decorative products, is set out on page 287.

You should draft a letter to Mr S Redmond in reply to the original request for credit facilities. Your letter should set out the information you require from the company in order to progress the granting of credit facilities. You should use the letterhead on page 298. Date your letter 10 April 2001.

Task 5

You have recently employed a trainee credit controller. Draft a memo to him setting out:

- six reasons why trade credit facilities might be refused

- how such a decision should be communicated to the applicant

You should use the memo on page 299. Date your memo 10 April 2001.

Task 6

An extract of the aged debtor analysis and the company's credit control policy is set out on page 288.

In a memo to Amy Williams, you should:

- set out the action to be taken with regard to each of the four customer accounts

- state how discussion should be conducted with overdue accounts

- recommend whether any provisions for doubtful debts are required

You should use the memo on page 300. Date your memo 10 April 2001.

DATA

LUCENT LTD – BALANCE SHEET AT 31 MARCH 2001

	£	£
Fixed assets		
Land and buildings		150,000
Plant and machinery	280,000	
Less: depreciation	120,000	
		160,000
		310,000
Current assets		
Stock		
Raw materials	60,000	
Finished goods	55,000	
Debtors	380,000	
Cash in hand at retail shop	1,000	
	496,000	
Current liabilities		
Bank overdraft	220,000	
Trade creditors for raw materials	120,000	
	340,000	
Net current assets		156,000
Total assets less current liabilities		466,000
Capital and reserves		
Share capital		100,000
Retained profits		366,000
		466,000

MEMO

To: Pat Smith, Assistant Accountant

From: Ross Morris, Production Director

Re: Budgetary Information

Date: 2 April 2001

___

I set out below the information you recently requested.

1. The cost of raw materials for each candle is 60 pence. No price increase is expected in the budgetary period.

2. Each candle takes six minutes of labour time to manufacture and we currently pay our production staff £5 per hour.

3. Our fixed production overheads are £25,000 per month. This includes depreciation of £5,000.

4. At 31 March 2001 our raw material stocks were sufficient to manufacture 100,000 candles and we also hold 50,000 candles in stock.

5. I plan to increase candle stocks by 5,000 each month but I shall maintain raw material stocks at their current level.

___

MEMO

To: Pat Smith, Assistant Accountant

From: Ben Mohammed, Sales Director

Re: Budgetary Information

Date: 29 March 2001

___

The sales information you requested is as follows:

1. Sales to the retail trade are expected to be 120,000 candles in April, 125,000 in May and 130,000 in June. In addition we expect to sell 5,000 candles from our own shop in each of the next three months.

2. Candles will be sold to the retail trade at £1.65. Sales made from our own shop will be made at £3 each.

3. Sales department costs are expected to be fixed at £12,000 per month including depreciation of £500 per month.

4. The costs for the shop are fixed and are £7,000 per month including depreciation of £800.

MEMO

To: Pat Smith, Assistant Accountant

From: Amy Williams, Financial Controller

Re: Budgetary Information

Date: 30 March 2001

In preparing the budgeted cash flow to June please incorporate the following assumptions.

1.   Although it is our policy for all trade customers to pay within 30 days, for budgetary purposes you should assume that 30% of retail trade customers pay one month after the date of sale and 70% pay two months after the date of sale.

2.   You should assume that the debtors at 31 March will pay as follows:

	£
In April	200,000
In May	180,000
	380,000

3.   All purchases of raw materials will be paid for one month in arrears as at present. All other costs will be paid in the month in which they are incurred.

4.   Sales from our own shop will be made for cash.

5.   Administration overheads should be budgeted to be £25,000 each month.

6.   Overdraft interest is charged by the bank each month and should be budgeted at the rate of 1% per month on the overdrawn balance at the end of the previous month.

FANCY GOODS LTD
20 High Street
Bristol BS1 2FG

Pat Smith
Assistant Accountant
Lucent Ltd
Tylers Trading Estate
Gloucester
GL15 3EW

21 March 2001

Dear Mr Smith

Request for credit facilities

I am seeking credit facilities for my chain of 10 decorative product shops. Although we have never purchased products from you I am keen to establish a trading relationship with you. To facilitate this I would be grateful if you could arrange for a credit facility of £10,000 on thirty days terms.

I look forward to receiving confirmation of this facility.

Yours sincerely

Stephen Redmond

Stephen Redmond
Director

AGED DEBTOR ANALYSIS

Customer	Amount Due £	Current £	31 – 60 Days	61 – 90 Days	91+ Days
Candles Ltd	12,500.65				12,500.65
Lux Ltd	3,250.00	2,250.00	850.00		150.00
Lights Ltd	1,475.00		475.00	1,000.00	
Flames Ltd	16,815.75	9,275.50	6,120.25	1,420.00	

CREDIT CONTROL POLICY

1. Invoices must be issued on the same day as goods are despatched.

2. An aged analysis of trade debtors is to be produced monthly.

3. Statements are to be despatched on the first working day of each month.

4. A reminder letter must be sent when a debt is 14 days overdue.

5. A telephone call to chase payment must be made when a debt is 21 days overdue.

6. The customer will be placed on the stop list when the debt is 30 days overdue and a meeting arranged with the customer to discuss the operation of the account.

7. A letter threatening legal action will be sent when the debt is 45 days overdue.

8. Legal proceedings to be commenced when a debt is 60 days overdue, subject to agreement with the Financial Controller.

ANSWER PAGES

Task 1

LUCENT LTD Cash flow forecast for the three months ending 30 June 2001			
	April £	**May** £	**June** £
Receipts			
Trade sales			
Own retail sales			
Total receipts			
Payments			
Trade suppliers			
Production wages			
Production overheads			
Sales department costs			
Retail shop costs			
Administration costs			
Overdraft interest			
Total payments			
Cash Flow for month			
Bank balance b/f			
Bank balance c/f			

Task 1: workings for cash flow forecast

Task 1: workings for cash flow forecast

Task 1: workings for impact of reduction in sales price

Task 1: workings for impact of reduction in sales price

Task 2

MEMO

To:

From:

Re:

Date:

Task 3

BRIEFING NOTES ON GILT EDGED SECURITIES AND BANK DEPOSITS

Task 4

LUCENT LIMITED

Tylers Trading Estate

Gloucester GL15 3EW

Task 5

MEMO

To:

From:

Re:

Date:

Task 6

MEMO

To:

From:

Re:

Date:

Answers to student activities

CHAPTER 1 – MANAGING CASH FLOWS

1.1 (a) Cash cycle = 5 months

(b) Cash cycle = 3 months.

1.2 The credit controller's absence accounts for an increase in debtors of £40,000, and an equal reduction in the bank balance.

The early delivery accounts for increased stock of £20,000 and an increase in creditors of the same amount.

The additional goods bought account for an increase in stock of £10,000, and a reduction in the bank balance of the same amount since the goods have been paid for.

These three issues together account for the differences between the budgeted and actual positions.

1.3 Statements 2, 3, 5, and 7 are true. The others are false.

CHAPTER 2 – PREPARING CASH BUDGETS

2.1 **Sonita's Business – Cash Budget for first four months' trading**

	1 £'000	2 £'000	3 £'000	4 £'000
Receipts				
Initial Investment	35			
Receipts from Sales	10	10	10	10
Total Receipts	45	10	10	10
Payments				
Purchases	9	-	8	7
Expenses	2	2	2	2
Fixed Assets	30	-	-	-
Drawings	1	1	1	1
Total Payments	42	3	11	10
Cash Flow for Month	3	7	(1)	0
Bank balance bf	0	3	10	9
Bank balance cf	3	10	9	9

Sonita's Business – Budgeted Balance Sheet as at the end of Month 4

	£	£	£
Fixed Assets			
	Cost	Dep'n	Net
Equipment	30,000	2,000	28,000
Current Assets:			
Stock		5,000	
Debtors		0	
Cash/Bank		9,000	
		14,000	
Less Current Liabilities:			
Trade Creditors		6,000	
			8,000
Total Net Assets			36,000
Financed by:			
Capital Invested			35,000
Add Budgeted Profit			5,000
Less Budgeted Drawings			(4,000)
Total Capital			36,000

2.2   (a)

	Jan	Feb	Mar	Apr	May	Jun
	£	£	£	£	£	£
Receipts						
Capital	10,000					
Debtors	-	1,250	3,000	4,000	4,000	4,500
Total receipts	10,000	1,250	3,000	4,000	4,000	4,500
Payments						
Van	6,000					
Creditors	-	4,500	4,500	3,500	3,500	3,500
Expenses	750	600	600	650	650	700
Total payments	6,750	5,100	5,100	4,150	4,150	4,200
Cash flow for month	3,250	(3,850)	(2,100)	(150)	(150)	300
Bank balance b/f	0	3,250	(600)	(2,700)	(2,850)	(3,000)
Bank balance c/f	3,250	(600)	(2,700)	(2,850)	(3,000)	(2,700)

(b) **Budgeted trading and profit and loss account**

	£	£
Sales		22,750
less cost of sales:		
opening stock	0	
purchases	23,500	
less closing stock	(3,250)	20,250
Gross profit		2,500
less:		
cash expenses	3,950	
depreciation	600	
		4,550
Net loss		(2,050)

(c) Budgeted Balance Sheet as at 30 June

	£	£	£
Fixed Assets			
	Cost	*Dep'n*	*Net Book Value*
Van	6,000	600	5,400
Current Assets			
Stock		3,250	
Debtors		6,000	
		9,250	
Less **Current Liabilities**			
Trade Creditors	4,000		
Bank Overdraft	2,700		
		6,700	
			2,550
Total Net Assets			7,950
Financed by:			
Capital Invested			10,000
less budgeted loss for six months			(2,050)
			7,950

CHAPTER 3 – PREPARING CASH BUDGETS – FURTHER ISSUES

3.1

(a)   The production budget in units for month 3 equals:

Budgeted Sales Units	2,600 units
– Opening Stock of Finished Goods	(600) units
+ Closing Stock of Finished Goods	500 units
Production budget	2,500 units

The raw materials usage budget is based on the raw material required to satisfy the production budget:

Raw Materials Usage = (2,500 units x 6 kilos per unit) = 15,000 kilos

The raw material purchases budget for month 3 will equal:

Raw materials usage budget	15,000 kilos
- opening stock of raw materials,	(1,500) kilos
+ closing stock of raw materials.	1,800 kilos
Raw materials purchases budget	15,300 kilos

(b)   The production budget would be used to prepare the labour utilisation budget. This in turn would provide data for the cash budget.

The raw materials purchases budget data (15,300 kilos, valued at the buying price) would be used in the cash budget, after any necessary lagging.

3.2   The Unit Company Cash Budget for January, April 20-7

	January £	February £	March £	April £
Receipts				
Receipts from year 20-6 sales	6,500	3,500	-	-
Receipts from year 20-7 sales	-	-	4,000	4,400
Total Receipts	6,500	3,500	4,000	4,400
Payments				
Raw Material Purchases	1,000	840	960	1,000
Labour	1,320	1,260	1,320	1,440
Fixed Overheads	800	800	800	800
Debenture Interest	1,200	-	-	-
Dividends	-	-	-	10,000
Total Payments	4,320	2,900	3,080	13,240
Cash Flow for Month	2,180	600	920	(8,840)
Bank balance brought fwd	12,000	14,180	14,780	15,700
Bank Balance carried fwd	14,180	14,780	15,700	6,860

		£
•	Finished Goods Stock	
	(Units: 20 + 89 Prod'n – 90 Sales = 19) 19 x £100	1,900
•	Raw Materials Stock	
	(Units: 30 + 92 Purchases – 89 Prod'n = 33) 33 x £40	1,320
•	Debtors	
	March + April Sales: (23 + 25) x £200	9,600
•	Bank – per cash budget	6,860
•	Raw Material Creditors	
	April Purchases 22 x £40	880

CHAPTER 4 – USING CASH BUDGETS

4.1

	January £	February £	March £	April £
Changes to Receipts	-	-	(5,000)	(4,000)
Changes to Payments for Fixed Assets	26,000	(24,000)		
Revised:				
Cash Flow for Month	(24,820)	21,640	(7,080)	(1,240)
Bank Balance bf	10,000	(14,820)	6,820	(260)
Bank Balance cf	(14,820)	6,820	(260)	(1,500)

4.2 Revised Cash Budget extract for the period July - October

	July £	August £	September £	October £
Payments				
Purchases	25,000	28,000	26,650	24,600
Labour	19,000	17,000	18,000	20,700
Rent	21,000	-	-	-
Expenses	10,080	10,093	10,133	10,140

CHAPTER 5 – MANAGING LIQUIDITY – THE UK FINANCIAL SYSTEM

5.1   Available cash (or a positive balance or overdraft facility with the bank) are essential if creditors are to be paid on time and money has to be collected from debtors. If creditors are not paid on time, credit may be withdrawn and in the worst case the business may become insolvent.

5.2   (a)   Paraphrase of definition on page 107.

(b)   It will need to raise finance, probably from a bank.

(c)   It should invest the funds (in an appropriately liquid fund) to obtain a return on its money.

5.3   (a)   Paraphrase of text on page 108.

(b)   aggregation of amounts, maturity transformation, low risk, known cost

5.4   (a)   retail

(b)   retail (note: also available through Building Society)

(c)   merchant

(d)   retail

5.5   Four from: Government banker, banks' banker, note printing, gold reserves, foreign currency reserves, influence on interest rates.

5.6   (a)   Treasury Bill

(b)   Gilts

5.7   Slightly higher risk

5.8   To provide liquidity to meet demand for customers withdrawing deposits. Also to provide security for borrowing from Bank of England.

5.9   Most likely – repo arrangement with Bank of England – tradeable securities in exchange for cash

CHAPTER 6 – MANAGING LIQUIDITY – OBTAINING FINANCE

6.1   (a)   See definition and features listed on page 121.

(b)   Two from:
– the customer only needs to borrow what is actually needed
– the customer only has to pay interest on what is actually borrowed
– flexibility – the overdraft limit may be changed with the minimum of formality

6.2   (a)   See definition and features listed on page 122. The cash flow advantage is in the timing of the advances against the invoices.

(b)   With invoice discounting the business continues to administer the sales ledger. With factoring, the finance company takes over the administration of the sales ledger.

(c)   Non-recourse factoring gives protection against bad debts, recourse factoring (which is cheaper) leaves the business with liability for bad debt losses.

6.3   See definition, features and advantages listed on pages 125 and 126.

6.4   (a)   The main difference is that with hire purchase the ownership of the assets passes to the customer when payments have been completed, whereas with a leasing contract ownership of the assets normally remains with the leasing company.

(b)   The payments for a finance lease are calculated so that they cover the whole cost of the asset and a rebate is then paid to the customer at the end of the lease period. The payments for an operating lease are lower – they cover the fall in value of the asset over the lease period, but no rebate is payable.

(c)   An asset such as computer equipment which the customer will want to keep and use after the repayments have been completed, but will not be of much resale value to the finance company.

(d)   A two year operating lease will be the best form of financing as the cars will be returned to the leasing company after the two years and can then be sold by the leasing company on the second-hand market. New cars and a new operating lease can then be provided for the company.

6.5   The table might be presented along the following lines (summary information shown here):

	bank overdraft	bank loan
period of finance	short-term (up to 12 months)	1 to 25 years
assets financed	working capital/liquidity	Fixed assets Permanent working capital
repayment	day-to-day operation of current account	Fixed and regular repayments monthly or quarterly
cost of finance	interest charged only on amounts borrowed, variable rate, arrangement fee	interest fixed, variable or capped, arrangement fee
security	full security, eg mortgage, guarantee(s), fixed and floating charge (company only)	full security, eg mortgage guarantee(s), fixed and floating charge (company only)

6.6   (a)   To ensure that it will be repaid as much as possible if the customer defaults on the loan.

(b)   A fixed charge is a charge (legal document) over specified assets given by a limited company. If the company defaults on the loan, the bank will have powers of sale over the assets.

A floating charge is a charge given by a limited company over assets which are not fixed but are floating, ie they may change from day to day. They include cash, debtors and stock (ie they are generally current assets).

(c)   A guarantee is a legal document. When you sign it you are undertaking to repay the company's borrowing if the bank makes demand on the company and the company is unable to repay that borrowing. The bank is likely to ask you to pledge assets such as your home to provide security to support the guarantee. You are therefore in real danger of losing your assets if the company runs into financial trouble and the bank has to make demand under the guarantee.

6.7 (a) bank = mortgagee, customer = mortgagor

(b) bank = baillee, customer = baillor

(c) bank = debtor, customer = creditor

6.8 (a) both the bank and the customer

(b) three from the 'undertaking' clauses illustrated on page 131

(c) three from the 'default' clauses illustrated on page 131

6.9 A mnemonic such as PARIS may be used. The following areas should be covered: personality of borrower (to include financial state of health, experience and commitment); the amount (correct amount, size compared with capital); repayment (how much, when, affordability), interest and fees charged (to cover risk and cost of lending), security (enough, not just lending on security).

CHAPTER 7 – MANAGING LIQUIDITY – INVESTING SURPLUS FUNDS

7.1 All the factors will increase the potential rate of return on the investment.

7.2 A rise in inflation normally also signals an increase in the general level of interest rates in the economy. The danger at this time for an investor in fixed-rate funds is that the investment, eg a gilt, will be 'locked in' at a low rate which will then effectively reduce the rate of return over time. One answer is to invest in funds that provide a variable rate of return, an index-linked gilt, for example.

7.3 Ken has a point about the excitement factor, but for a private or public sector organisation, which is constrained by external and internal regulations requiring safe and low-risk investment, the shares cannot be recommended. They are subject to market trends and are higher credit risks: the share price can fall substantially, and, if the worst scenario is realised, the listed company can become insolvent, with little or no money left for shareholders.

7.4 (a) The interbank market is comprised principally of deposits placed by banks with each other, the local authority market with deposits made with local authorities. The difference in the rates reflects the difference in risk. The local authorities are quasi-governmental and, as such, very low risk; the banks are certainly creditworthy, but as commercial organisations do not carry the same high credit rating (state risk) as local authorities.

(b) A certificate of deposit is a paper security which is tradeable (minimum £50,000, up to three months) and repayable on maturity. An interbank deposit is not tradeable as no paper certificate is involved – it is a straight deposit/loan. The amounts are normally larger and the rate of return higher.

(c) A treasury bill is a three month tradeable security issued on behalf of the Government to fund Government borrowing. It is therefore very low risk and attractive to private and public sector Treasuries looking for a safe investment. This low risk status means that the return on treasury bills is lower than the return on interbank deposits (which are commercial risk).

7.5 (a)   Secure long-term investment.

(b)   Interest yield relates the interest rate stated on the investment (coupon rate) to the current market price. Redemption yield relates the coupon rate to the period up to the redemption date and takes into account the change in price of the investment over that period; as such it is a much better way of comparing the gilt yield with the yield on other investments. The numerical difference between interest yield and redemption yield reflects the unreliability of the interest yield, ie the fact that interest yield only takes account of income (interest) whereas the redemption yield takes account of both income and capital elements.

(c)   The market price of a gilt will reflect the difference between the stated rate (coupon rate) and the prevailing market interest rate. If the coupon rate is higher than market rates for that type of investment, then so is the price (eg the Treasury 8% 2009); if the coupon rate is lower than market rates, then so is the price (eg the Treasury 4.25% 2036). It could also be pointed out that the 'long' date of the Treasury 4.25% 2036 would normally command a higher rate of return than the coupon rate provides.

7.6 See suggested procedures on page 150.

CHAPTER 8 – GRANTING CREDIT – ASSESSING THE CUSTOMERS

8.1 Letter to Bart Attman, Director, Toppo Toys Limited, address as letterhead. Text should acknowledge their request and politely ask for bank reference (plus authority for bank) and two trade references, while at the same time acknowledging current cash trading. See page 159 for similar letter. References will still be required because there is a need to comply with the Credit Policy Manual.

8.2 (a)   Company financial details (accounts); payment record, details of directors, records of any insolvency proceedings.

(b)   Advantages: speed of response, reliability of information, comprehensive information. Disadvantages: cost, possibility that some information may be out of date.

8.3 Unless GML Importers has written authority from its customer to release information, to do so would be a breach of the duty of confidentiality and also of the Data Protection Act 1998 which protects the rights of 'data subjects'. The request should be politely declined.

CHAPTER 9 – GRANTING CREDIT – SETTING UP THE ACCOUNT

9.1 (a)   Period of availability, credit limit, payment date, discounts, payment details, interest penalties.

(b)   No. These are terms and conditions which relate to future trading, but do not themselves constitute a contract. The sales transactions are individual contracts which refer back to these terms.

9.2 (a) 27 May (b) 30 June (c) 2 June

9.3 (a) 18.54%

(b) (i) No. The figure is higher than the cost of borrowing and therefore unattractive.

(ii) Yes. The figure is lower than the cost of borrowing and therefore attractive.

9.4 Yes. Late Payment of Commercial Debts (Interest) Act 1998 gives authority.

9.5 (a) Not a contract. There is no value which passes and no intention to create legal relations. You would probably have to repaint it yourself, perhaps with your friend's help!

(b) This is a contract as all three elements are present. It is your fault for picking up the wrong paper. You could try and change it, if you think it is worth the effort.

(c) Not a contract. There is no value which passes because the pen is free. As the supplier is hoping for an order they would undoubtedly want to send a replacement. As the pen is faulty you may not feel inclined to place an order.

(d) Not a contract. There is no acceptance of the offer. The goods are offered for sale but the acceptance (the order) has not been communicated. You are going to have to order again.

9.6 2 Prices quoted in brochures and catalogues need to be confirmed with the supplier and can be changed by the supplier at the time of ordering. They do not include VAT which will be charged at the current rate.

3 Credit limits can be approved, changed or withdrawn by the supplier. Bank and trade references will be requested.

4 Invoices must be paid within 30 days of the date of the invoice. If payment is not made, the supplier has the right to suspend deliveries and may at the same time use other methods to recover the amount owing.

5 The supplier will retain the ownership of goods sold until payment has been made in full.

CHAPTER 10 – MONITORING AND CONTROLLING THE SALES LEDGER

10.1

DOWZEE LIMITED: AGED DEBTORS ANALYSIS

Account	Account number	Credit Limit	Balance	up to 30 days	31 - 60 days	61 - 90 days	91 days & over
TOTALS			52,129.50	18,982.00	15,786.50	10,891.00	6,500.00
Percentage			100%	36%	30%	21%	13%

(a)   See percentages above.

(b)   The liquidity of the company will be restricted as a result of the overdue accounts. Note that only 36% of the total outstanding is within the limit. 30% is over 30 days overdue and 34% over 60 days overdue. This situation may also conceal some potential bad debts which, should they materialise, will reduce liquidity on a permanent basis.

(c)   Problems can be identified as the lack of a formal Credit Control Policy, the lack of standard chaser letters and any structure for reinforcement of debt collection.

(d)   Solutions would be to rectify this lax situation. This would involve the drawing up of a formal Credit Control Policy, the drafting of standard chaser letters and the establishment of procedures for debt collection.

10.2   A doubtful debt is a debt which is thought <u>unlikely</u> to be repaid. A provision may be raised in the accounting records for a doubtful debt.

A bad debt is a debt which is thought will <u>definitely not</u> be repaid. A bad debt will normally be written off in the accounting records.

10.3   Credit insurance is insurance taken out to protect an organisation against loss of money incurred through customer default. Examples include cover arranged for the whole turnover, a group of key customer accounts and single customer accounts.

10.4   (a)   Factoring involves the management of the client's sales ledger; with invoice discounting the client continues to operate the sales ledger. The sales ledger customers see that a factor is involved because they have to make payment to the factor; they do not realise if invoice discounting is taking place.

(b)   Recourse factoring does not include bad debt protection. Loss of money through customer default is borne by the client (ie there is 'recourse' to the client). Non-recourse factoring means that any loss through bad debts will be borne by the factoring company. The factoring company has 'no recourse' to the client for the money.

10.6   (a)

Aged Debtors Analysis as at 31 July					
Customer	Total due	1 - 30 days	31 - 60 days	61 - 90 days	91 days and over
R Brooklyn	1,625.00	825.00			800.00

(b/c)   The £825 current amount is within the credit terms agreed with the customer and so should not prove a problem. The £800 which is over 90 days outstanding could be a disputed invoice, in which case the dispute needs to be sorted out and the amount paid. For example the customer may claim that there is an overcharge on the invoice, or the goods were unsatisfactory, or there was a short delivery. Another possibility is that the amount is a potential bad debt, in which case the company will need to take firm action such as stopping the account and threatening legal action. Given that there are no other overdue amounts outstanding, the disputed invoice is possibly the more likely answer.

CHAPTER 11 - COLLECTING DEBTS AND DEALING WITH INSOLVENCY

11.1 (a) Fastrak College is in a difficult position here because it can be argued that there is no underlying contract:

1 the offer of the course was not accepted as it should have been in a formal signed document

2 no formal contract document was issued by Fastrak as it would normally have been

Legal action is therefore out of the question as there is no contract on which to sue. Fastrak can nevertheless attempt to trace Bob and demand the money, but it will have no legal backing for doing so. It could also attempt to recover the course materials, but the value of these is likely to be minimal.

(b) The debt will initially have to be placed in a provision for doubtful debts account and probably eventually written off as a bad debt. Fastrak will need to tighten up its internal control procedures and ensure that courses are only issued after payment has been received and the formal contract issued.

11.2 The **advantages** of employing a debt collection agency: psychological advantage of using a new method of debt collection which causes customer to pay up, admin cost savings, the agency only charges for what it collects.

The **disadvantages** of employing a debt collection agency: loss of control over the debt collection process, paying someone else to do what you should be able to do yourself, possible loss of customer if heavy tactics used.

11.3 The memo could include the following points:

(a) R Bootle Limited. There is no real chance of recovering this debt. It should be written off as a bad debt in line with company policy.

(b) Tessa Sims. Employing a debt collection agency to chase this debt should achieve results as it will stir the customer into action. A solicitor's letter is another possibility, but employing a solicitor could in the long run prove more costly.

(c) R Patel. A letter threatening legal action and placing the account on stop will hopefully persuade the customer to pay. A provision for doubtful debts should be made.

(d) Ken Chang. There is little chance of receiving any significant payment from the bankruptcy, although a claim should be made. The debt should be written off as a bad debt in line with company policy.

(e) Ron Pumkiss would appear to have sufficient assets to repay the debt. The most appropriate remedy would be a warrant for execution issued by the court which will involve the bailiffs being sent in. Just the threat of this may well persuade Ron to pay.

11.4 (a) For processes, see text pages 218 and 221-222.
     (b) The differences include:
      - County Court process does not involve other creditors and so there is a better chance of obtaining full repayment of debt; the bankruptcy process involves all the other creditors and the eventual repayment is likely to be much less
      - the effect on the debtor will be different: a County Court judgement will be a black mark on the debtor's credit rating whereas a bankruptcy is more serious and means the loss of most major assets and a black mark on the character of the debtor.

Index